A History of Spain

PALGRAVE ESSENTIAL HISTORIES
General Editor: Jeremy Black

This series of compact, readable and informative national histories is designed to appeal to anyone wishing to gain a broad understanding of a country's history.

Published

A History of Spain   *Simon Barton*
A History of the British Isles (2nd edn)   *Jeremy Black*
A History of Israel   *Ahron Bregman*
A History of Ireland   *Mike Cronin*
A History of the Pacific Islands   *Steven Roger Fischer*
A History of the United States (2nd edn)   *Philip Jenkins*
A History of India   *Peter Robb*
A History of China   *J.A.G. Roberts*

Further titles are in preparation

A History of Spain

Simon Barton

First published 2004 by
PALGRAVE MACMILLAN
Houndmills, Basingstoke, Hampshire RG21 6XS and
175 Fifth Avenue, New York, N.Y. 10010
Companies and representatives throughout the world

PALGRAVE MACMILLAN is the global academic imprint of the Palgrave Macmillan division of St. Martin's Press, LLC and of Palgrave Macmillan Ltd. Macmillan® is a registered trademark in the United States, United Kingdom and other countries. Palgrave is a registered trademark in the European Union and other countries.

ISBN 0–333–63257–5 hardback
ISBN 0–333–63258–3 paperback

This book is printed on paper suitable for recycling and made from fully managed and sustained forest sources.

A catalogue record for this book is available from the British Library.

Library of Congress Cataloging-in-Publication Data
Barton, Simon, 1962–
     A history of Spain/Simon Barton.
          p. cm.—(Palgrave essential histories)
     Includes bibliographical references and index.
     ISBN 0–333–63257–5 (cloth)
          1. Spain—History. I. Title. II. Series.
DP66.B37 2003
946—dc22

                                                           2003066374

10   9   8   7   6   5   4   3   2   1
13   12   11   10   09   08   07   06   05   04

Typeset by Cambrian Typesetters, Frimley, Camberley, Surrey
Printed and bound in Great Britain by Creative Print & Design (Ebbw Vale), Wales

To Alexander and Victoria,
for whom Spain is in their blood

Contents

CONTENTS

Maps

Preface

This book seeks to offer to a general readership a clear and concise overview of the historical development of Spain, from its origins to the modern era. 'Spain', of course, is shorthand, in that for much of the period under study a plethora of political entities co-existed within the geographical area now occupied by the modern Spanish state. In writing this work, I have been hugely indebted to the labours of many scholars of Spanish history, some (but by no means all) of whose works are listed at the end of this book. Needless to say, the severe constraints on space have forced me to be highly selective in the range of material covered and I am acutely aware that the scope and emphases of the work will not be to the liking of all. In particular, Spain's splendid literary and artistic heritage is not dealt with in any depth here. None the less, if this book at least encourages the reader to delve more deeply into Spain's strikingly rich and diverse history, I shall be well satisfied.

I should like to record a deep debt of gratitude to all those friends who have offered advice or have uncomplainingly agreed to read the drafts of chapters I have placed before them. In this respect, I am particularly grateful to Isabel Cáceres, Roger Collins, Simon Doubleday, John Edwards, Richard Fletcher and Tim Rees. Special thanks go to Jeremy Black, who first invited me to write this volume and who has been a constant source of advice and inspiration during its preparation; to Geri Smith, whose steadfast support ensured that the book was completed; and to Terka Acton and her team at the publisher's, who have patiently borne with me despite my persistent and doubtless infuriating failure to meet deadlines.

Every effort has been made to contact the copyright holders of material used in the text, but if any have been inadvertently missed, the publisher will be pleased to make the necessary arrangements.

A NOTE ON PLACE-NAMES

Place names are given in their modern Castilian forms, with the exception of a handful of widely used anglicized versions, such as Aragon, Castile, Catalonia, Majorca, Minorca, Navarre and Seville.

Introduction

Among the regions of Western Europe, none can match the physical contrasts of Iberia, which in terms of its extremes of topography, climate and natural vegetation is virtually a subcontinent unto itself. Writing in the early fifth century AD, the historian Orosius observed that 'by the disposition of the land, Hispania as a whole is a triangle and, surrounded as it is by the Ocean and the Tyrrhenian Sea, is almost an island'. Five hundred years earlier, the Greek geographer Strabo had likened the distinctive landmass of the Iberian peninsula to a bull's hide stretched out at the southernmost tip of Europe. Yet, while the external boundaries of the peninsula are strikingly clear-cut, with most of the periphery bounded by water, the physical landscape of the interior is far from being so. If one studies a map of the peninsula, two features immediately catch the eye. First, there is its sheer size: at over 580,000 square kilometres, of which the state of modern Spain occupies roughly 85 per cent, Iberia covers an area very nearly twice that of the British Isles. Second, there is its altitude: after Switzerland, this is the highest region in Europe. At the centre of the peninsula, occupying roughly one half of the total landmass, lies the vast, arid tableland known as the *meseta*. The *meseta* is bisected by the imposing sierras of the Central System – the Serra da Estrela, the Sierra de Gredos and the Sierra de Guadarrama – and is ringed by a series of other formidable mountain barriers: the Cantabrian Cordillera to the north; the Iberian mountains to the north-east and the Sierra Morena and the Cordillera Bética to the south. On the fringes of these mountain ranges there lies a narrow coastal plain which seldom exceeds 30 kilometres in width, although in a few places, for example along the Ebro and Guadalquivir river valleys, or in the Atlantic coastlands of southern Portugal, this low-lying terrain stretches much further inland. In the extreme north-east, stretching from the Bay of Biscay to the Mediterranean, the rugged (though not impenetrable) mountain chain of the Pyrenees guards the land link between the peninsula and the rest of Europe; to the far south, Spain is divided from Africa by the Straits of Gibraltar, which at their narrowest are barely 15 kilometres wide. There are five principal rivers, none of them easily navigable: four of

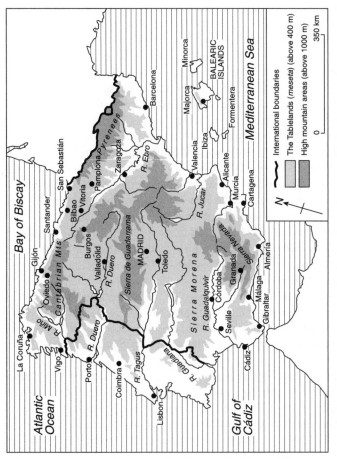

Map 1   The Iberian peninsula, physical features and main towns.   Adapted from John Hooper, *The New Spaniards* (Harmondsworth, 1995), p. xiv.

xiii

them (the Duero, Tagus, Guadiana and Guadalquivir) drain westwards and southwards towards the Atlantic Ocean; the Ebro, in north-eastern Spain, which has the greatest volume of water, flows towards the Mediterranean.

The climate of the peninsula is no less varied than its physical geography. The coastal territories of the north and north-west – from central Portugal to the Pyrenees – share a temperate Atlantic climate with abundant rainfall; the rest of the peninsula is semi-arid. Drought is commonplace. The northern *meseta* experiences violent contrasts of temperature, as bitterly cold winters are followed by searingly hot summers: 'nine months of winter and three of hell', as the Castilian proverb pithily has it. Mediterranean vegetation, such as the olive tree, cannot survive in a climate of such harsh extremes. Further to the south and east, however, particularly along the Mediterranean coast, winters are generally mild and frost-free, while summers are oppressively hot and rainfall is low. The subtropical climes of southern Spain have far more in common with North Africa than with the fierce continental climate of the *meseta*. These climatic variables have dictated the economic development of the regions of the peninsula. Thus, the agricultural potential of the rugged, acid soils of 'wet Spain' to the north is severely limited, with the result that horn has always prevailed over corn, with cattle and sheep rearing providing one of the mainstays of the local economy. On the arid plains of the *meseta*, by contrast, cereal crops are extensively grown to the north, while olives and vines dominate to the south, in addition to which the steppelands of La Mancha and Extremadura provide ample pasturage for cattle, sheep and goats. The rich, alluvial soils of the Ebro and Guadalquivir deltas, and the Mediterranean coastal plain, 'the garden of Spain', yield abundant produce.

Spain's 'geographical convulsions', as Laurie Lee aptly described them, and her striking contrasts of climate and vegetation, have profoundly shaped her political, economic and cultural development and endowed the peninsula with an astonishing regional diversity. From the earliest times, for example, the fertile soils of the Guadalquivir valley and the Levante (eastern Spain) proved a powerful magnet to incoming waves of settlers. It was no accident that the principal Roman cities were founded in these areas of prime agricultural land, which could supply an ample surplus of wealth for taxation. As will also become evident in the pages that follow, the narrow sea crossing between southern Spain and north-west Africa has tended to act less as a barrier than as a bridge, facilitating plentiful contact between the two regions. By contrast, the mountain chains which gird and bisect the *meseta* have long acted as an obstacle to communication between the prosperous, low-lying periphery and the peoples of the interior, with the result that until the advent of the locomotive and the motor car, the local economies of much of the centre and north developed as virtual 'islands' of production, many effectively marooned from one other. For many centuries, Catalonia, to the north-east, which is separated from the rest of the peninsula by the peaks of the Iberian mountain range, enjoyed far closer political, economic and cultural links with its near neighbours across the Pyrenees and in the Mediterranean than it did with the peoples of the *meseta*.

Even if political unity has been frequently held up by some as a natural goal, Spain's 'geographical handicap', as Claudio Sánchez-Albornoz once referred to it, has in fact tended to encourage the development of regionalist and separatist movements and has compounded the difficulty that governments through the centuries have encountered in forging a strong unitary state. It was for this reason that Richard Ford felicitously described Spain as 'a bundle of small bodies tied together by a rope of sand', while in his influential essay 'Invertebrate Spain' (*España Invertebrada*), the philosopher José Ortega y Gasset considered that Spain was 'not so much a nation as a series of watertight compartments'. For many historians, Spanish history is to be understood above all in terms of a permanent struggle between centre and periphery: the desire of a central government to overcome regional particularism and bring about a truly united nation; and the no less strenuous efforts of the regions to maintain their identity and to keep central government at arm's length.

*   *   *

Just precisely when Spain as a nation was born has been much debated. While the dynastic union cemented by Isabella I of Castile and Ferdinand II of Aragon in 1479 has traditionally been presented as the key moment, some historians have claimed that it is possible to trace the origins of the Spanish nation right back to the unitary kingdom forged by the Visigothic monarchy in the late sixth and early seventh centuries. Support can also be found for the view that Spain as a national entity is the product of relatively modern times: for example, it has been argued that it was only after Philip V swept away the privileges and institutions of the constituent realms of the Crown of Aragon, between 1707 and 1716, that Spain became truly united for the first time. But political unity is one thing, national consciousness quite another. Given the persistence of strong regionalist feelings in the peninsula to this day – notably in the Basque Country and Catalonia – some would contend that Spain as a nation is still to be born.

Until relatively recently, the old adage 'Africa begins at the Pyrenees' was deeply engrained in the consciousness of historians of all nationalities. Spain, it was widely believed, was a nation apart: physically joined to Europe, yet strikingly different, not only in terms of her topography, climate and ecology, but of her culture, mind-set and, above all, her historical 'trajectory'. For many observers, the essential 'difference' of Spain lay in the fact that the Iberian peninsula was the only region in the medieval West (apart from Sicily) to experience an Islamic conquest and that the subsequent interaction, or 'symbiosis', as Américo Castro would have it, of Muslim, Christian and Jewish cultures, from the eighth century onwards, left a profound imprint on Spain and the Spanish psyche. However, other historians angrily rejected the notion that the Muslims had any significant influence upon the Spanish Christian realms, arguing instead that the medieval Reconquest (*Reconquista*), the centuries-long military struggle waged by the Christian states to reclaim the peninsula from Muslim rule, was the forge in which Spain as a nation had been wrought.

The fall in 1492 of Granada, the last stronghold of independent Islamic power, brought the Reconquest to a close and was followed almost immediately by a remarkable phase of imperial expansion, which in the space of barely fifty years catapulted Spain to the status of major world power. But she was not to enjoy her pre-eminent position for long. During the second half of the seventeenth century, Spanish hegemony in Europe was broken, Portugal (annexed by Philip II in 1580) cast off Spanish rule for good, and to compound matters Spain was to suffer invasion by foreign armies in 1704 and 1808. By the nineteenth century, Spain had seemingly become a peripheral nation in every sense, synonymous with political volatility, social inequality, religious intolerance and economic underachievement, even if foreign travellers to the peninsula, such as Théophile Gautier, Prosper Mérimée and Washington Irvine, intoxicated with the ideals of the Romantic movement, were captivated by what they saw as Spain's 'exoticism' and pre-modern simplicity.

By the end of the nineteenth century, the loss of the last remnants of Spain's overseas empire fuelled a growing mood of introspection and pessimism among the Spanish intelligentsia. There was a widespread perception that, compared to the great industrialized powers of Western Europe, Spain had somehow failed as a nation and 'missed the train of progress'. Not only was Spain's imperial past widely condemned as a tragic error, but the very 'historical unity' of Spain began to be called into question. Increasingly, writers (both in Spain and abroad) chose to attribute Spain's decline from great power status to the long-standing conflict between the 'Two Spains', that is, between the forces of tradition and innovation. For Spanish conservatives, Spain's decline was the fault of those who had infected the nation with the foreign ideas of the Enlightenment and undermined the traditional Catholic values that had sustained Spain's rise to greatness. For their part, Protestants and liberals were adamant that it was Spain's failure to keep up with Europe and to do away with 'medieval' obscurantist attitudes and institutions, embodied most powerfully by the Inquisition, that lay at the root of her imperial decline, her stunted industrial revolution and the grave social and political conflicts of the nineteenth and twentieth centuries. 'If Spain is the problem', wrote Ortega y Gasset, 'Europe is the solution.' It was because Spain's 'historical destiny' was seemingly so far out of step with that of the rest of Europe, so the argument ran, that she failed in modern times to develop a stable parliamentary democracy, or to achieve much needed social and economic reform.

During the course of the past 25 years or so, however, such black-and-white interpretations of the Spanish past have come to seem increasingly inappropriate and passé. Rapid economic growth since the 1960s has ensured that today Spaniards enjoy a standard of living that is broadly on a par with that of their European neighbours. The restoration of democracy in 1977 has helped to curb the endemic volatility that was once a hallmark of Spanish political life and, as a fully paid-up member of NATO and the European Union, Spain has been firmly integrated into the community of Western democratic nations. Now, far from emphasizing the exceptionalism of Spain's past, many commentators are at pains to point out how profoundly Europeanized Spain was and is. Historians today no longer seek, like the intellectuals of the 'Generation of '98' and their successors, to identify Spain's *Volksgeist*, or national spirit, in order to understand her history, but rather to delineate and make sense of the bewilderingly complex series of political, social, economic and cultural substrata which together have formed the modern Spanish nation. It may well be that Ramón Menéndez Pidal was right when he stated that Spain was 'a nation with an imperfect sense of nationality', but the same could undoubtedly be said of many of the states of modern Europe. As Juan Pablo Fusi has rightly observed, the creation of national identity is an 'indeterminate process, dynamic and open, which lacks a point of departure and a point of arrival'; like our perceptions of the past, it is constantly evolving.

1

The Pride and Ornament of the World: Prehistory to AD 1000

ORIGINS

The ethnic origins of the population of the Iberian peninsula are shrouded in mystery and controversy. However, thanks to the remarkable excavations currently taking place in the Sierra de Atapuerca, high up in the north-eastern corner of the Castilian *meseta*, we can at least be sure that communities of hominids (ultimately of African origin) had already begun to establish themselves in the peninsula around 800,000 years ago. *Homo antecessor*, as he has been dubbed by anthropologists, probably relied principally on hunting to sustain himself, although the grisly forensic evidence from Atapuerca, where human bones bearing cut marks have been discovered, suggests that he also routinely resorted to cannibalism. Whether any relationship existed between *Homo antecessor* and the other hominid forms that subsequently settled in the peninsula has yet to be established. Among the latter were the cave-dwelling Neanderthals, who during the Middle Palaeolithic period (*c.*100,000–40,000 BC) founded numerous settlements on Iberian soil, with particularly important concentrations in Cantabria, the Western Pyrenees, Catalonia and the Levante.

During the Upper Palaeolithic period (*c.*40,000–10,000 BC), when Europe lay in the grip of the last Ice Age, and mammoth, woolly rhinoceros and bison still roamed the peninsula, the Neanderthals were gradually displaced by a new wave of immigrants, the so-called Cro-Magnon humans, from whom modern man, *Homo Sapiens Sapiens*, descends. Like the Neanderthals, the Cro-Magnon newcomers were primarily cave-dwellers, who made extensive use of stone and bone tools and weapons, and who lived as hunters, fishers and food-gatherers. What set these peoples apart from their Neanderthal cousins, their strikingly different physical constitution aside, was their incipient artistic creativity, manifested from around 15,000 BC in a series of colourful cave paintings of animals. Many of these paintings are to be found in the northern regions of Asturias and Cantabria, such as the spectacular collection that was discovered in the caves of Altamira near Santander.

As the Ice Age slowly retreated, from around 5000 BC, and the climate warmed, patterns of human settlement in the peninsula (and elsewhere in Europe) were slowly transformed by the diffusion of cultural influences from the eastern Mediterranean. What has been dubbed the 'Neolithic Revolution' saw formerly highly-mobile groups of humans gradually abandon their hunter-gatherer lifestyle and adopt livestock husbandry and agriculture as the principal means to sustain themselves. The foundation of sedentary communities, the first of which appear to have been established in Catalonia, the Levante and Andalusia, was accompanied by technological advances: pottery, often richly decorated, began to be widely used; linen and wool were woven; and lithic technology was further perfected by the development of polished-stone weapons and tools.

Maritime contact with the wider Mediterranean world was to be influential in introducing new technologies and cultural influences to Iberia. From the middle of the second millennium BC, copper working gradually began to be introduced into the south-eastern and south-western regions of the peninsula, where some of the most important deposits of metal ores were to be found. Excavations at Los Millares in the province of Almería have revealed evidence of a prosperous fortified farming and stock-breeding settlement which flourished on the site between c.2500 and 1800 BC, where craftsmen produced a wide range of copper tools, including axes, chisels and knives. Copper smelting was followed in the second millennium BC by the introduction of bronze technology. Between c.1700 and 1200 BC, the principal Bronze Age societies were again located in the south-east and south-west, but there was also a concentration of bronze-using communities on the plains of La Mancha, where a series of *motillas*, or heavily fortified mounds, have been excavated, and in the Levante. The archaeological evidence from thriving Early Bronze Age settlements such as El Argar in the province of Almería, where bronze weapons and ornaments were produced on a large scale, points to considerable disparities in levels of wealth among the population and to the development of social stratification. Yet the impact of metallurgy was not felt uniformly across the peninsula: copper and bronze initially circulated in such small quantities that flint tools and weapons remained in wide-spread use, and it would be some time before the new technology had spread widely to the scattered and sparsely populated communities of the interior. Even in those communities where metallurgy was most highly developed, farming and livestock breeding remained the main-stay of the local economy.

Archaeologists have pointed to a significant 'realignment' of Bronze Age societies during the period after *c*.1200 BC. As some settlements were abandoned, new farming villages were established across the northern and southern *meseta*s, probably in response to rising population levels; bronze-working skills became common-place, although flint tools still predominated; and highly decorated pottery circulated widely among the communities of the Duero basin and further afield. Meanwhile, increased production of bronze weapons in Atlantic Europe led to a growing demand for supplies of Iberian copper and tin, and to the development of a flourishing two-way trade route along the western and southern coastal waters of the peninsula. By *c*.850 BC, it is evident that some Bronze Age commu-nities were enjoying a far higher degree of material wealth than had been the case hitherto. Evidence of this is provided not only by the large hoards of gold and bronze artefacts (including jewellery and weapons) that have been discovered in good number along the west-ern and southern seaboard of the peninsula, but also by the engraved stelae, or decorated stone slabs, principally from the south-west, many of which depict warriors surrounded by their weapons and other chattels, including chariots, slaves, dancers and even musical instruments. To the north-east, in the region of Catalonia and the Ebro valley, meanwhile, a distinctive Late Bronze Age culture predominated between *c*.1100 and 700 BC. These are the Urnfield settlements, so-called because their inhabitants cremated their dead and preserved the ashes in biconical pottery urns. This funerary prac-tice closely mirrors that followed by the Hallstatt culture of Central and Western Europe at this time, prompting speculation that 'Urnfield invaders' may have constituted the first wave of Celtic settlers to enter the peninsula. Alternatively, it is conceivable that what took place in north-eastern Spain at this time was a peaceful transfer of religious ideas and practices from beyond the Pyrenees, rather than the violent imposition of new societal customs and ideologies.

3

PHOENICIANS, GREEKS AND CARTHAGINIANS

During the first millennium BC, the population of the peninsula was to be subjected to a series of other powerful external cultural influences. According to later tradition, Phoenician seafarers from the eastern Mediterranean established their first foothold on Spanish soil around 1100 BC at *Gadir* (modern Cádiz), 'at the farthest extremity of the inhabited world', in the words of Diodorus of Sicily. However, archaeological evidence currently suggests that the foundation of Cádiz probably took place some three hundred years after that. Attracted chiefly by the rich deposits of metal ores (principally gold, silver, copper and tin) of the peninsula, which they sought for export to the Assyrian Empire in the Near East, Phoenician merchants soon founded a series of settlements along the southern coast of Spain, from Cádiz in the west as far as Villaricos in the province of Almería in the east. It has often been assumed that these colonies were little more than simple trading posts, but excavations carried out at El Cerro del Villar and Toscanos near Málaga have revealed the existence of two sizeable self-sufficient Phoenician settlements, each of which must have housed a population of at least 1000 inhabitants. From bases such as these, the Phoenicians were able to establish close commercial relations with the indigenous peoples of the interior, obtaining the precious metals they craved, as well as grain, meat and salt, in exchange for wine, oil, textiles, perfumes and other luxury goods.

Greek traders were also active in the peninsula. Greek ceramics, perfume and wine began to be imported into southern Spain from about 630 BC onwards. Around 575 BC a group of merchants from the Phocaean colony of Marseille founded a trading centre at *Emporion* (modern Ampurias) on the far north-east coast of Spain; this may have been followed by a similar settlement at nearby *Rhode* (Rosas). Ampurias and Rosas acted as important distribution points for Greek ceramics and Italian metalwork, in particular, and enabled Greek merchants to enter into close commercial relations with the communities of the interior. Greek manufactures also circulated widely along the eastern and southern seaboard, but Greek traders appear to have relied heavily on Phoenician middlemen to distribute their goods and it is unknown whether they were able to establish any further colonies or trading bases along the Iberian coastline.

Together, between *c*.750 and 550 BC, the Phoenicians and Greeks wrought a major change in the material culture of the indigenous societies of southern and eastern Spain. Quite apart from the wealth of metalwork, ceramics and other luxury goods that entered the southern areas of the peninsula at this time, iron working and the potter's wheel were introduced, mining production increased, and urbanization and agricultural expansion received a notable impulse. The Phoenicians also introduced writing to the peninsula. The earliest inscriptions in a semi-syllabic script derived from the Phoenician alphabet are to be found on numerous grave stelae in what is now southern Portugal. However, no lengthy literary compositions or documents survive and all attempts to decipher the meaning of this indigenous writing system have been unsuccessful hitherto.

The Iberian civilization which was subjected to these 'orientalizing' cultural influences stretched in a great arc from the southern Atlantic seaboard to the eastern Pyrenees and beyond; politically, however, it was divided into a mosaic of competing tribal kingdoms and city-states. Most celebrated of all among the diverse Iberian polities was the realm of Tartessos, whose fabulous wealth due to its abundance of precious metals was recorded and exaggerated by later Greek writers. While the origins and history of Tartessos itself remain hazy in the extreme, it is clear enough that the commercial exchange that took place between the Phoenicians and the indigenous Iberians was accompanied by a process of lively cultural cross-fertilization. Two masterpieces of Iberian sculpture executed in the fourth century BC, the funerary statues known as the *Dama de Baza* and the *Dama de Elche*, both of which represent richly robed and bejewelled goddesses or priestesses, appear to have been inspired by Punic religious imagery. Phoenician influences can also be glimpsed in Iberian architectural styles, tombs, metalwork and votive offerings.

Beyond the orbit of the Iberian civilization, three principal cultural groups may be identified. The western Pyrenees were the stronghold of the Basques, a pre Indo-European people, whose origins remain controversial. Northern and western Spain were dominated by iron-using Celtic tribes, some of whom appear to have established themselves in the peninsula during the sixth century BC, whose heavily fortified settlements with distinctive round houses, known as *castros*, became a prominent feature of the landscape. In Aragon, the upper Ebro valley and the plains of the eastern *meseta*, meanwhile, contact between Celtic and Iberian peoples gave rise to a distinctive 'Celtiberian' culture, whose art forms assimilated both Celtic and Iberian traditions; by the fourth century BC, moreover, these tribes had

5

begun to embrace the urbanizing traditions of their Iberian neighbours to the south and east.

The fall of Tyre, the last of the independent Phoenician city-states of the eastern Mediterranean, to the Babylonian king Nebuchadnezzar in 573 BC, led to the abandonment of many of the trading centres that had earlier been founded in southern Spain. Those that remained were eventually taken over by Carthage, a Phoenician colony which had been founded on the Bay of Tunis c.750 BC. Initially, it seems, the Carthaginians were content simply to consolidate or expand the trading centres which the Phoenicians had established in the coastal regions of southern Spain. However, defeat in the First Punic War (264–41 BC) by Rome, followed by the loss of her territories in Sicily, Corsica and Sardinia, encouraged Carthage to extend her territorial presence in the peninsula. Between 237 and 228 BC, under the leadership of Hamilcar Barca and his son-in-law and successor Hasdrubal, the Carthaginians brought the peoples of southern, eastern and central Iberia under their authority, and established an important naval base at 'New Carthage' (Cartagena). Carthaginian expansionism in the peninsula was viewed with consternation by Rome, her arch-rival for political and economic supremacy in the western Mediterranean, so much so that when Hamilcar's son Hannibal besieged and sacked the town of Saguntum (Sagunto) in 219–18 BC, Rome dispatched an expeditionary force under Gnaeus Cornelius Scipio to the peninsula. The titanic military struggle that ensued, during the course of which Hannibal's troops reached the very gates of Rome and brought their adversary to the brink of defeat, dragged on until 206 BC, when the Carthaginians were forced to evacuate the peninsula.

ROMAN HISPANIA

Victory over Carthage left Rome in control of eastern and southern Iberia. However, the difficulty of the terrain, the obduracy of the indigenous tribes, who frequently rose up in rebellion, and above all the lack of any coherent long-term military strategy on the part of the Roman authorities, who were seemingly content to maintain an endemic state of conflict in the region in order that governors might have the opportunity to enrich themselves and enhance their own careers, ensured that another two centuries of campaigning were to be necessary before the tribes of the entire peninsula were brought to heel. The campaign to quell the rebellion of the Lusitani in the west of the peninsula between 147 and 139 BC, and what the Greek historian Polybius called the 'war of fire' to reduce the Celtiberian town of Numantia (near modern Soria) in 142–33 BC, which culminated in the mass-suicide of many of the Numantine inhabitants and the total destruction of the town, were but two of the most serious military operations that Rome was to undertake during this long and arduous period of conquest. Besides, the peninsula was not immune to the internecine conflicts that periodically convulsed the Roman Republic during the first century BC. Most notorious of all, the struggle for political supremacy between the supporters of Julius Caesar and Pompey, which unfolded between 49 and 45 BC, was finally resolved when Caesar defeated his enemies on the battlefield of Munda in Andalusia. Even after the pacification of Spain was officially deemed complete, with the defeat of the Cantabrian tribes in 19 BC, revolts against Roman rule still flared up periodically.

For all that, Hispania, as the peninsula was known to the Romans, became a largely peaceful and prosperous region which was fully integrated into the political, administrative and economic structures of the Empire. In 197 BC, the territory then under Roman rule had been divided into two vast provinces: Hispania Citerior, which comprised the east and the central *meseta*; and Hispania Ulterior, which included the south and west. Subsequently, under the emperor Augustus (27 BC–AD 14), the peninsula was redivided into three administrative areas: Baetica (approximately modern Andalusia and southern Extremadura), based upon its capital at Córdoba; Lusitania (the far west of the peninsula), whose capital was Mérida; and Hispania Tarraconensis (which comprised the rest of the peninsula), whose administrative centre, as the name suggests, was Tarragona. A network of towns, linked by roads and bridges, served to bind the peninsula more tightly under Roman rule, and acted as a conduit of Roman ideas and methods into the interior. Some of these towns were newly founded colonies for veteran legionaries, like Italica (Santiponce, near Seville) and Emerita Augusta (Mérida); others had their origins in the military bases established by the Romans, such as those founded at the height of the Cantabrian wars at Asturica (Astorga), Legio (León) and Lucus Augusti (Lugo); and yet others were developed on existing urban centres, such as Tarraco (Tarragona), Carthago Nova (Cartagena) and Gades (Cádiz). The imprint of Roman civilization gradually made itself felt in the form of the Latin language (from which the modern Iberian languages, with the exception of Basque, derive), law, religion, art, public engineering works, education, coinage and so on. The early imperial period, that is, from the beginning of the reign of Augustus in 27 BC to the death of Hadrian in AD 138, saw a remarkable surge in building activity, much of it promoted by members of the local aristocracy keen to demonstrate their Romanizing credentials. The vast, imposing granite aqueduct that still bestrides the city centre of Segovia and the majestic bridge that spans the Tagus at Alcántara near Cáceres, to name only two of the most spectacular public buildings that stand to this day, speak volumes for the power and sophistication of Roman imperial rule in the peninsula.

Urban growth went hand in hand with a substantial increase in agricultural production, as improved irrigation techniques helped to bring large areas of marginal land under the plough. Rome looked to the peninsula to provide the Mediterranean market with horses, grain, *garum* (a fish sauce), olive oil, wine, wool and, not least, precious metals. Contemporary writers laid particular emphasis upon the mineral wealth of the peninsula. According to the elder Pliny, who was responsible for the collection of revenues from Hispania Citerior in around AD 72–4, the mines of the north-west – such as the vast open-cast workings at Las Médulas near Astorga – yielded over 20,000 pounds of gold per annum. Hispania was also regarded by Rome as an important source of military manpower: soldiers from the peninsula served throughout the Empire, such as the unit of mounted infantry recruited from the Basque tribe of the Varduli, which in the third century AD was stationed at High Rochester to the north of Hadrian's Wall. Far from being simply an important reservoir of raw materials and manpower, however, Hispania made its own distinguished contribution to the political and cultural life of the Roman Empire. No fewer than four emperors – Trajan (98–117), Hadrian (117–38), Theodosius I (378–95) and Magnus Maximus (383–88) – hailed from the peninsula, while among the most distinguished literary luminaries of the Spanish provinces were the two Senecas, Lucan, Martial, Quintilian and the Christian poet Prudentius.

The patina of Roman culture was not spread evenly across the peninsula. Like the conquest of Hispania itself, 'Romanization' was a slow, gradual and piecemeal process. While some areas, such as the prosperous Levante and the Ebro and Guadalquivir valleys, became thoroughly assimilated from an early date, adopting Latin speech and Roman dress and customs, yet others, notably the remote, mountainous regions of

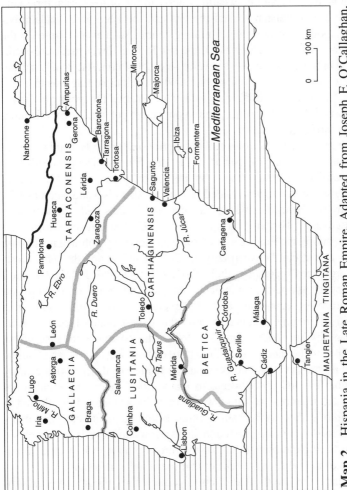
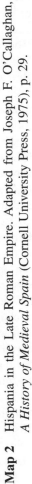

Map 2 Hispania in the Late Roman Empire. Adapted from Joseph F. O'Callaghan, *A History of Medieval Spain* (Cornell University Press, 1975), p. 29.

9

the north and north-west retained their tribal structures, religious beliefs and pastoral lifestyles. In much of the peninsula, it has been said, cultural assimilation was little more than a 'superficial veneer, barely masking the indigenous subculture'. The most substantial and prosperous Roman urban and rural settlements were situated in the main areas of economic wealth, chiefly in the prime agricultural land of the Mediterranean coastal regions and the Ebro and Guadalquivir valleys, or else near to major mining centres such as Río Tinto (in the modern province of Huelva). Of the few Roman towns that were established in the north and west, several – notably León, Astorga, Lugo and Braga – were chiefly military bases whose principal role was to guard over Rome's vital economic interests, notably the gold and silver mines of León and Asturias, and to police the potentially volatile territories further to the north.

The relative tranquillity and prosperity of Roman Hispania were to be disturbed during the period of the later Empire. The peninsula was subjected to external attacks by Berber tribesmen from Mauretania (modern Morocco), who raided Baetica in AD 171–3 and again in 177, and by migrating Germanic war-bands of Franks and Alamani, who crossed into Hispania from Gaul c.262 and sacked Tarragona. Furthermore, the Empire as a whole was racked by political instability, to the extent that between 260 and 269, Hispania and the other western provinces repudiated their allegiance to Rome. Political turmoil disrupted trade and communications and contributed to a significant downturn in economic activity: exports of foodstuffs and wine declined; mining production fell; the debasement of the imperial coinage by successive emperors led to the complete collapse of the currency in the second half of the third century AD; and the great public building projects that had been such a feature of the previous century became few and far between. In many cities, increasing numbers of civic and religious buildings were gradually abandoned or allowed to fall into decay, and urban centres began to contract. That many Hispano-Roman citizens found it necessary to bury large hoards of coins during the second half of the third century AD is itself symptomatic of the sense of insecurity that prevailed at this time.

During the late third and fourth centuries AD, the imperial authorities attempted to shore up the creaking administrative structures of government. Under the emperor Diocletian (284–305), the provincial boundaries of the Empire were redrawn in an attempt to tighten administrative control over the territories and ensure the efficient collection of taxes. Within Hispania itself, Tarraconensis was subdivided into three smaller provinces: Gallaecia (the north-west of the peninsula), whose capital was to be Braga, in what is now northern Portugal; Carthaginensis (which encompassed the centre and the south-east), based upon its capital at Cartagena; and Tarraconensis (the north and north-eastern districts), whose administrative centre remained Tarragona. As if to underline the determination of the imperial authority to strengthen its control over the provinces of Hispania, it may have been at this time that many of the most important administrative centres (for example, Barcelona, Lugo and Zaragoza) were fortified with massive town walls and towers. However, these measures do not appear to have restored the waning confidence of the Hispano-Roman élite in the late imperial state. During the fourth century AD, as the burden of taxation on the urban aristocracy increased yet further, many wealthy individuals sought to secure exemption from service on town councils. Civic pride gave way to private ostentation, as many among the élite channelled their wealth into lavish private town-houses or, increasingly, sumptuous rural villas. The latter were the residential and administrative centres of vast estates, which not only employed large numbers of labourers and craftsmen, but also, in some cases, their own private armies.

Perhaps the most significant development in Hispania during the period of the later Empire was the introduction and diffusion of Christianity. In his *Epistle to the Romans*, St Paul had spoken of his intention to travel to Hispania, but when and how the new religion took root in the peninsula is uncertain. It has been speculated that returning soldiers, who had previously served in Mauretania, may have played a significant part in spreading the faith. At any rate, by the middle of the third century Christian communities had sprung up in many parts of the peninsula and bishoprics had been created in León, Mérida and Zaragoza. The ecclesiastical council held at Elvira (near modern Granada) c.300 was attended by some twenty bishops in all. These communities were to suffer persecution at the hands of the emperors Decius (249–51), Diocletian and Galerius (305–12), but after the conversion of the emperor Constantine (306–37) in 312, and the adoption of Christianity as the official religion of the Empire, the Christian church in the peninsula went from strength to strength. Ecclesiastical buildings, such as churches, baptisteries, hospitals and episcopal palaces, were erected in most of the major Hispano-Roman towns, and many among the landed aristocracy embraced the faith and converted residential sections of their villas into chapels. Free from the fear of persecution, Christian writers were able to flourish, such as the poets Iuvencus (*fl. c.*330) and Prudentius (*fl. c.*400), and the historian Orosius (*fl. c.*418), author of the *Seven Books of History against the Pagans*, an influential history of the world from the Creation to his own times. One of the most prominent among the Hispano-Roman Christians was the wealthy land-owner Priscillian of Avila, who championed an ascetic movement which attracted widespread support in Hispania and south-western Gaul, until he was executed for heresy by command of the emperor Magnus Maximus in 385.

THE TWILIGHT OF ROMAN RULE

By the early fifth century AD, Roman imperial authority in the West had begun to disintegrate. In 409, a confederacy of peoples of Germanic origin – the Alans, Sueves and the Hasding and Siling Vandals – who had entered the Empire across the Rhine frontier only three years before, crossed the Pyrenees and established themselves in the peninsula. In the aftermath, according to Orosius and the Galician chronicler Bishop Hydatius (d. 469), war, famine and disease caused large-scale loss of life among the local population. Far from amounting to a full-scale 'barbarian' invasion, however, it is likely that these forces were brought into Hispania at the express invitation of the Roman general, Gerontius, who had raised up a rebel emperor, Maximus, in Barcelona and was desperate to free regular army units for campaigning in neighbouring Gaul. But when the Roman troops did not return to the peninsula after 411, and the regime of Maximus and Gerontius promptly collapsed, political authority in much of the region was appropriated by the Germanic newcomers. The Sueves and Hasding Vandals established themselves in Gallaecia, the Alans in Lusitania and Carthaginensis, and the Siling Vandals in Baetica; only Tarraconensis remained under Roman rule. None the less, the imperial government was not ready to relinquish Hispania without a fight. In 416, another Germanic people, the Visigoths, who had earlier sacked Rome in 410 and then established themselves in south-western Gaul, crossed into Hispania as allies of Rome and inflicted a crushing defeat on the Alans and Siling Vandals, who were forced to retreat north to Gallaecia, where they merged with the Hasding Vandals. Two years later, however, the Visigoths were recalled by the

Romans to Gaul, where they were re-established as federates in Aquitaine.

The inability of Rome to recover her lost provinces in Hispania, and the decision of the Hasding Vandals to cross the Straits of Gibraltar in 429, in order to establish themselves in the Roman provinces of North Africa, allowed the Sueves to emerge as the dominant power in the peninsula. Under their kings Rechila (438–48) and Rechiarius (448–56), the Sueves established their capital at Mérida, after that city was conquered in 441, and extended their authority over Lusitania, Baetica and Carthaginensis. But any hopes Rechiarius may have entertained of reuniting the peninsula under his rule were dashed in 456 when he was defeated and killed near Astorga by a Visigothic expeditionary force led by Theoderic II (453–66), acting apparently at the behest of the Roman imperial authorities. The Suevic kingdom quickly unravelled until it had been reduced to only Gallaecia, allowing Visigothic forces to seize control of Baetica, Lusitania and Carthaginensis. Subsequently, as the Western Roman Empire steadily descended into insignificance, the various 'barbarian' groups who had established themselves in the West by treaty with the Roman government, and who had effectively taken over the functions of the imperial army, jockeyed with one another to carve out their own independent centres of power. In the mid-470s, what remained of Roman authority in Hispania was ended for good when the armies of Theoderic's brother, Euric (466–84), overran Tarraconensis, as well as most of southern Gaul. In 476, the emperor Romulus Augustulus (475–6) was deposed and the Roman Empire in Western Europe was finally extinguished.

THE KINGDOM OF THE VISIGOTHS

The campaigns of Theoderic II and Euric left almost the whole of the peninsula, with the exception of the Suevic territory in Gallaecia, under Visigothic control. Yet, Hispania initially remained peripheral to Visigothic interests. It was not until their dominions in south-western Gaul had been almost obliterated, after a series of catastrophic defeats at the hands of the Franks and Burgundians between 507 and 531, that Visigothic settlement in the peninsula appears to have begun in earnest. Yet the Germanic newcomers never represented any more than a very small minority of the population of Iberia as a whole. That the

13

precarious Visigothic realm in Hispania survived at all at this time of military crisis was thanks to the intervention of the Ostrogothic king of Italy, Theoderic the Great (493–526), who halted the Frankish and Burgundian advance and brought the remaining Visigothic dominions in Hispania and Septimania (the area around Narbonne and Carcassonne) under his overlordship. When his grandson and successor in the Visigothic lands, Amalaric (526–31), born of the marriage of Theoderic's daughter to Alaric II of the Visigoths (484–507), was defeated by the Franks and murdered in 531, the old Visigothic royal dynasty, which had held power almost without interruption since the late fourth century, came to an end. In 541, Frankish armies crossed the Pyrenees, captured Pamplona and subjected Zaragoza to siege. It was only thanks to determined resistance by Amalaric's successor, Theudis (531–48), an Ostrogothic general who had previously administered the Visigothic territories on Theoderic's behalf, that the Frankish advance was halted.

The transition from Imperial to Visigothic rule did not result in the wholesale destruction of Roman civilization in the peninsula. On the contrary, the Visigoths were firm admirers of Roman ways, so much so that it has been said that the kingdom they founded in Hispania was in effect 'Roman Spain under changed management'. The fact that the newcomers adopted the Latin language and the Christian religion (albeit of the non-Catholic Arian form), issued a coinage inspired by imperial models, and admired the literary and intellectual heritage of antiquity is proof enough of the enthusiasm with which the Visigothic rulers embraced the Roman legacy. Visigothic government also owed much to imperial precedent: the structures of Roman provincial administration were in large part preserved, as were the mechanisms of fiscal organization; some of the Hispano-Roman officials who had served the previous regime remained in post; and sets of laws were promulgated (such as the *Breviary of Alaric* of 506) which were closely based upon Roman codes. In some areas, moreover, local infrastructure was maintained. At Mérida, an inscription records that in 483, during the reign of King Euric, the Roman bridge over the Guadiana was repaired by command of the Visigothic official Count Salla and the local bishop, Zeno. For the most part, however, the physical contraction of urban centres and the gradual abandonment of Roman public buildings, which had already begun during the period of the late Empire, continued unchecked. At Tarragona, the lower town was all but abandoned during the late fifth and sixth centuries and the old forum used as a quarry. Yet, even as Roman buildings were allowed to fall into decay, new structures were being erected. During the second half of the sixth century, for example, the bishops of Mérida promoted the construction of a number of ecclesiastical and charitable buildings within that city. For his part, King Leovigild (569–86) revived the Roman urban tradition by founding two new towns: one at Reccopolis (near Zorita de los Canes to the east of Madrid) in 578, which, according to the bishop of Gerona and contemporary chronicler John of Biclaro, 'he endowed with splendid buildings, both within the walls and in the suburbs'; the other at Victoriacum (probably modern Olite) in Navarre in 581.

The economic horizons of Visigothic Hispania were markedly more circumscribed than they had been under Roman rule. Although the commercial ties which bound the peninsula to the rest of the Mediterranean were not entirely sundered after the fall of the Western Empire, the disruption and fragmentation of the former imperial trading network undoubtedly caused the already diminishing volume of trade to decline yet further. The mines, which had lured the Romans to the peninsula in the first place, experienced a marked slump in production, and the celebrated *garum* factories of southern Spain closed down altogether. What little is known of the organization of rural society under the Visigoths suggests a similar process of continuity and change. The disengagement of the Hispano-Roman élite from urban life and the progressive ruralization of the economy, which was under way well before the arrival of Visigoths, continued unabated. Some villas that had been built during the period of the Late Empire were abandoned or destroyed during the fifth century invasions, but many others continued to function much as before, and yet others, such as the substantial Visigothic residence at Pla de Nadal near Valencia, were built from scratch. Agricultural techniques remained largely unchanged, but the dislocation of the lucrative imperial export markets meant that villa estates, still worked by slaves and serfs, began to contract and became largely geared towards self-sufficiency. Some of these great estates remained in the hands of the still powerful Hispano-Roman aristocracy; many others were appropriated by the monarchy or by the secular and ecclesiastical magnates among the Visigothic élite. A number of landowners erected churches and monasteries on their rural estates, some of which survive to this day, such as that of San Juan de Baños near Palencia, which was founded by King Reccesuinth (649–72) in 661.

The Hispano-Gothic magnates stood at the apex of Visigothic society. The ruling monarch, lacking a standing army, relied upon the contingents of troops provided by such magnates to wage war on his enemies. The king also looked to the great nobles to serve in his household and advise him on matters of state, and he entrusted them with the governorship of towns and provinces throughout the realm. At a local level, the growing power and independence of the landowning class was reflected in various ways. Some estate owners appropriated the right to levy taxation and carry out judicial functions on their own lands; others began to fortify their rural residences and raise private armed retinues. The Ostrogoth Theudis, who married a wealthy Hispano-Roman heiress in the early sixth century, is reported to have commanded a personal militia of some 2000 men. At the same time, a growing sense of insecurity, exacerbated by rural lawlessness and regular outbreaks of plague, drought and famine, prompted many free peasant families to place themselves and their lands under the protection of these local lords, as a result of which further swathes of the countryside passed into the hands of the already powerful secular and ecclesiastical magnates.

The middle of the sixth century was marked by endemic political instability, as rival factions among the Visigothic nobility competed for the throne. Theudis was murdered in 548 and his successor, the general Theudisclus (548–9), met the same fate after only 18 months, an event that prompted Bishop Gregory of Tours (d. 594) to observe acidly that 'the Goths had adopted the detestable custom of killing with the sword any of their kings who displeased them, and of replacing him on the throne by someone whom they preferred'. The death of Theudisclus marked the end of the Ostrogothic protectorate in the peninsula. In 551, a bloody struggle for supremacy erupted between the reigning king Agila (549–54) and the nobleman Athanagild, who had raised the flag of rebellion in Seville. Agila was murdered by his own followers in Mérida in 554, which allowed Athanagild (554–68) to seize the throne, but not before a Byzantine expeditionary force which had been sent to assist him had brought a narrow enclave of territory, stretching along the Mediterranean coast from Medina Sidonia near Cádiz to Cartagena, under the authority of the emperor Justinian. At the same time, political infighting at the centre of the kingdom encouraged some notables in the localities to repudiate Visigothic royal authority. In the south, for example, Córdoba rebelled against King Agila in 550 and managed to survive as an independent city-state for a further 22 years;

in the north, the emergence of a number of local autonomies is recorded, such as the 'senate' of landowners which asserted its independence in Cantabria.

It was not until the second half of the sixth century that the Visigothic monarchy in Iberia became established on a firmer footing. The principal architect of this achievement was King Leovigild, who during the course of the 570s and 580s waged relentless war on what John of Biclaro called 'the usurpers and despoilers of Spain'. Victories over the Byzantines in 570 and 571, which led to the recapture of Málaga and Medina Sidonia respectively, were followed by a series of successful campaigns to subdue the rebellious localities, including Córdoba, which was brought to heel in 572. In 579, Leovigild had to confront an armed revolt in Baetica led by his own son Hermenegild, who with Byzantine support remained defiant for over four years. However, Hermenegild surrendered in 584 and was murdered the following year. Shortly afterwards, Leovigild defeated the Sueves and subjugated their kingdom for good. When Leovigild died in 586, he held sway over most of the peninsula, with the exception of the small Byzantine enclave in southern Spain. The latter was to be gradually eroded by Leovigild's successors on the throne, until it was extinguished by King Suinthila (621–31) in 624.

Military operations apart, Leovigild introduced a number of other measures designed to reinforce the authority of the monarchy. Toledo, strategically situated at the centre of the peninsula, which Athanagild had already chosen as his capital, was confirmed as the political and religious centre of the Visigothic realm, and would remain so until the early eighth century. Leovigild also sought to enhance his own prestige by adopting many of the trappings of monarchy, including royal regalia and ceremonial inspired by Byzantine custom, and by issuing coinage that was no longer a pale imitation of late Roman and Byzantine styles, but proudly bore his own name, title and image. The decision to found new towns at Reccopolis and Victoriacum and, perhaps, to issue a new law-code, were also clear echoes of imperial practice. Is it not conceivable that by vigorously asserting his authority in this manner Leovigild was seeking to create his very own 'Byzantium' in the peninsula?

Leovigild's quest for political unity was matched by a desire to bring about religious uniformity within his kingdom. The Visigothic ruling élite were adherents of Arianism – a Christian heresy which believed that Christ was subordinate to God the Father – and were thus

at odds with the Catholicism of the majority Hispano-Roman population. The Sueves, it may be noted in passing, had already renounced
Arianism and converted to Catholicism under the influence of Bishop
Martin of Braga *c*.560. However, Leovigild's attempts to broker a
doctrinal settlement between the rival Arian and Catholic Churches, at
a council held in Toledo in 580, or even to bribe or cajole Catholic
bishops into the Arian fold, met with only limited success. During the
course of the sixth century, it appears that significant numbers of
Goths had already begun to abandon the Arian Church. One who did
so was Leovigild's own son Hermenegild, although whether the latter's
conversion to Catholicism was the inspiration for his decision to rebel
against his father in 579, or rather was subsequent to it, remains uncertain. Pope Gregory the Great was to declare Hermenegild a martyr to
the Catholic cause, but this view was not shared by contemporaries
such as John of Biclaro or Bishop Isidore of Seville, for whom the
rebellion of 579 was an unwelcome threat to the political stability of
the realm. In the event, the religious question was subsequently
resolved by Leovigild's son and successor Reccared I (586–601), who,
under the guidance of Bishop Leander of Seville, embraced
Catholicism in 587 and formally proclaimed the conversion of the
entire Visigothic kingdom to the faith at the Third Council of Toledo
in May 589. The transition from Arianism to Catholicism was not
universally welcomed: Reccared had to confront no fewer than four
separate rebellions led by Arian bishops and their supporters among
the Visigothic nobility. But, deprived of royal support, theirs was a lost
cause: when the last of these insurrections was crushed in 590, all
support for Arianism swiftly evaporated.

For John of Biclaro, Reccared's decision to embrace Catholicism,
which 'restored all the people of the Goths and the Sueves to the unity
and peace of the Christian Church', marked a watershed in the history of
the peninsula. Thereafter, Church and monarchy would act together in
close mutual support. During the last quarter of the sixth century, the see
of Seville, through its influential bishops Leander and his brother
Isidore, was the dominant force in the government of the realm; on
Isidore's death in 636, the bishops of Toledo came to the fore. At a series
of ecclesiastical councils held in Toledo during the seventh century, the
bishops of that city promoted a number of measures designed to enhance
the authority of the monarchy, bring about uniformity in ecclesiastical
organization and liturgy, and bolster their own supremacy over the other
bishops of the Visigothic Church. The bishops also strove to consolidate

the position of Toledo as the ceremonial centre of the kingdom and they bound the monarchy ever-more closely to themselves by devising a series of inauguration rituals, such as unction, which they alone could administer.

The growing authority and influence of the ecclesiastical élite was matched by an intellectual activity unparalleled anywhere in the Latin West. Many Iberian bishops maintained close links with the Byzantine Empire and with the North African Church, and were thus fully integrated into the cultural mainstream of the Mediterranean world. Churchmen were not only responsible for a number of distinguished liturgical and scriptural compositions, but for works of hagiography, polemic, grammar, poetry and history. Roman culture was far from forgotten, but the literary output of the luminaries of the Visigothic Church – men of the calibre of Fructuosus of Braga, Braulio of Zaragoza, Eugenius, Ildefonsus and Julian of Toledo, and Valerio of the Bierzo – owed far more to the example of the Church Fathers than to the pagan writers of the Roman Golden and Silver Ages. The most illustrious of them all was Isidore of Seville, 'the glory of Spain, the pillar of the Church', in the words of Braulio. Isidore's vast literary output included two histories of the Goths, a biographical study of 46 popes, bishops and authors, various exegetical writings and his encyclopaedic *Etymologies* which, in 20 books, summarized the learning of antiquity and was to enjoy widespread readership in literary circles across Europe. Yet, intellectual pursuits were not the exclusive preserve of the clergy. King Sisebut (611/12–19), who was rather guardedly described by Isidore of Seville as 'imbued with some knowledge of letters', may have composed a *Life* of St Desiderius of Vienne, and both he and King Chintila (636–9) were accomplished poets in their own right.

For all the determination with which the Visigothic monarchs sought to preserve the unity of their kingdom, their own grip on power was sometimes fragile. Between the death of Reccared in 601 and the demise of the Visigothic state a little over a century later, no fewer than 16 monarchs occupied the throne. Some, like Leovigild, Sisenand (631–6), Chindasuinth (642–53) and Egica (687–702), ensured a smooth succession by enthroning their sons as co-rulers during their own lifetimes. But the hereditary principle did not take root. Gundemar (610–11/12), Sisebut, Suinthila, Wamba (672–80) and Ervig (680–7) were all elected to the throne by the palatine magnates; Witteric (603–10), Sisenand and Chindasuinth seized power by force.

Weak or incompetent rulers, such as those who were unable to provide effective military leadership, were particularly vulnerable to deposition by aristocratic factions. The Fourth Council of Toledo, held at the behest of Sisenand in 633, sought to protect the king from revolt by threatening would-be usurpers with excommunication and by establishing that henceforward his successor should be elected by the bishops and lay magnates of the realm. These provisions were further refined at the councils held in Toledo in 636 and 638. In practice, however, the ecclesiastical authorities were usually pragmatic enough to offer their support to whomever came to occupy the throne: the overthrow of the established ruler was regarded in itself as an act of divine will and conferred legitimacy on the usurper.

Chindasuinth and his son Reccesuinth are chiefly remembered for their legislative achievements. The *Liber Iudicorum,* or 'Book of the Judges', which was begun by Chindasuinth and completed and promulgated by Reccesuinth in 654, was the culmination of a tradition of law-giving by the Visigothic monarchy that went back to the late fifth century. Divided into 12 books and comprising a relatively comprehensive collection of criminal, civil and commercial legal procedures, the *Liber* was the largest and most ambitious of any the law-codes issued by the 'barbarian' successor states to the Western Roman Empire, and its provisions would remain in use in much of the peninsula until the thirteenth century. The *Liber* was applicable to every citizen in the land, whether of Hispano-Roman or Germanic origin, although it is likely that any legal differentiation between the two communities had already long since disappeared. Intermarriage between the Gothic and Roman élites, formally outlawed until the time of Leovigild, was probably already common practice by the sixth century. The assimilation of the Hispano-Roman aristocracy into the political, military and administrative structures of the kingdom, not to mention the disappearance of the Catholic-Arian divide, helped speed the process of inter-ethnic integration. By the end of the seventh century, all could regard themselves as members of a common Gothic nation, regardless of their origins.

The development of a common sense of Gothic identity among the Christian peoples of the peninsula occurred at a time when the minority Jewish population was becoming the target of sustained persecution. Jews had probably begun to settle in the peninsula during the first century AD, although we know remarkably little about the communities they established. The repression of the Jews from the late sixth century onwards was prompted by the determination of the Visigothic authorities to uphold religious orthodoxy within the kingdom, and took place against a backdrop of rising anti-Jewish feeling within the Mediterranean world as a whole. In 613, King Sisebut issued a decree which obliged all the Jews in his realm to convert to Christianity, on pain of exile and confiscation of property. This draconian policy was to be the subject of criticism at the Fourth Council of Toledo in 633, but further measures designed to undermine the legal and social standing of Jews were issued at this and later councils. Under King Reccesuinth, Jewish religious customs, such as marriage ceremonies and dietary laws, were proscribed; Jews were also debarred from initiating legal proceedings against Christians, and Jewish converts to Christianity were subjected to supervision. In 694, King Egica accused the Jews of conspiring to overthrow him and ordered that the entire Jewish population be reduced to slavery and their property confiscated. Whether these legal measures were ever fully enacted is very much a moot point. At the beginning of the eighth century, despite the raft of decrees that had gone before, the Jewish communities in the peninsula had far from disappeared.

THE 'RUIN OF SPAIN'

Writing *c*.625, Bishop Isidore of Seville prefaced his *History of the Kings of the Goths* with this extravagant paean of praise to his homeland:

Of all the lands from the west to the Indies, you Spain, O sacred and always fortunate mother of princes and peoples, are the most beautiful . . . You are the pride and ornament of the world, the most illustrious part of the Earth, in which the Gothic people are gloriously prolific, rejoicing much and flourishing greatly. Indulgent nature has deservedly enriched you with an abundance of everything fruitful . . . Rightly did golden Rome, the head of the nations, desire you long ago . . . Now it is the most flourishing people of the Goths, who in their turn, after many victories all over the world, have eagerly seized you and loved you: they enjoy you up to the present time amidst royal emblems and great wealth, secure in the good fortune of empire.

Isidore's confidence in the security of the Visigothic kingdom was to prove misplaced, however. In 711, a Berber expeditionary force led by the Muslim governor of Tangier, Ṭāriq b. Ziyād, crossed the Straits to southern Spain. Christian and Muslim accounts of the invasion are at variance as to what precisely happened next. According to the latter, having disembarked at the rocky promontory which still bears Ṭāriq's name, *Jabal Ṭāriq*, or Gibraltar, the invaders moved inland and in July 711 inflicted a decisive defeat on a Visigothic army led by King Roderic (710–11/12). By contrast, a near-contemporary Christian source, conventionally known as the *Chronicle of 754*, relates that a number of clashes between local forces and the Muslims occurred, before Roderic was finally defeated and killed in the 'Transductine mountains', perhaps in the vicinity of Medina Sidonia, in 712. Having defeated Roderic, the Muslim armies went on to occupy Córdoba and the capital, Toledo. The Toledan clergy are reported to have fled the capital with the valuables of their churches, which probably included the jewel-encrusted gold liturgical crown presented by King Reccesuinth, which was unearthed along with other fabulous treasures at Guarrazar near Toledo in 1849.

Encouraged by Ṭāriq's success, in 711 or the following year (depending upon which version of events we follow), the Arab governor of *Ifrīqīya* (North Africa), Mūsā b. Nuṣayr, crossed the Straits with substantial reinforcements. He captured Seville and Mérida, then advanced north-east via Toledo, subdued Zaragoza with great bloodshed, and brought the entire Ebro valley under his authority. When Mūsā was recalled to Damascus by the Umayyad caliph, late in 712 or the following year, his son, 'Abd al-'Azīz, was entrusted with the governorship of the region and the task of reducing the remaining strongholds of Christian power. By 720, almost the whole of the peninsula, with the exception of the most mountainous districts of the western and central Pyrenees, had been brought under Islamic authority. This Muslim territory in Iberia would henceforth be known as al-Andalus. Córdoba, which lay at the hub of a number of important lines of communication, was established as the centre of government.

The Muslim invasion of the Iberian peninsula was the logical extension of a spectacular movement of conquest and expansion, which in the space of barely a century, after the death of the prophet Muḥammad in 632, led to the creation of a vast Islamic empire – stretching from the Atlantic seaboard and the Pyrenees in the west, as far as Central Asia and the Punjab in the east – under the supreme authority of the Umayyad caliph in Damascus. During the second half of the seventh century, the Arab campaigns to subdue the Berber heartlands of the Maghreb, and the Byzantine garrisons that still clung on to coastal enclaves like Tripoli and Carthage, had proved long and difficult. Once subdued, however, many of the conquered Berber tribes had converted to Islam and were recruited into the Arab-led armies which overran the western Maghreb between *c*.680 and 710. Once the Muslims had reached Tangier in 703, it was not surprising that they should have turned their attention to the rich lands of the peninsula to the north.

To contemporaries and to subsequent generations, the sudden demise of the Visigothic kingdom in Hispania was a traumatic and deeply puzzling event. The Toledan author of the *Chronicle of 754* gave vent to his anguish in this way:

Who can bear to relate such perils? Who can count such terrible disasters? Even if every limb were transformed into a tongue, it would be beyond human capability to describe the ruin of Spain and its many and great evils.

Christian writers were quick to portray the sudden collapse of the Visigothic state as an act of divine punishment for the sins of her rulers and people. The Anglo-Saxon missionary Boniface, writing in 746–7, attributed the defeat to the gross moral turpitude of the Visigoths; a late ninth-century Asturian chronicler pointed the finger of blame at the womanizing King Wittiza (702–10), whom he accused of having compelled the local clergy to marry. Muslim writers found fault with King Roderic, who had reputedly seduced the daughter of the governor of Ceuta, Count Julian. The count, in an act of calculated revenge, so the story went, had conspired to bring about the overthrow of Roderic by ferrying the Muslim army across the Straits into Spain.

Such moralizing perspectives find little favour with historians today. The fact that the Visigothic monarchy was overthrown with such apparent ease, was not because its ruling class was in any way 'decadent', nor because its fall was pre-ordained. It is true, however, that when Ṭāriq crossed the Straits in 711, he encountered a kingdom riven by political divisions. On the death of King Wittiza in 710, the succession had been disputed between Achila (710–13) and the supporters of Roderic. Roderic was elected king by a section of the Visigothic aristocracy and established himself in Toledo, but Achila won support in the north-east of the peninsula and in Septimania. Roderic's ability to stand up to the Muslim invasion of 711 was probably severely compromised by the need to campaign against both Achila and the Basque tribes at roughly the same time. There are also reports that a number of leading magnates defected from Roderic's camp, while a grievous shortage of fighting men appears have undermined the ability of the major cities to mount any effective resistance to Muslim attack. Parallels are often drawn between the sudden demise of the Visigothic kingdom and the equally dramatic fall of Anglo-Saxon England to the Normans in 1066. The defeat and death of Roderic, the decimation of his military entourage and the palatine aristocracy, and the fall of the capital, Toledo, all in quick succession, caused paralysis at the heart of the Visigothic government and left what remained of the ruling élite without the will or the means to co-ordinate further resistance.

With their king dead and no clear successor at hand, some members of the Visigothic hierarchy fled across the Pyrenees. Bishop Sindered of Toledo, 'like a hireling rather than a shepherd', in the barbed words of the *Chronicle of 754*, abandoned his flock altogether and travelled to Rome. Other magnates sought refuge in the remote mountainous regions in the north of the peninsula; yet others were executed outright. The landed estates of those who fled or resisted were seized and distributed among the army of conquest which began to settle in the new lands. Yet, a significant number of Visigothic notables sought to preserve their power and status by speedily coming to terms with the Muslims. One such man was Theodemir (d. 744), lord of Orihuela, Alicante and a handful of other towns in south-east Spain, who on 5 April 713 agreed a treaty with 'Abd al-'Azīz. The communities under Theodemir's rule were guaranteed their safety and freedom of worship, in return for a pledge of loyalty and an annual tribute of one dinar per head and quantities of wheat, barley, grape juice, vinegar, honey and oil. Similar terms were probably offered and accepted elsewhere. However, it is unlikely that these Christian enclaves retained their autonomous status for long: part of the territory ruled by Theodemir and his son Athanagild, for example, may have been allotted to newly arrived Syrian soldiers in 744. Some leading Visigothic families later became *muwallad*s, or converts to Islam, such as the Banū Qasī dynasty of Tudela in the Upper Ebro valley, and the Banū 'Amrūs of Huesca, who came to prominence at the end of the eighth century and were to hold sway in these areas for some time to come. The pacification of the peninsula was further eased by intermarriage between the Muslim conquerors and leading members of the Visigothic aristocracy: thus, 'Abd al-'Azīz took as his wife King Roderic's widow, Egilona.

Agreements such as these enabled the Muslims to concentrate their military forces where they were most needed. In 720, the last Visigothic positions in Catalonia and Septimania were overrun, and Muslim armies began to conduct a series of plundering raids deep into southern France. In 725, Carcassonne was captured and raiding parties penetrated as far east as Autun in Burgundy. However, further territorial expansion north of the Pyrenees was severely constrained by a shortage of manpower and the need to attend to the administration of the newly conquered territories in al-Andalus. The defeat by Charles Martel of the Franks near Poitiers, probably in late 733, did not spell the immediate death-knell for Muslim ambitions in France, as is often supposed, but it is certainly the case that the Islamic presence in Septimania came under increasing pressure from the Franks thereafter, until Narbonne, their last foothold north of the Pyrenees, was finally relinquished in 759.

AL-ANDALUS

The beginnings of Islamic rule in the peninsula were far from auspicious. It is reported that the governor 'Abd al-'Azīz, acting on the advice of Queen Egilona, began to wear a crown in imitation of Visigothic practice and attempted to set himself up as the ruler of an independent al-Andalus. However, in 715 'Abd al-'Azīz was assassinated by his followers in Seville, perhaps with the connivance of the caliph. During the next 40 years, al-Andalus was to be ruled by a succession of *wali*, or governors, most of whom were directly appointed by the governors of *Ifrīqīya*, and all of whom ultimately owed allegiance to the Umayyad caliph in Damascus. To guard against further secessionist plots, these governors were rarely retained in post for more than one or two years. At a local level, a number of *qāḍī*s, or judges, attended to the fiscal and military administration of the districts under their command. Yet, although the caliph was remembered in the Friday sermon in the mosque and his name appeared on the coins that were issued under his authority, the lines of communication between Damascus and Córdoba were so long that in practice he wielded only limited influence over peninsular affairs. The Muslim settlers of al-Andalus were determined not to relinquish their hold on the spoils of conquest, to the extent that it is debatable whether the one-fifth share of booty, to which the caliph was traditionally entitled, was ever sent to Damascus at all.

The Islamic invaders were a far from united or homogenous force. In the aftermath of the conquest, Muslim settlement in the peninsula occurred largely along tribal or ethnic lines. The Arab minority settled chiefly in the major towns, such as Córdoba, Seville and Zaragoza, and in the rich agricultural lands of the Guadalquivir valley, Murcia and the middle Ebro; the Berber tribes, who made up the bulk of the army of conquest, were established in the pasture lands of the central *meseta* and Extremadura, and there were other important concentrations of Berber population in the hill country of Andalusia and Valencia. Subsequent friction between Berber and Arab was caused less by any perceived imbalance in the division of spoils after the conquest, than by a sense among Berber ranks – both in the peninsula and in the Maghreb – that they had been reduced to subordinate status within Islamic society. Wealth and power in most of al-Andalus was the preserve of an Arab élite of landowners, military governors and civil administrators; most of the Berbers, it has been said, constituted a 'rural proletariat', or else found humble employment as artisans in the towns of al-Andalus. In 740, the Berbers of the Maghreb, incensed by the decision of the Arab authorities to levy the *kharāj*, or land tax, upon them, when as fellow believers they should have been exempt, rebelled against Umayyad rule. The following year, the revolt spread to the peninsula and the Berber garrisons began to evacuate the territories they had earlier occupied in the northernmost regions of Galicia, Asturias and the northern *meseta* and advanced on Córdoba. The caliph Hishām (724–43) dispatched an army of Syrian troops to the Maghreb to restore order, but these forces were heavily defeated by the Berbers of northern Morocco. In 742, the remnants of the vanquished Syrian army crossed to al-Andalus to help the governor 'Abd al-Malik b. Qaṭan pacify the rebellious Berber tribes. The Berbers were soon subdued, but the Syrian newcomers, who were organized in military units called *jund*s, then refused to leave and were eventually allowed to settle in the south of the peninsula, in return for which they were required to render military service to the governor.

The consequences of the upheaval of 741–2 were widely felt. First, the arrival of the Syrians exacerbated the inter-ethnic tensions and resentments that already festered within Andalusi society. While most of the original Arab settlers were descended from the Yemeni confederation of tribes, the Syrian newcomers belonged to that of their arch-rivals of longstanding, the Qaysis. Conflict between the two major Arab factions broke out immediately in 742 and would become a prominent feature of Andalusi politics for generations to come. Second, the Berber uprising led to the evacuation of the Muslim garrisons that had been established north of the Duero and allowed the Christians of Asturias, who in 718 or 722 had rebelled against Islamic rule, to consolidate their independence. The movement of the Berbers southwards accelerated after 750, as a period of prolonged drought and famine devastated the Duero valley. They left behind a vast swathe of lightly populated territory which thereafter would act as a buffer zone between the emerging states of the Christian north and al-Andalus. Although Muslim armies would return to raid the Christian principalities at regular intervals in the future, there would be no attempt to reconquer the far north of the peninsula.

THE UMAYYAD EMIRATE

Since 661, the Umayyad caliphate had enjoyed supreme authority over the entire Islamic world. However, this supremacy was soon to be challenged by those who believed that the caliphate rightly belonged to the descendants of the Prophet Muḥammad and who resented the dominance of ethnic Arabs in the Umayyad state. In 750, the Umayyads and their Syrian supporters were overthrown by a rival dynasty, the 'Abbasids, who in 762 moved the centre of the Islamic empire from Damascus to Baghdad. In an attempt to reinforce the authority of his dynasty, the first 'Abbasid caliph, al-Saffāḥ (749–54), conducted a brutal political purge of his enemies, in the course of which most of the leading members of the Umayyad ruling family were executed. Among the few to survive the blood-bath was a grandson of the former caliph Hishām, 'Abd al-Raḥmān, who took refuge in the Maghreb and then crossed to al-Andalus in 755. Thanks to his ability to attract support among the Yemenis and other ethnic groups, 'Abd al-Raḥmān seized Córdoba, refused allegiance to the 'Abbasids and proclaimed himself emir, or prince, of an independent al-Andalus in July 756.

From his power-base in the Guadalquivir valley, 'Abd al-Raḥmān I (756–88) gradually extended his authority over the southern and central districts of the peninsula. However, Umayyad pretensions to rule throughout al-Andalus were to be fiercely resisted and 'Abd al-Raḥmān had to face numerous challenges to his power, some of them orchestrated by agents of the 'Abbasid caliphate. The emir and his successors had particular difficulty imposing their writ over the largely autonomous frontier territories known collectively as the *thughūr*, or 'front teeth' of al-Andalus: the Lower March, based on Mérida; the Middle March, whose centre was Toledo; and the Upper March in the Ebro valley, whose capital was Zaragoza. In these regions, power lay chiefly with the Berber tribes, with prominent local Arab families, and with *muwallad* notables of Visigothic descent. Not only was friction and conflict between these ethnic groups commonplace, but all of them vigorously resisted any attempt by the Umayyads to bend them to their will. In this way, inter-ethnic rivalries and tribal divisions helped to fuel the intense spirit of local autonomy which had been such a feature of peninsular society since the end of the Roman Empire. A strong and charismatic emir might temporarily override local separatism of this sort by subtle diplomacy and force of arms, but Andalusi society remained markedly fissile. The reign of 'Abd al-Raḥmān's grandson, al-Ḥakam I (796–822), was particularly troubled in this regard. There were rebellions in Zaragoza, Toledo and Mérida, and the emir also had to face two serious challenges to his rule in Córdoba itself: a conspiracy hatched by leading members of the local Arab élite, which was defused in 805; and a major uprising in the southern suburb of the city, which was suppressed with considerable brutality in 818.

The long reign of al-Ḥakam's son, 'Abd al-Raḥmān II (822–52), saw the Umayyad emirate begin to consolidate its grip on power. The increased financial solvency of the Umayyad state, made possible by efficiencies in tax collection, allowed the emir to expand the bodyguard of mercenaries, some of whom were *ṣaqāliba* (slaves of Slavonic or Northern European origin), which had first been established by al-Ḥakam I, and to fund a state bureaucracy. The latter, under the overall responsibility of the *ḥājib*, or chief minister, was subdivided into departments of finance, justice, foreign relations and administration of the marches, each under the control of a *wazīr*, or vizier. The court was closely modelled on that of the 'Abbasid caliphs of Baghdad and the emir himself became an increasingly remote and inaccessible figure. On the political front, the emir demonstrated his readiness to defend the frontiers of al-Andalus: the Christian principalities of the north were subjected to a number of attacks, and a Viking raiding-party which sacked Seville in 844 was repelled. 'Abd al-Raḥmān's reign also witnessed a more determined effort by the emirate to assert its authority over the quasi-autonomous marcher territories. Governors and garrisons loyal to the Umayyad regime were installed in Mérida, Toledo and Zaragoza, but the hinterland of these cities remained firmly under the control of local chiefs. In the Upper March, for example, the *muwallad* Banū Qasī, who had established close ties with the Christian kingdom of Pamplona, remained in effective control of the Ebro valley under their leader, the self-styled 'third king of Spain', Mūsā b. Mūsā (d. 862).

The fragile nature of Umayyad control over the provinces was graphically demonstrated during the second half of the ninth century. In the Middle March, the Toledans repudiated the authority of the emir Muḥammad I (852–86), after his accession to the throne, and were to remain largely independent of Umayyad control until the early tenth century. In the Upper March, the Banū Qasī continued to alternate between rebellion and submission, until they were finally displaced from power by a rival family, the Tujībīds, in 907. And in the Lower March, the *muwallad* Ibn Marwān rebelled against the emir in 868 and again in 874/5, and with the assistance of King Alfonso III (866–910) of Asturias established an autonomous principality based upon the newly founded settlement of Badajoz, which was to remain under the control of Ibn Marwān's family until 930. By far the most serious threat to Umayyad authority, however, was the rebellion led by another renegade *muwallad*, 'Umar ibn Hafṣūn, who was able to maintain an independent principality, based upon his strongpoint at Bobastro near Málaga, under the very noses of the emirs of Córdoba, between 881 and his death in 917. During the reign of the emir 'Abd Allāh (888–912), centralized Umayyad power began to evaporate. In much of al-Andalus, local potentates raised themselves up as semi-independent princes and began to fortify their residences, levy taxation and raise private armies; inter-ethnic disputes between Arabs, Berbers and *muwallad*s flared up in numerous places; and the increasingly dangerous Ibn Hafṣūn, whose authority was by now recognized by *muwallad* elements across much of southern Iberia, raided the area around Córdoba itself in 891.

The emergence of an Islamic society in al-Andalus was a slow and uneven process. The Berber and Arab soldiers who carried out the conquest and began the process of land redistribution among their ranks constituted only a very small minority of the population of the peninsula as a whole. The majority Christian population and the Jews were regarded by Islamic law as *dhimmīs*, or 'Peoples of the Book', and were therefore guaranteed free practice of their faith. In return, *dhimmīs* were required to pay an annual poll-tax (*jizya*) to the Muslim authorities and curbs were also placed on church building and on intrusive religious practices such as processions, chanting or bell ringing, although these do not appear to have been strictly enforced. Although the subordinate position of *dhimmīs* in Islamic society meant that theoretically they were not able to wield authority over Muslims, in practice a number of Christians and Jews pursued careers in the Cordoban bureaucracy as secretaries, translators and tax collectors. Yet, while no attempt was made to impose Islam upon the conquered, the incentives to convert were not inconsiderable. *Muwallads* were able to integrate themselves more successfully into Muslim society, the opportunities for the acquisition of wealth and power were considerably greater, and the burden of taxation was appreciably lighter. Thus, Gómez b. Antoniān is reported to have converted to Islam early in the reign of Muḥammad I because he wished to become chief secretary to the emir, a post from which *dhimmīs* had hitherto been excluded. The rate of conversion to Islam is impossible to gauge with any accuracy; yet, when the Arab geographer Ibn Ḥawqal visited the peninsula in 948, he observed that Christians still formed the majority of the rural population.

Even if they did not embrace Islam, the Christian communities of al-Andalus became increasingly Arabized, in language as well as custom, as a result of which they are usually known as Mozarabs. The word derives from the Arabic *musta'rib*, meaning 'Arabized', although the term does not appear to have been used by Andalusi Muslims themselves. Cultural assimilation, together with a possible rise in the rate of conversion to Islam by the middle of the ninth century, caused considerable disquiet in some Christian quarters. Writing in 854, Paulus Alvarus of Córdoba lamented the fact that Christian youths seemed to display far more enthusiasm for the language and learning of the Muslims than they did for their own Latin traditions. Discontent may have been further fuelled by the fact that the fiscal burden on the Mozarabic community had increased markedly in the preceding decades. Some disenchanted Mozarabs responded to the progressive Islamicization of al-Andalus by emigrating to the Christian principalities of the north. Another, more radical, group of Christians, most of them drawn from a handful of monasteries around Córdoba, deliberately courted 'martyrdom' at the hands of the Islamic authorities by publicly denouncing Islam or by encouraging *muwallad*s to apostatize, both of which were punishable by death in Islamic law. Between 851 and 859, when the leader of the movement, Bishop Eulogius of Toledo, was himself executed, some 48 Christians, most of them monks and clerics, were put to death. However, the 'martyrdom movement', with its emphasis upon confrontation and self-sacrifice, did not command widespread support among the Christian ecclesiastical hierarchy or the wider Mozarabic community, and after Eulogius's execution it soon subsided.

'THE OTHER SPAINS'

The Muslim armies of the early eighth century may have destroyed the unitary Visigothic kingdom in the peninsula, but they did not extinguish all resistance to the invader. During the eighth and ninth centuries, there emerged a cluster of embryonic Christian principalities in the north of the peninsula which would eventually develop into large and powerful kingdoms, and would ultimately challenge Islam for political supremacy. This long and complex process of conflict and expansion, which was to culminate in the Christian conquest of the last Muslim stronghold in the peninsula, Granada, in 1492, is conventionally known to historians as the *Reconquista*, or Reconquest. The term is in many respects a misnomer, in that it implies a state of permanent animosity and conflict between two rival faiths. In reality, the reconquest of Muslim territory did not always dominate Christian strategic thinking: relations between the Christian states and al-Andalus were by no means consistently hostile and political alliances between the two were commonplace.

Our knowledge of the emergence and expansion of the mountain kingdom of Asturias is almost entirely dependent upon the testimony of two brief Latin chronicles probably begun at the end of the ninth century: the *Chronicle of Albelda* and the *Chronicle of Alfonso III*. They relate that in 718 (or 722), a group of Asturians rose up in revolt under the leadership of one Pelayo – the former sword-bearer of Kings Wittiza and Roderic according to one account, and of royal descent according to another – and defeated and killed the Arab governor of Gijón in battle at Covadonga at the foot of the Picos de Europa mountains. 'From then on', the *Chronicle of Albelda* declared, 'freedom was restored to the Christian people . . . and by divine providence the kingdom of Asturias was born.' For all their differences of detail and emphasis, the message of the Asturian chronicles was clear: the sins of the Visigoths may have allowed the Muslims to invade and triumph, but God had no intention of allowing His people to be vanquished altogether. Asturias was the Visigothic kingdom reborn, not just in spirit, but in personnel, too. However, there is no clear-cut evidence that significant numbers of Visigothic nobles took refuge in Asturias after 711, let alone that Pelayo, their leader, was of royal lineage; equally, although posterity would portray the victory at Covadonga as the first step in the Christian reconquest of the peninsula, contemporaries are unlikely to have regarded it as such.

That the fledgling Asturian monarchy was able to maintain its independence after Pelayo's rebellion, and even to expand its borders thereafter, owed less to the military skill of the insurgents than to the fact that in the immediate aftermath of the Muslim invasion, the governors of al-Andalus preferred to devote most their energies towards military operations in southern Gaul. The Christians were further assisted by the Arab-Berber conflict of the 740s and the devastating famine of the 750s, both of which led the Berber tribes to evacuate the military outposts they had established in the northernmost regions of the peninsula. This breathing-space allowed the Asturian kingdom to survive and thrive. By the marriage of Pelayo's daughter, Ermesinda, to Alfonso, son of Duke Pedro of Cantabria, the region to the east of Asturias was incorporated to the Crown. Under Alfonso I (739–57) and his son Fruela I (757–68), the Asturian kingdom began to extend its authority into neighbouring Galicia and the western Basque regions, and the same monarchs reputedly carried out a number of raids southwards into the Duero valley, during the course of which large numbers of Christians are said to have migrated north. However, another century would then elapse before the territorial expansion of the Asturian kingdom was renewed. There are reports of internal disorder, principally the result of disputed successions to the throne or revolts against the monarchy by dissident nobles. The region was also subjected to regular raids by Muslim armies and by a Viking fleet which attacked the Galician coast in 844.

The outbreak of renewed internal strife within al-Andalus during the second half of the ninth century enabled the Asturian kingdom to begin to expand southwards on to the plains of the *meseta*. The process was begun by Ordoño I (850–66), during whose reign several of the old Roman towns, such as León and Astorga, were resettled, and was continued by his son Alfonso III, who oversaw the repopulation of the Duero valley from Porto in the west to Burgos in the border region of Castile in the east. By the time the court chroniclers of the late ninth century came to write up their accounts of the deeds of the Asturian kings, a triumphalist spirit prevailed, so much so that the author of the so-called *Prophetic Chronicle* of 883/4 could confidently predict that the expulsion of the infidel from the peninsula was just around the corner. As if to underline the self-confidence of the Asturians, when Alfonso III was deposed by his son García I (910–13/14) in 910, the decision was taken to move the chief royal centre of the kingdom from the mountain fastness of Oviedo to the plains of León: thenceforth the rulers of this expanding kingdom were to be styled kings of León.

By proclaiming the political continuity between the Toledo of the Visigothic kings and the Oviedo of Alfonso III, the court chroniclers of the late ninth century sought to establish the legitimate rights of the Asturian kings to rule over the whole of the peninsula. However, political realities on the ground were considerably more complex. At roughly the same time as the inhabitants of Asturias were throwing off the yoke of Muslim domination, other centres of Christian resistance were emerging. In the western Pyrenees, a small independent principality based upon the old Roman town of Pamplona came into being by the second quarter of the ninth century, although its origins are utterly obscure. Like the Asturians and Cantabrians, the Basque tribes had fiercely resisted the centralizing pretensions of the Visigoths, and Muslim and Frankish attempts to impose their own authority over the region met with a similar lack of success. In 740, the Arab governor of Pamplona and his troops were forced to withdraw after a rebellion by its citizens. In 778, the king of the Carolingian Franks, Charles the Great (Charlemagne), captured Pamplona in the course of a military campaign in the Upper Ebro. However, forced to withdraw, the rearguard of his army was subsequently ambushed and annihilated by the Basques as it made its way through the pass of Roncesvalles, a military disaster which was later to be commemorated in the famous French epic poem, the *Chanson de Roland*. In 806, the Franks again captured Pamplona and at the same time established a marcher county in the valley of the River Aragón; however, after a second heavy defeat in 824, Frankish attempts to create a military march in the western Pyrenees were abandoned. In the ensuing power vacuum, there emerged a small, independent kingdom of Pamplona – later to be known as the kingdom of Navarre – under the leadership of a local lord named Iñigo Arista (d. 851), whose dynasty would remain in power until it was overthrown by Sancho Garcés I (905–25) of the rival Jimeno family in 905. It was Sancho Garcés who in 925 brought the area of the Rioja Alta, including Nájera, which became the new royal centre, under his control. The county of Aragon also came under the orbit of the kings of Pamplona and would remain there until it was elevated to the status of an independent kingdom in its own right in 1035.

At the eastern end of the Pyrenees, Frankish military incursions proved rather more successful. Charlemagne's son, Louis of Aquitaine, captured Barcelona in 801 and established a Frankish protectorate over the territory between that city and the Pyrenees, whose boundaries were to remain largely unchanged until the eleventh century. This protectorate, known as the *Marca Hispanica*, or 'Spanish March', was divided up into a number of counties, such as Ausona (Vich), Barcelona, Besalú, Cardona, Cerdanya, Gerona, Pallars, Ribagorza and Urgell, which were placed under the command of royal appointees recruited from the ranks of the Frankish aristocracy. Although the boundaries of the 'Spanish March' barely altered after the conquest of Barcelona in 801, the number of counties within it fluctuated over the succeeding centuries and it was by no means uncommon for a number of the territories to be held under the authority of a single figure. The counties of the march enjoyed considerable autonomy and were frequently in rebellion against the Frankish Crown. When Frankish power subsequently began to wane during the second half of the ninth century, the counties of the Spanish March gradually drifted into independence. By far the most prominent of the independent dynasts who emerged at this time was Wifred I 'the Hairy' (870–97/8), count of Barcelona, Gerona and Ausona, whose descendants would eventually rule over all of the march. Yet, formal political ties with the Frankish Crown were not immediately sundered. The counts of Barcelona and their lay and ecclesiastical magnates continued to date their charters by the regnal years of the Frankish kings, and Catalan monasteries thought it worthwhile to have their charters confirmed by Frankish rulers. It was not until the Carolingian dynasty was finally overthrown by the Capetians in 987 that the polite political fiction that linked the Catalan counties to the Frankish empire was formally brought to an end.

The Christian societies of northern Iberia were neither wealthy nor sophisticated. Their rudimentary economy was based overwhelmingly

on subsistence agriculture and pastoral activities; royal centres such as
Oviedo, León and Pamplona fulfilled important administrative and
ceremonial functions, but they were little more than small fortified
settlements; trade was sluggish and based on barter; and industry was
almost non-existent until the tenth century, when there are the first
signs of small-scale artisan activity in such places as León and Burgos.
The Christian rulers did not have the wherewithal to sustain a professional army or a state bureaucracy and relied upon a small entourage
of warrior nobles and ecclesiastical magnates to defend and administer the realm on their behalf. However, these were expanding societies.
Demographic growth in the north, accompanied by the arrival of
Mozarabic immigrants from the south, prompted the Asturian kingdom to expand on to the plains of León in the ninth century. A slow,
piecemeal movement of colonization ensued, as small groups of peasants began to establish themselves in the numerous river valleys that
cross the northern *meseta*, until they had reached the banks of the
Duero by the beginning of the tenth. It was a similar story in the region
of the 'Spanish March', which was extensively repopulated by settlers
from the Pyrenean area and by Mozarabic immigrants from al-Andalus
during the course of the ninth and tenth centuries.

The emigration of Mozarabs from the south appears to have begun
during the late eighth century; however, the movement of population
accelerated during the second half of the ninth, during the turbulent
reign of 'Abd Allāh, and reached a peak during the early decades of the
tenth. It was chiefly through the agency of the Mozarabs that the
cultural traditions of the Visigoths began to take firm root in the
Christian north. Alfonso II of Asturias (791–842) is reported to have
established 'the ceremonial of Gothic rule as it had been in Toledo,
both in church and palace alike', in his chief royal centre, Oviedo.
Mozarabic monks established new communities in the Christian
realms or took up residence at existing monastic houses: for example,
the monastery of Samos, near Lugo, in Galicia, was entrusted to the
care of two monks from al-Andalus by King Ordoño I of Asturias in
857. These monks brought with them their own distinctive artistic
traditions which were very different from those then in vogue in
Asturias. They can be seen in the various 'Mozarabic' monastic
churches – whose horseshoe arches, slender columns and small
double-arched windows are reminiscent of Islamic architectural styles
– which were erected in the territory of León during the early decades
of the tenth century, such as those of San Miguel de la Escalada

(founded 913), San Cebrián de Mazote (*c*.915) and Santiago de Peñalba (*c*.937); they can also be seen in the 'Mozarabic' manuscript illuminations, characterized by abstract bidimensional drawing and striking use of colour, which embellish the various tenth- and eleventh-century copies of the Scriptures and the monk Beatus's *Commentary on the Apocalypse* of *c*.786. At a more prosaic level, Mozarab immigrants were probably responsible for introducing the irrigation techniques of the Muslim world to the north of the peninsula, with the result that the Christian settlers who occupied the Duero basin were able to bring far larger areas of land under the plough and to increase agricultural yields.

Kings and counts were enthusiastic patrons of the Church, founding or endowing monasteries and commissioning elaborate altar goods, such as the bejewelled 'Cross of the Angels' which was presented to the church of Oviedo by Alfonso II in 808. Alfonso also demonstrated his support for the emerging cult of St James, whose supposed body was discovered by Theodemir, bishop of Iria Flavia, some time between 818 and 842 in the place that came to be known as Santiago de Compostela.

Literate culture in the Christian north was overwhelmingly the preserve of clerics and monks. In the north-west of the peninsula, monasteries like those of Samos in Galicia, Sahagún near León and San Millán in the Rioja acted as repositories of the learning of the Visigothic age; they seem to have had only limited contact with intellectual currents further afield and made little by way of original contribution to intellectual culture. By far and away the most important area of cultural activity in the Christian north was the Spanish March, whose monasteries and churches were exposed to the cultural influences of both the Carolingian world and al-Andalus. Catalan monasteries adopted the *Rule of St Benedict*, rather than the Visigothic *Rule of St Fructuosus* which still predominated further to the west, and the Roman rite displaced the traditional Visigothic liturgy. Chief among the monasteries of the march was that of Ripoll, founded by Wifred the Hairy in 880, which became one of the most distinguished centres of learning in Western Europe. Its well-stocked library, which included collections of works by classical authors, as well as Arabic mathematical and astronomical treatises, attracted scholars from beyond the Pyrenees, such as the monk Gerbert of Aurillac, later Pope Sylvester II, who visited Ripoll some time during the 960s.

THE CALIPHATE OF CÓRDOBA

When 'Abd Allāh died in 912, the authority of the emirate did not extend far beyond Córdoba and its hinterland, and the days of the Umayyad state in al-Andalus appeared to be numbered. However, under the able and vigorous leadership of 'Abd Allāh's grandson, 'Abd al-Raḥmān III (912–61), the Umayyad dynasty was to undergo an extraordinary recovery in its fortunes. The immediate priority for the new emir was to neutralize the rebellious elements within al-Andalus who had earlier rejected Umayyad authority. One by one, the rebels who had tried to establish independent lordships in the south were forced back into obedience. The contumacious Ibn Hafṣūn died in 917 and his sons and supporters were finally brought to heel in 928. Subsequently, between 929 and 937, the recalcitrant marches were also subdued.

'Abd al-Raḥmān also led a number of military expeditions against the Christian principalities of the north. He did not seek to conquer the Christian states, but to assert his authority over them and deter future raids against Muslim territory; he also sought to enhance his prestige among his own subjects, make his presence felt among the troublesome governors of the frontier marches, and enrich himself and his followers with the spoils of war. Among the most successful of these raids was that of 920, during the course of which the emir defeated the armies of Ordoño II of León (913/14–24) and Sancho Garcés I of Navarre at Valdejunquera near Pamplona; four years later the city of Pamplona itself was sacked by the emir's forces. The only Christian monarch to stand up successfully to the Umayyad offensive was Ramiro II of León (930–51), who reinforced Christian control over the Duero valley and inflicted a humiliating defeat on 'Abd al-Raḥmān III at Simancas near Valladolid in 939. After the death of Ramiro II, however, and for the rest of the tenth century, the Umayyad state held the upper hand in its dealings with the Christian principalities, which became little more than client kingdoms. In 958, Sancho I of León (956–66), ousted by his subjects because he was reputedly too obese to mount a horse, travelled in person to Córdoba in the hope that 'Abd al-Raḥmān's physicians would help him shed the excess pounds; he also obtained the military backing with which he reclaimed the Leonese throne from the usurper Ordoño IV (958–9) the following year. The prolonged period of political dissension in the Leonese kingdom enabled the lay magnates of the realm to become increasingly entrenched in power: most notably of all, Count Fernán González (d. 970), who by playing off the rival factions against one another was able to establish the county of Castile as an effectively independent principality.

In January 929, 'Abd al-Raḥmān had himself proclaimed caliph and adopted the titles of 'Commander of the Believers' and 'Defender of the Faith of Allah', thereby making himself both the spiritual and temporal head of the Sunni community in al-Andalus and further afield. The assumption of the caliphal title by 'Abd al-Raḥmān III appears to have been prompted partly by awareness that the power of the 'Abbasid caliphate in Baghdad was rapidly on the wane. More particularly, it was designed as a counterweight against the rising power of the Shi'ite Fatimid dynasty at Kairouan (in modern Tunisia), whose ruler 'Ubayd Allāh had himself adopted the caliphal title in 909 and had begun to extend his influence into the western Maghreb. Fatimid expansion was a threat not only to Umayyad authority and prestige, but also to the trading networks that linked al-Andalus to the Mediterranean, and most notably to the trans-Saharan route along which gold, salt and slaves flowed from West Africa via Sijilmassa to the peninsula. 'Abd al-Raḥmān III backed up his claim to temporal and spiritual authority over the Maghreb with a number of military and diplomatic initiatives. He ensured Umayyad dominance in the western Mediterranean by building a new fleet in 956 and by establishing naval bases and coastal fortifications along the Mediterranean and Atlantic seaboard; he also secured an important strategic presence on the North African coast with the conquest of the strongpoints of Melilla (927), Ceuta (931) and Tangier (951). At the same time, the Umayyad caliph established a network of alliances with some of the chieftains of the Berber tribes of the Maghreb, who were implacably opposed to the Shi'ite Fatimids. Faced with such vigorous resistance, the Fatimid regime shifted its strategic objectives away from the Maghreb towards the east: in 969, Egypt was conquered and a new Fatimid capital was established at Cairo.

Thanks in large part to the customs duties that were levied on the booming commercial sector, the various levies on personal wealth and property, and the taxes paid by non-Muslims, public finances were buoyant under the caliphate, with annual revenues reportedly in the region of six and a quarter million gold dinars. The lion's share of this wealth was probably designated to the military budget. The caliph was able to put bigger and better equipped armies into the field (to which he recruited large numbers of Berber and Christian mercenaries, in order to reduce his dependence on traditional tribal levies), to erect fortresses and coastal bases, and to build and equip a fleet. The prosperity of al-Andalus was also reflected by the resumption of the minting of gold coins by the caliphate. The state bureaucracy was reorganized and the caliph sought to reduce his dependence on the old families of al-Andalus by recruiting large numbers of *muwallads*, Christians, Jews and *saqāliba* to high office within the bureaucracy. The Jewish scholar and physician Hasdāi b. Shaprūt, who carried out diplomatic negotiations on behalf of the government, was but one among a number of eminent Jews to hold influential positions at the Umayyad court; the Christian Recemund, who served as secretary under 'Abd al-Raḥmān III, was sent as an ambassador to the court of the emperor Otto I of Germany in 955–6 and was rewarded with the bishopric of Elvira. The caliph also promoted a number of ambitious building projects: the Great Mosque of Córdoba was further extended and embellished, and a vast and luxurious palace complex, set amid fountains and gardens, was erected at Madīnat al-Zahra (reputedly named after one of the caliph's concubines) on the outskirts of Córdoba. The latter became the nerve-centre of the state bureaucracy and the mint, and home to a lavish court which was serviced by a veritable army of functionaries and servants. Such was the power of the Umayyad state by the middle of the tenth century, that foreign rulers eagerly sought to establish diplomatic relations with the caliphate. In 953, for example, Otto I of Germany sent John, abbot of the monastery of Gorze in Lorraine, to the caliphal court in an attempt to secure Umayyad help to curb Muslim piracy in the western Mediterranean. There were further diplomatic contacts between Córdoba and Germany in 974, and ambassadors from the Byzantine emperors of Constantinople are recorded to have visited Córdoba in 949 and 972.

The burgeoning wealth of the caliphate owed much to its flourishing agrarian base. In the two centuries that followed the Muslim invasion, the rural economy was gradually transformed and revitalized. Large latifundia were broken up, peasant tenants were offered more favourable share-cropping arrangements, and Roman irrigation systems were substantially upgraded with the introduction of Middle Eastern technologies such as the *noria* (water wheel). The diffusion of irrigation allowed for more intensive exploitation of the land, increased productivity and the introduction of a wide range of new crops, including citrus fruits, bananas, artichokes, cotton, rice, hard

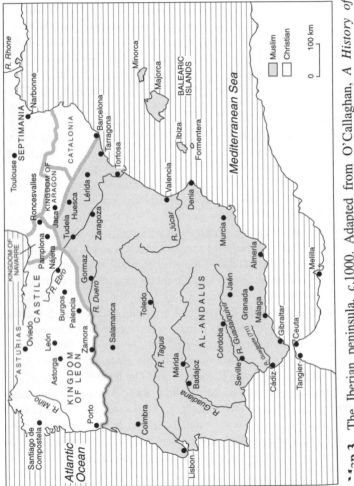

Map 3 The Iberian peninsula, c.1000. Adapted from O'Callaghan, *A History of* ... *Spain*, p. 108.

wheat, sorghum and sugar-cane. In highland areas, olive groves, vines, fig trees and cereals predominated, although the area of land designated for the latter appears to have contracted under Muslim rule, with the result that grain had to be imported from North Africa. The effects of what has been described as a 'green revolution' in al-Andalus were widely felt: population levels began to rise; increased profits from agricultural surpluses acted as a stimulus to industrial and commercial activity; and urban centres, always the fulcrum of Islamic society and economy, began to expand. Among the latter, by far the greatest was Córdoba, dubbed 'the navel of al-Andalus', which by the tenth century had become one of the great cities of the Mediterranean world with a population of around 100,000. The towns of al-Andalus became important centres of industrial activity, producing textiles (particularly linens, cottons and silks), ceramics, glassware, metalwork, leather goods and paper. These manufactured goods, together with metals, minerals and timber, and agricultural commodities such as olive oil and dried fruits, found ready buyers both in the peninsula and much farther afield, as al-Andalus became fully integrated into an international commercial network that spanned not only the Mediterranean, but the entire Islamic world. Andalusi woven textiles were exported to Egypt and perhaps as far afield as Khurasan and India; Málaga figs were enjoyed in Baghdad. Al-Andalus imported spices, flax, raw wool, perfumes and precious stones, among other things, and it also acted as an important centre of transit trade, redistributing furs from Northern Europe, Russia and Central Asia, gold from the western Sudan, and slaves from Christian Spain and Eastern Europe.

Córdoba was not merely the seat of Umayyad government, it was also the cultural epicentre of al-Andalus. The Great Mosque was an important seat of learning, where scholars and students devoted themselves to the study of the traditions of the Koran and the Malikite branch of Islamic law. The Umayyad rulers themselves were enthusiastic patrons of the arts and their courts were attended by poets, musicians and scholars. During the reign of 'Abd al-Raḥmān II, the Umayyad court embraced the cultural influences of the eastern Islamic world. The exiled Persian scholar and musician Ziryāb became the arbiter of good taste to Cordoban high society, to which he introduced new fashions in hairstyles, clothes and cuisine, as well as such innovations as the guitar, toothpaste and underarm deodorants. As Andalusi culture became progressively 'orientalized' during the ninth century, increasing numbers of Iberian Muslims sought to further their studies in Baghdad and other cultural centres of the Middle East. The reigns of 'Abd al-Raḥmān III and his son and successor, al-Ḥakam II (961–76), witnessed a notable flowering of cultural activity. Important works were produced in the fields of science, geography, history, philosophy and grammar. Arabic translations of Greek scientific treatises and Persian astronomy circulated widely. The personal library of al-Ḥakam II alone is reputed to have comprised some 400,000 volumes, although few scholars today give much credence to this figure.

In the political-military sphere, al-Ḥakam II continued the policies that had been pursued with such success by his father. The powerful families of the marcher regions were integrated more fully into the Umayyad state. Diplomatic envoys from the Christian north and further afield continued to beat a path to the Umayyad court. Substantial numbers of Berber mercenaries were recruited to the state army. By a combination of diplomacy and force, the Christian realms of the north were kept firmly in check. In 965, the fortress of Gormaz, which still towers impressively above the valley of the Duero near Soria, was substantially extended and reinforced; ten years later it would withstand a three-month siege by the kings of León and Navarre. In north-western Morocco, the power of the Idrisids was neutralized in 972–3 and an Umayyad protectorate was established in the region.

On al-Ḥakam II's death in 976 he was succeeded by his 14-year-old son, Hishām II (976–1009). A power struggle then ensued between the caliph's regents, one of whom, Muḥammad ibn Abī 'Āmir, better known to history by his later honorific al-Manṣūr, 'the Victorious', successfully eliminated his chief rivals within government (the former ḥājib al-Muṣḥafī and the general Ghālib) and took power into his own hands. The caliph, Hishām, was sidelined from government and relegated to little more than a ceremonial role. Thenceforth, until his death in 1002, al-Manṣūr's authority as chief minister to the caliph and *de facto* ruler of al-Andalus was to go largely unchallenged. As a mark of his status, al-Manṣūr erected a palace complex of his own, Madīnat al-Zāhira ('the Glittering City'), on the eastern outskirts of Córdoba, to which he moved the offices of government in 981. He won the approval of the conservative religious authorities by further extending the Great Mosque of Córdoba and having part of al-Ḥakam's library burned. The state army was further expanded with the recruitment of large numbers of ṣaqāliba and Berber soldiers, with the result that the role of the traditional *jund*s was diminished. The size and strength of the armies that al-Manṣūr had under his command ensured that central control over the provinces of al-Andalus was never seriously called into question, just as they also enabled him to win considerable personal prestige, as well as impressive quantities of booty, by virtue of the devastating plundering expeditions in the name of *jihād* that he led at regular intervals into Christian territory: among the centres sacked by al-Manṣūr were Barcelona (985), Coimbra (987), León and Zamora (988), Carrión and Astorga (995), and Pamplona (999); monasteries, such as those of Sant Cugat del Vallès (985), Sahagún and Eslonza (988) and San Millán de la Cogolla (1002), were also despoiled. Most famously of all, in 997 the holy city of Santiago de Compostela in the far north-west was attacked, its cathedral was plundered, and its doors and bells carried off to adorn the Great Mosque in Córdoba. Al-Manṣūr's subjects could not fail to be impressed by the martial prowess of the self-styled champion of Islam, just as the Christians to the north were suitably cowed, offering tribute and contingents of troops to the *ḥājib* as a mark of their obedience. Under al-Manṣūr's rule, 'Abd Allāh b. Buluggīn of Granada would observe a century later, 'Islam enjoyed a glory which al-Andalus had never witnessed before, while the Christians suffered their greatest humiliation.' Yet, it was to prove a brittle authority. A remarkable shift in the balance of power between Muslim and Christian was at hand.

2

The Ascendancy of Christian Iberia, AD 1000–1474

When al-Manṣūr died in August 1002, as he returned from yet another successful raiding expedition into Christian territory, al-Andalus appeared to be at the peak of its power. Yet, when his son and successor as chief minister (*ḥājib*), al-Muẓaffar, followed his father to the grave six years later, unitary political authority in al-Andalus suddenly collapsed and in 1031 the western Umayyad caliphate passed into history, never to be resurrected. Although Muslim Iberia was subsequently to regain short-lived unity under two Berber movements – the Almoravids and Almohads – the balance of power in the peninsula thereafter shifted decisively away from al-Andalus towards the increasingly self-confident and expansionist states of the Christian north.

THE FALL OF THE UMAYYAD CALIPHATE

The collapse of the Umayyad caliphate was in large part a consequence of the policies that had been pursued by al-Manṣūr and al-Muẓaffar. The isolation from government of the caliph, Hishām II, had diminished the prestige of the caliphate and undermined the established basis of authority in al-Andalus. Furthermore, the continued expansion of the state army and the recruitment of increasing numbers of Berbers and *ṣaqāliba* into its ranks, had not only placed a heavy strain on the public purse, but had also introduced into Andalusi society a volatile foreign element which owed its loyalty to its paymasters in Córdoba rather than to the caliphate itself. The immediate catalyst of the political crisis, however, was the decision of al-Muẓaffar's

brother and successor as *ḥājib*, 'Abd al-Raḥmān, to have himself appointed heir to the caliphal throne late in 1008. Faced with the imminent
extinction of their dynasty as a political force, a group of prominent
Umayyads launched a rebellion the following February, in the course
of which they murdered 'Abd al-Raḥmān, ousted Hishām II, and
proclaimed another member of their family, Muḥammad
al-Mahdī, caliph in his stead.

Far from restoring Umayyad authority, the insurrection of 1009
unleashed a period of intense political upheaval. As rival factions
competed for the caliphate, unitary political authority crumbled and al-
Andalus fragmented into a mosaic of regional successor states, known
as *taifas* (from the Arabic word for 'party' or 'faction'). After the fall
of the caliphate, 'Abd Allāh b. Buluggīn, ruler of the *taifa* of Granada
between 1073 and 1090, observed, 'every military commander rose up
in his own town and entrenched himself behind the walls of his own
fortress, having first secured his own position, created his own army
and amassed his own resources. These persons vied with one another
for worldly power and each sought to subdue the other.' Some of those
who seized power belonged to Arab and Berber families of longstanding wealth and influence, like the 'Abbādids of Seville; others were
newly established Berber warlords, like Zāwī b. Zīrī, who was to establish his seat of government in Granada; yet others were *ṣaqāliba*, who
founded a handful of short-lived lordships in the Levante. Although
some still considered that the caliphal institution was worth resuscitat-
ing, a feverish atmosphere of plot and counter-plot ensured that no one
was able to hold on to power for long. By the time the last of the
caliphs, Hishām III (1027–31), was sent packing in 1031, Córdoba
itself had been reduced to the status of a minor *taifa* statelet like any
other.

In the immediate aftermath of the collapse of Umayyad authority,
there were about three dozen of these *taifa* states. By the middle of the
eleventh century, however, the political map of al-Andalus had begun
to simplify somewhat, as many of the lesser *taifas* were swallowed up
by their more powerful neighbours. Most predatory of all was the
'Abbādid kingdom of Seville, which by 1070 had brought a dozen
smaller *taifas* in western Andalusia and the Algarve under its rule.
Taifa politics took place against a constantly shifting background of
petty dynastic rivalries, local diplomatic manoeuvring and small-scale
military conflict. Diplomatic relations with overseas powers dried up
and offensive campaigns against the northern Christian realms became

few and far between. Indeed, lacking substantial armies of their own, the feuding *taifa* monarchs looked to the Christian states to provide them with the military muscle they needed in their regular territorial squabbles with their rivals, and were willing to pay handsomely to do so. Thus, contingents of Castilian and Catalan soldiers were recruited by the competing factions during the power struggle for Córdoba in 1009–13.

For much of the first half of the eleventh century, however, the Christian rulers made little attempt to profit – territorially or otherwise – from the collapse of the caliphate. To the north-west, Alfonso V of León (999–1028) had to face up to repeated challenges to his authority by rebellious elements within the local aristocracy and repel the Viking marauders whose raids regularly devastated the Galician coastline. At the eastern end of the Pyrenees, the Catalan counties suffered a progressive breakdown in public order after 1020, as the authority of the counts of Barcelona was attacked head on by the great nobles and a 'new aristocracy' of petty castellans. Meanwhile, Sancho III 'the Great' of Navarre (1004–35), the self-styled 'Emperor of Spain', used diplomatic skill backed up by military force to extend his authority over his Christian neighbours. Navarrese claims to peninsular overlordship evaporated on Sancho's death, however, and his territories – Navarre, Aragon, Ribagorza and Castile – were partitioned between his four sons. Two years later, one of these sons, Ferdinand I (1035–65), who had been enthroned as the first king of Castile, defeated and killed his brother-in-law, Vermudo III of León (1028–37), in battle at Tamarón, thereby uniting León and Castile under his rule. In 1054, Leonese-Castilian pre-eminence in the north was reinforced when Ferdinand defeated and killed his brother, García III of Navarre (1035–54), at Atapuerca near Burgos.

His position secure, Ferdinand I was at last in a position to exploit the political and military weakness of the Muslim *taifas*. His best-publicized territorial conquests – Lamego (1057), Viseu (1058) and Coimbra (1064) – came in what is now northern Portugal at the expense of the *taifa* of Badajoz. For the most part, however, the exaction of tribute, not territorial expansion, appears to have been Ferdinand's primary objective. The rulers of Barcelona and Aragon were the first to demand payments of tribute, known as *parias*, from the *taifa* kings, but the practice was perfected by Ferdinand I – who by the time of his death was in receipt of regular *paria* payments from the *taifas* of Zaragoza, Toledo, Badajoz and Seville – and by his son

Alfonso VI (1065–1109). The Christian rulers operated what has aptly been dubbed a 'protection racket', offering their military services to the *taifa* monarchs in return for sizeable annual payments of gold and silver. By the terms of the treaties that were agreed between al-Muqtadir of Zaragoza (1046–82) and Sancho IV of Navarre (1054–76), in 1069 and 1073, for example, the former undertook to pay the latter the sum of 1000 gold *dinars* every month (the equivalent of about 20 kilograms of gold annually), in return for military protection 'either against Christians or against Muslims'. Tribute payments might also include luxury goods, such as jewellery, textiles and ivories, while in 1063 al-Mu'taḍid of Seville (1042–69) even surrendered the mortal remains of St Isidore to Ferdinand I. The readiness with which Christian lords were willing to take up arms against their fellow Christians in defence of their *taifa* tributaries demonstrates the primacy of political pragmatism over ideology at this time. When, for example, Ramiro I of Aragon (1035–63) attempted to capture the Zaragozan town of Graus in 1063, he was defeated and killed by an army sent by Ferdinand I of León-Castile to protect his Muslim vassal al-Muqtadir.

The influx of *parias* brought unheard of wealth to the previously impoverished Christian kingdoms. It enabled their rulers to reward their supporters lavishly, put bigger armies into the field, and commission costly works of art, such as the exquisite jewelled gold and agate chalice that was fashioned for Ferdinand I's daughter, Urraca, and granted to the royal church of San Isidoro in León. Muslim tribute also allowed the Christian kings to indulge in church and castle building on an unprecedented scale. Among the various building projects promoted by Sancho Ramírez I of Aragon (1063–94) during the 1070s, for example, were the cathedral of Jaca, the imposing castle and church complex at Loarre north-west of Huesca, and a number of bridges on the pilgrim-road to Santiago de Compostela. Count Ramón Berenguer I of Barcelona (1035–76), who received regular payments of *parias* from the *taifas* of Lérida, Tortosa and Zaragoza, used much of his new-found wealth to purchase lands, castles and rights, with which he was able to consolidate his hegemony over the Spanish March and bring the trans-Pyrenean counties of Carcassonne and Razès under his control. The count was also the first Christian ruler in the peninsula to issue his own gold coinage. Religious institutions were the other great beneficiaries of *parias*. Most famously of all, the Burgundian abbey of Cluny was promised a huge annual donative of

1000 gold pieces by Ferdinand I of León-Castile in around 1063, and twice that amount by Alfonso VI in 1077, in return for the spiritual intercession of the monks.

Enterprising noblemen also profited from the same system of *parias*. Most enterprising of all, was the Castilian Rodrigo Díaz, better known to posterity as El Cid (an epithet probably derived from the Arabic *sayyid*, 'lord'). By all accounts a soldier of some genius, Rodrigo's exploits on the field of battle, against Christian and Muslim alike, won him great wealth and fame. In 1081, driven into exile by Alfonso VI, he took up employment as a mercenary in the service of the *taifa* of Zaragoza and won decisive victories over Count Berenguer Ramón II of Barcelona (1076–96) and Sancho Ramírez I of Aragon. Subsequently, during a second spell of exile between 1089 and 1094, El Cid operated as a freelance soldier of fortune in the east of the peninsula, exacting prodigious sums in *parias* from the *taifas* of the region, before going on to carve out an independent principality for himself based on Valencia in June 1094. El Cid has traditionally been portrayed as one of the great heroes of Spanish history. Later literary works, notably the Castilian epic poem the *Cantar de mio Cid* (*c.*1207), keen to present a suitable role model for the warrior nobility of Castile to imitate, emphasized that El Cid's conquests had been carried out on behalf of his liege lord Alfonso VI, and that he held them as the king's loyal vassal. But earlier, and more reliable, evidence strongly suggests that between 1094 and 1099 El Cid, the self-styled 'prince of Valencia', remained very much his own man.

The ease with which ambitious soldiers of fortune like El Cid were able to operate in Muslim territory is illustrative of what has been called the 'permeability' of the Christian-Muslim frontier zone during the eleventh century. Transhumant shepherds crossed the border area in search of lush pasturelands for their flocks; Jewish merchants journeyed to the expanding market towns of the Christian north to sell their precious cargoes of silks and other luxuries; diplomatic envoys shuttled back and forth between Christian and Muslim rulers; go-betweens (later known as *alfaqueques*) crossed the frontier to ransom prisoners of war; and political exiles of the highest rank found succour in the courts of the Muslim south: thus, Alfonso VI, ousted from the throne of León by his sibling, Sancho II of Castile (1065–72), in January 1072, found asylum at the court of al-Mam'ūn of Toledo (1043–75).

Given the vast amounts of gold and silver that flowed annually into the coffers of the Christian monarchs, there could have been little immediate incentive to abandon the policy of systematic tribute-taking. Some, however, were beginning to look to the longer term. Count Sisnando Davídez, who was sent by Alfonso VI of León-Castile to negotiate the resumption of tribute payments with 'Abd Allāh b. Buluggīn of Granada in about 1075, is reported to have declared:

> Al-Andalus originally belonged to the Christians, until they were conquered by the Arabs . . . Now . . . they want to recover what was taken from them by force, something they will achieve by weakening you and wasting you away with time. When you no longer have money or soldiers, we will seize the country without the least effort.

A decade later, in May 1085, these predictions were partly fulfilled, when Alfonso VI deposed the ruler of the *taifa* of Toledo, al-Qādir (1075–85), and brought the latter's kingdom under his own authority. At a stroke, the kingdom of León-Castile expanded by roughly a third and Alfonso VI was able to put in train the gradual repopulation of the lands between the Duero and the Tagus. The city of Toledo itself was the ancient capital of the Visigoths and the primatial see of the Spanish Church. For a monarch like Alfonso VI, who, from 1077, had begun to make clear his hegemonic pretensions in the peninsula by styling himself 'Emperor of all the Spains', the conquest of that city was an act that was imbued with immense symbolic significance.

THE ALMORAVID INVASION

The fall of Toledo sent a tremor of fear through the Muslim population. 'O people of al-Andalus, spur on your mounts; it will be nothing but a blunder to stay on here . . . We are surrounded by an enemy who will not leave us alone: How can we live in a basket together with snakes?', lamented the poet Ibn al-'Aṣṣāl. These fears were reinforced the following year when Alfonso VI's armies subjected Zaragoza to siege and captured the fortress of Aledo south-west of Murcia. In Toledo, the terms of surrender, which had allowed the inhabitants freedom to practise their own religion, were soon flouted when the city mosque was converted into a cathedral. Fearing that their own days as independent rulers were numbered, the remaining *taifa* rulers sent a desperate appeal for military assistance across the Straits to the Berber chieftain Yūsūf b. Tāshufin (1061–1106), leader of the Islamic sect known as the

Almoravids (*al-Murābiṭūn*). The *taifa* kings had deep misgivings about seeking Berber intervention, for they had little in common with the unsophisticated and puritanical Almoravids, but desperate times called for desperate measures: 'If I have to choose, I would rather tend camels in Morocco than be a swineherd in Castile,' was the pithy comment of al-Muʿtamid of Seville (1069–91) on his predicament.

The Almoravid movement, which was born among the nomadic Ṣanhāja Berber tribes of the western Sahara, had been founded some time after 1039 by a Malikite scholar, ʿAbd Allāh b. Yāsin. With its compelling brand of austerity and revivalist vigour, summed up by its slogan 'the spreading of righteousness, the correction of injustice and the abolition of unlawful taxes', the movement enjoyed a spectacular growth in popularity. Under Ibn Yāsin's successor, Abū Bakr (1056–87), and the latter's cousin, Yūsuf b. Tāshufin, Almoravid authority spread southwards into the gold-producing kingdom of Ghana and northwards on-to the plains of Morocco, where in 1070 a new capital for the dynasty was founded at Marrakesh. In June 1086, in response to the appeals of the beleaguered *taifa* rulers, Yūsuf crossed the Straits at the head of a large army and landed at Algeciras. The following October, he won a crushing victory over Alfonso VI at Sagrajas near Badajoz. Although the Almoravids were to reap no territorial advantage from their success, Yūsuf returned to campaign in the peninsula in 1088, when he tried and failed to take Aledo, and in 1090, when he mounted an unsuccessful attack on Toledo. By now, believing that the *taifa* rulers had betrayed Islam by leading a licentious lifestyle and by levying non-Koranic taxes on their subjects with which to pay *parias* to infidels, and suspecting (correctly) that some of them had secretly reopened negotiations with Alfonso VI, Yūsuf resolved to make himself the master of al-Andalus. Between 1090 and 1094, all of the *taifa* rulers of western and southern al-Andalus were toppled and their territories absorbed into the Almoravid empire. Only El Cid in Valencia was briefly able to halt the Almoravid advance towards the Levante, but in 1102, three years after his death, his widow Jimena was forced to evacuate the city and the region was overrun by Yūsuf's forces. In 1110, the last outpost of independent Muslim power in the peninsula, the *taifa* of Zaragoza, was subdued by Yūsuf's son and successor, ʿAlī b. Yūsuf (1106–43).

Simultaneously, Almoravid armies had begun to launch a series of attacks against Christian positions. By the end of the eleventh century, all the territories that had belonged to the former *taifa* kingdom of

Toledo as far north as the Tagus had been conquered, although the embattled city of Toledo remained in Christian hands. Furthermore, the supply of *parias* had been abruptly cut off, leaving Alfonso VI and his fellow Christian rulers severely short of cash. Alfonso VI did what he could to halt the Almoravid advance, capturing the strategic fortress-town of Medinaceli in 1104, but in May 1108 these efforts were undone when a Leonese-Castilian army was annihilated at Uclés, east of Toledo.

The defeat at Uclés did not signal the complete collapse of the Tagus frontier. However, the death in battle of Alfonso VI's son and heir, the Infante Sancho, was to trigger an acute political crisis. On the king's death in July 1109, the throne of León-Castile passed to his eldest daughter, Urraca, whom he had earlier betrothed to Alfonso I 'the Battler', king of Aragon (1104–34). However, the marriage soon broke down and Urraca found herself embroiled in a bitter struggle for power involving not only her estranged husband, but the supporters of the queen's son by her first marriage to Count Raymond of Burgundy, Alfonso Raimúndez, and those who were loyal to Count Henry of Portugal and his wife Teresa, the illegitimate daughter of Alfonso VI. Between 1110 and 1117, dynastic war raged throughout León and Castile and near anarchy reigned in town and country alike. It says much for the determination of Urraca that in the face of such adversity she maintained herself on the throne, but the price she paid was heavy: to the east, large areas of Castile, as well as the Rioja and the Sorian highlands, were brought under Aragonese control; to the west, the county of Portugal, under the leadership of Countess Teresa, who had begun to style herself queen, drifted out of the Leonese orbit altogether and emerged as an independent political entity in its own right.

While Alfonso VI was engaged in his titanic struggle for ascendancy with the Almoravids, the Christian realm of Aragon, which had only come into being as a kingdom on the death of Sancho III of Navarre in 1035, was steadily consolidating its position as the foremost power in the north-east of the peninsula. Under the rule of the first king of Aragon, Ramiro I, and that of his son, Sancho Ramírez I, their principal strategic objective was the southwards expansion of their kingdom at the expense of the *taifa* of Zaragoza. Through Sancho's efforts, a string of important Zaragozan border fortresses fell into Aragonese hands during the 1080s, including Graus (1083), Montearagón (1088) and Monzón (1089). In 1096, victory in battle at Alcoraz over al-Musta'īn of Zaragoza (1085–1110) allowed Sancho's son and successor, Peter I (1094–1104), to conquer the strongpoint of Huesca; five years after that, the city of Zaragoza itself was the object of an unsuccessful attack.

At the eastern end of the Pyrenees, the Catalan counts of Barcelona were equally ambitious to extend their territory and influence at the expense of the *taifas* of al-Andalus. However, Barcelona's designs on the Levante were to be frustrated, first by El Cid, who blocked two advances against Valencia by Berenguer Ramon II, in 1085 and 1089, and then by the Almoravids, who defeated Count Ramon Berenguer III (1097–1131) at Mollerusa in 1102. None the less, the latter was able to consolidate his power in the Spanish March by the acquisition of the county of Besalú and the territory of Vallespir in 1111, and by the annexation of Cerdanya, Conflent and Bergà in 1117. He also strengthened his authority over the trans-Pyrenean counties of Carcassonne and Razès and extended his influence along the southern coast of Languedoc through his marriage to Countess Douce, heiress to the county of Provence, in 1112.

THE 'EUROPEANIZATION' OF CHRISTIAN IBERIA

Prior to the eleventh century, the Christian realms of the peninsula had remained relatively isolated from the political and cultural mainstream of Western Europe. With the exception of the Catalan counties of the Spanish March, whose history as an appendage of Frankish empire had ensured regular trans-Pyrenean contacts, the Christian rulers are not known to have engaged in regular diplomacy with their counterparts elsewhere in Europe. Outside Catalonia, the Iberian Church was conservative and inward-looking: contact with the papacy in Rome was non-existent; the Visigothic or 'Mozarabic', rather than the Roman, liturgy ruled supreme; monasteries were governed by Visigothic rules, not the Benedictine variety which had taken root in most of the rest of the Latin West; and there was apparently only dim awareness of cultural movements beyond the Pyrenees. During the course of the eleventh century, however, the peninsula's relationship with the rest of Western Christendom was to be spectacularly transformed.

One of the key factors in this transformation was the pilgrimage to Santiago de Compostela. Some time between 818 and 842, what was believed to be the tomb of the apostle St James the Great was discovered near Iria Flavia in Galicia, at the place now known as Santiago de

Compostela. With the enthusiastic support of the local clergy and the Leonese monarchy, a cult began to grow up on the site and stories of the miracles that had been worked at the shrine of the apostle circulated widely. By the middle of the tenth century, foreign pilgrims were beginning to visit the shrine-church at Compostela and the flow of pilgrim traffic to the tomb of the apostle grew steadily thereafter. The pilgrim-road to Compostela ran from four principal starting-points in France – Tours, Vezelay, Le Puy and St Gilles du Gard – and converged at Puente la Reina in the western Pyrenees, from where the so-called *camino francés*, or French road, ran westwards across northern Spain through important staging-posts such as Pamplona, Burgos, León and Astorga, before reaching the holy city of Compostela itself. The influx of so many foreign pilgrims not only brought great wealth to the church and city of Compostela, but it also left a lasting impression on the communities through which it passed. Kings, clerics and laymen competed to enhance the facilities available to the passing pilgrims, mending roads and building bridges, churches, hostels and hospitals.

Parallel to this process, the papacy was beginning to take a far closer interest in Iberian affairs. The reform movement championed by Popes Alexander II and Gregory VII sought to sever the bonds that tied the Western Church to the secular world, advance the authority of Rome over lay powers, and ensure uniformity of religious discipline and ritual throughout the Latin West. The monks of Cluny, who owed a special vow of obedience to the papacy, stood in the vanguard of this programme of reform. Cluniac influence was particularly strongly felt in Navarre and in León, where, as we have seen, Ferdinand I and Alfonso VI secured themselves a place in the liturgical commemorations of the Cluniacs by making lavish annual payments of Muslim gold. Incoming French Cluniacs established a network of important monastic centres in the west of the peninsula, while others were appointed to key positions in the ecclesiastical hierarchy. Most prominent of all the Cluniacs, was Bernard of Sédirac, who held the abbacy of Sahagún between 1080 and 1076, and was subsequently appointed to the archbishopric of Toledo after the conquest of that city.

Through the efforts of the Cluniacs and the papal legates who visited the peninsula at regular intervals after 1067, the Iberian Church was subjected to a far-reaching programme of reform. The Visigothic liturgy, regarded by the papacy as 'confused' or even heretical, was replaced in the western kingdoms by the Roman rite between 1071 and 1080; the Benedictine rule supplanted Visigothic ones; a new canon law was introduced; traditional 'Mozarabic' techniques of manuscript illumination died out; and the Visigothic script was gradually replaced in favour of the 'Carolingian' minuscule used elsewhere in the Latin West. At the same time, contacts between the peninsular Church and the papacy intensified, as bishops increasingly sought papal adjudication in territorial disputes with their episcopal neighbours, and came to regard Rome as a source of privileges with which they might bolster their authority. It was thanks to an intensive campaign of lobbying conducted at the papal court by Bishop Diego Gelmírez, for example, that Santiago de Compostela was elevated to the status of an archbishopric in 1120.

Piety was not the only force that drew outsiders to the peninsula. Rumours of the immense wealth flowing north in *parias* from the *taifa* kingdoms led some nobles from beyond the Pyrenees to view the frontier with al-Andalus as a potential source of wealth. Thus, it was the prospect of plunder, not piety, that encouraged a force of French knights to help Catalan and Aragonese troops besiege and conquer the Zaragozan fortress-town of Barbastro in 1064. Family ties with peninsular dynasties also encouraged French nobles to travel to Spain. Among the leaders of the French military force that campaigned inconclusively around Tudela in 1087, were Duke Odo of Burgundy, nephew of Alfonso VI's second wife Constance, and Raymond of St-Gilles, whose mother Almodis had married Count Ramón Berenguer I of Barcelona. The 1087 expedition achieved little in military terms, yet two members of the Burgundian ducal house – Raymond of Amous and his cousin Henry of Châlon – were subsequently betrothed to Alfonso VI's daughters, Urraca and Teresa respectively.

The peninsula was also a magnet for foreign colonists of more modest rank and horizons. French settlers established themselves in the hinterland around Toledo and Zaragoza after the conquest of those cities in 1085 and 1118 respectively, while foreign merchants and artisans set up shop at numerous points along the pilgrim-road to Compostela in order to cater for the needs of the faithful who passed through in droves. At Estella, south-west of Pamplona, French settlers were awarded a special *fuero*, or charter of privileges, by Sancho Ramírez I of Aragon in 1090, and the same *fuero* was later extended to other towns in the vicinity. The foreign, though mostly French, incomers, be they pilgrims or permanent settlers, left a profound cultural imprint too. It can be glimpsed in the innovative sculptural forms which came into vogue in places as far apart as Jaca and Sahagún, and in the churches, palaces and other buildings designed in the popular 'Romanesque' style – characterized by thick stone walls, round arches and square or octagonal bell towers – which sprang up in large numbers from Catalonia to Portugal. Towards the end of the twelfth century, elements of the French 'Gothic' style, with its distinctive pointed arches, also began to be incorporated. The cathedrals of Burgos and Toledo, begun in 1222 and 1226 respectively, are two of the most spectacular examples of the new style.

RECONQUEST AND CRUSADE

The Almoravid assault on Christian Iberia took place at a time when the nobility in much of Western Europe was beginning to be persuaded by Church leaders that military activity could have a penitential value if it were directed against the enemies of Christendom. At the Council of Clermont, in November 1095, Pope Urban II appealed for an 'armed pilgrimage' to liberate the Christians of the Holy Land from the yoke of Islam, promising those who took part in the crusade the remission of all the sins they confessed. For the laity, Guibert of Nogent later observed, it represented 'a new way to attain salvation'. Concern that the burgeoning popularity of the new crusading ethic among the Christian nobility of the Iberian realms might lead excessive numbers of knights to take the cross and journey to the Holy Land appears to have surfaced early on. In a letter he composed some time between 1096 and 1099, Pope Urban urged Counts Bernat of Besalú, Guislabert of Roussillon and Guillem of Cerdanya not to travel to Jerusalem, but to devote their energies towards the recovery of Tarragona, promising that those who died while doing so would receive remission of their sins and the prospect of eternal life: 'it is no virtue to rescue Christians from Muslimsin one place, only to expose Christians to the tyranny and oppression of the Muslims in another', the pope concluded.

Thereafter, the notion of Reconquest, which had first been articulated by the Asturian court chroniclers of the late ninth century, was yoked to the crusading movement. Pope Paschal II granted crusading indulgences to the joint Catalan-Pisan expedition that was launched against Majorca in 1114; and Gelasius II did the same to the Franco-Aragonese campaign which besieged Zaragoza in 1118. At a council celebrated at Santiago de Compostela in January 1125, Archbishop Diego Gelmírez issued this impassioned call-to-arms:

Just as the soldiers of Christ and faithful sons of the Holy Church opened the way to Jerusalem with much toil and bloodshed, so we should become soldiers of Christ and, defeating his wicked enemies, the Saracens, beat a shorter and much less difficult path through the regions of Spain to the same Sepulchre of the Lord.

The new-found crusading enthusiasm was exemplified by Alfonso I of Aragon, who in later life led a series of successful campaigns against the Muslims of the Ebro valley. In December 1118, supported by a contingent of French crusaders who had fought on the First Crusade to the Holy Land, he conquered the city of Zaragoza after a seven-month siege. The following year, Alfonso's forces advanced south of the River Ebro and overran the strongpoints of Tudela and Tarazona; in 1120, the Almoravids were defeated at Cutanda, as a result of which Alfonso was able to occupy Calatayud and Daroca. In 1122, Alfonso underlined his crusading credentials by founding a 'militia of Christ' based at Belchite, south-east of Zaragoza, whose members were promised remission of their sins if they devoted themselves permanently to the armed struggle with Islam. The militia of Belchite, like that founded by the king at nearby Monreal in around 1124, was inspired by the Orders of the Temple and the Hospital of St John, which had earlier been founded in the Holy Land for the protection of pilgrims travelling to Jerusalem. The Templars and Hospitallers soon acquired properties and influence in the peninsula, particularly in Aragon, but initially played little part in the campaigns that were waged by the Christian rulers. As a result, during the second half of the twelfth century a number of indigenous military orders were founded, the most powerful of which were those of Calatrava (1158), Santiago (1170) and Alcántara (1176). In Portugal, the Order of Évora, later called the Order of Avis, was founded by 1176. During the succeeding decades, these orders would come to play a leading role in the war against Islam and in the defence and administration of the territories of the southern frontier.

During the final years of his reign, Alfonso I campaigned to extend Aragonese authority over the Middle Ebro, but in July 1134, in the course of siege operations at Fraga near Lérida, the king was heavily defeated by an Almoravid army and died the following September. The consequences of the king's death were widely felt across the Christian north. The kingdom of Navarre, which had been overrun and partitioned by Alfonso VI of León-Castile and Sancho Ramírez I of Aragon

in 1076, re-emerged as an independent state under the rule of García
Ramírez IV (1134–50), although the definitive loss of the Rioja to León-
Castile meant that the route to any further expansion into Muslim territory was barred. Within Aragon proper, the local nobility refused to
accept the terms of Alfonso I's extraordinary will, which had bequeathed
his kingdom to the Templars, the Hospitallers and the Church of the
Holy Sepulchre, and instead offered the throne to his brother, Ramiro II
'the Monk' (1134–7). In 1137, the latter betrothed his infant daughter,
Petronilla, to Count Ramón Berenguer IV of Barcelona (1131–62), who
thereafter was to act as protector of the kingdom of Aragon. The count's
marriage to Petronilla in 1150 brought about the definitive dynastic
union of Aragon and the Catalan counties. In the west of the peninsula,
meanwhile, Queen Urraca's son, Alfonso VII of León-Castile
(1126–57), was able to recover the remaining territories that had been
occupied by the Aragonese during the war of 1110–17, and even brought
Zaragoza temporarily under his lordship. It was a mark of Alfonso VII's
restored authority that in May 1135 he had himself crowned emperor in
León. However, his pretensions to peninsular hegemony were to be
resisted by the other Christian states, not least by the now independent
kingdom of Portugal, whose ruler, Afonso I (1128–85), son of Count
Henry and Queen Teresa, was formally recognized as king by Alfonso
VII in 1143.

In the meantime, Almoravid authority within the peninsula had begun
to crumble. The emergence in Morocco of a rival Berber movement, the
Almohads, during the course of the 1120s, had given rise to a bitter
struggle for power in the Maghreb which steadily drained the resources
of the empire. Within al-Andalus, the austere Berber-speaking
Almoravids, who constituted little more than a tiny, though powerful,
military aristocracy, were despised as uncouth foreigners, and popular
discontent with the regime was fuelled by the imposition of non-Koranic
taxes and by the failure of the Almoravid authorities to protect them
from Christian attacks, which were mounting in intensity and range by
the day. Between 1144 and 1147, as the war against the Almohads
reached its climax, a series of local uprisings led to the disintegration of
Almoravid political authority in al-Andalus. In its place, there emerged
a new clutch of successor-states – some 14 of them – whose leaders, an
assortment of army generals, functionaries and religious leaders sought
to establish themselves as independent dynasts.

It was against this background of profound political turmoil within
al-Andalus and heightened crusading enthusiasm within Christendom

as a whole, which culminated in the proclamation of the Second Crusade in December 1145, that the Christian rulers of the peninsula launched a series of co-ordinated attacks against the Muslim south. In May 1146, Alfonso VII briefly held Córdoba and the following January seized Calatrava on the Guadiana. In October 1147, the emperor's forces combined with contingents from Navarre, Barcelona, Montpellier and Genoa to conquer the prosperous port city of Almería; a week later, Lisbon fell to a joint assault by Portuguese troops and a force of Anglo-Norman, Flemish and German crusaders who, *en route* for the Holy Land, had been invited to lend a hand. In 1148, Count Ramón Berenguer IV of Barcelona, supported by a Genoese fleet and a contingent of the crusaders who had fought at Lisbon, overran Tortosa at the mouth of the Ebro; the following year the count extinguished the Muslim presence in the Ebro valley for good by capturing Lérida, Fraga and Mequinenza.

The Iberian conquests of 1147–9 were viewed by contemporaries elsewhere in Europe as part of a concerted attack against the enemies of Christendom by a single Christian 'pilgrim army'. For the French troubadour poet Marcabru, Spain was a *lavador*, or cleansing place, where knights might purify their souls and win salvation, as well as honour, wealth and merit. Within Christian Iberia itself, the mood was one of heady optimism. In January 1151, at Tudején on the eastern border of Castile, Alfonso VII and Ramón Berenguer IV agreed a treaty which prefigured the dismemberment of Navarre and the partition of all the territories of al-Andalus between the two rulers: Valencia, Denia and Murcia were to be the preserve of the count, who would hold them as the emperor's vassal; Alfonso VII would get the rest. But the treaty never came to fruition. Not only was Alfonso VII unable to secure the military support from overseas which might have enabled him to complete his conquests in al-Andalus, but in 1156–7 the Almohads conducted a series of major offensives which led to the evacuation of all the Christian-held strongpoints south of the Sierra Morena, including Almería itself. Another two generations were to elapse before the conquest of the Guadalquivir valley would once again become a practical proposition.

THE RISE AND FALL OF THE ALMOHAD EMPIRE

The Almohad movement was founded around 1120 by one Ibn Tūmart

(d. 1130), who was born and raised among of one of the Berber Maṣmūda tribes of the Atlas Mountains. Having served his education in Córdoba and Baghdad, Ibn Tūmart returned to the Maghreb in 1118 and began to campaign against what he saw as the moral laxity of the Almoravid regime; three years later he declared himself to be the Mahdī, or divinely guided leader, who would restore Islamic orthodoxy to the Berber peoples. Ibn Tūmart's doctrine was underpinned by a belief in the absolute unity and oneness of God, for which reason his supporters came to be known as *Muwaḥḥidūn*, from which the term 'Almohad' derives. From his power-base in the Atlas, Ibn Tūmart began to preach his message of moral purification among the tribes of the Maṣmūda and engaged in a protracted battle for ascendancy with the Almoravids, which was to culminate in the fall of Marrakesh to his successor, the first Almohad Caliph, 'Abd al-Mu'min (1130–63), in March 1147. Subsequently, between 1146 and 1173, the Almohads gradually brought the various successor-states that had cast off Almoravid rule in al-Andalus under their control, and transferred the capital of the region from Córdoba to Seville.

This period of political flux in the Muslim territories of al-Andalus and the Maghreb was matched by similar upheaval among the Christian states of the north. On the death of Alfonso VII of León-Castile in 1157, his 'empire' was divided between his two sons, Sancho III (1157–8) and Ferdinand II (1157–88), who were granted kingdoms in Castile and León respectively. When Sancho followed his father to the grave in 1158, a power struggle broke out between rival Castilian aristocratic families (the Laras and Castros) to secure custody of Sancho's infant son Alfonso VIII (1158–1214). Simultaneously, Castile came under attack from Ferdinand II and Sancho VI of Navarre (1150–94). Castile and León would remain at loggerheads until they were finally reunited, this time for good, under Ferdinand III (1217–52) in 1230. In the interim, violent disputes flared up periodically and towns and castles along the border between the two frequently changed hands; but there were to be no major territorial gains for either side. At the same time, the emerging state of Portugal remained a constant thorn in the side of the Leonese, while Castile became embroiled in a protracted border dispute with Navarre.

During the second half of the twelfth century, the Almohad caliphs led a number of expeditions against the Christian states. The raids caused widespread destruction, but the Almohad armies lacked the necessary experience in siegecraft to enable them to capture any major

strongpoints, besides which their campaigns were frequently undermined by logistical problems. The expedition of 1172, when a substantial Almohad army tried and failed to capture the insignificant fortress
town of Huete near Cuenca, was symptomatic of the wider problem. In
stark contrast to the highly militarized communities on the Christian
side of the frontier, the Andalusi population centres lacked any significant military capability, with the result that operations against the
Christian north were virtually paralysed whenever the caliph and his
army returned to the Maghreb. The need to quell frequent revolts in
North Africa meant that neither Yūsuf I (1163–84) nor his son Ya'qūb
(1184–99) were able to devote much attention to Iberian affairs. As a
result of this military weakness, Christian armies were able to attack
along a wide front throughout the 1170s and 1180s. Regular plundering raids and hit-and-run attacks, which carried off slaves and cattle,
and destroyed vineyards and olive groves, had devastating consequences for the exposed Muslim communities along the frontier, to the
extent that in some places, such as at Alcacer do Sal south of Lisbon,
the Almohad authorities had to pay monthly subsidies to persuade the
inhabitants to stay put. Christian raiding expeditions were interspersed
by occasional campaigns of conquest. In 1171, Alfonso II of Aragon
(1162–96) conquered Teruel, and six years later helped Alfonso VIII
of Castile to take Cuenca. In March 1179, the two monarchs set a seal
on their alliance at Cazola when – like their counterparts at Tudején 28
years before – they agreed to partition al-Andalus between themselves.
By the terms of the treaty, the king of Aragon was freed from any
feudal obligation to his namesake, though the territory of Murcia was
thereafter reserved for Castile.

In the final decade of the twelfth century, the Almohads launched a
series of major military offensives. In July 1195, the caliph Ya'qūb
inflicted a crushing defeat on Alfonso VIII at Alarcos near Calatrava.
The following year, with Almohad support, the kings of León and
Navarre, who apparently feared the hegemonic pretensions of Alfonso
VIII far more than the threat of Islamic expansionism, launched
damaging raids of their own into Castilian territory. Castile survived
the crisis, not least because renewed unrest in Tunisia led the caliph to
agree to five-year truce in 1197. At the same time, the papacy, disillusioned by the loss of Jerusalem in 1187 and the failure of the Third
Crusade to the Holy Land, launched a series of diplomatic initiatives
designed to put an end to the infighting between the peninsular
monarchs and rekindle the flame of crusade. These diplomatic efforts

intensified in 1211, when the caliph Muḥammad al-Nāṣir (1199–1213) captured the headquarters of the Order of Calatrava at Salvatierra in La Mancha. Alfonso VIII of Castile, Peter II of Aragon (1196–1213) and Sancho VII of Navarre (1194–1234) pledged support for a crusade against the Almohads, and Archbishop Rodrigo Jiménez of Toledo and Alfonso VIII's physician, Arnaldo, were sent to France to drum up support for the forthcoming campaign. By the spring of 1212, the Christian coalition was in place. Despite the desertion of the majority of the French crusaders after the capture of Calatrava in June, Alfonso VIII and his allies advanced south across the Sierra Morena and on 16 July 1212, at Las Navas de Tolosa, won a decisive victory over the caliph's army.

The battle of Las Navas de Tolosa is traditionally seen to have marked the beginning of the end of the Almohad empire in the peninsula. However, in the immediate aftermath of the campaign, the Christian states were unable to derive much advantage from their success, preoccupied as they were with their own internal affairs. Peter II of Aragon's intervention in the Albigensian crisis led to his death in battle with the crusading army of Simon de Montfort at Muret near Toulouse in September 1213. This set-back not only threatened traditional Catalan-Aragonese interests in southern France, but also left Peter's five-year-old son James I (1213–76) on the throne and ushered in a period of intense political infighting among the Aragonese barons. Peter's death, followed by those of the caliph Muḥammad and Alfonso VIII in 1214, encouraged the Aragonese and Castilians to agree a hasty truce with the Almohads. In Portugal, where the death of Sancho I (1185–1211) had left his inexperienced son Afonso II (1211–23) on the throne, the only military success of note was the capture of Alcacer do Sal in 1217 by a fleet of German crusaders bound for Egypt. On the death of Alfonso VIII's young son, Henry I (1214–17), the latter's nephew Ferdinand III was proclaimed king of Castile, despite the opposition of the Lara family and that of his father Alfonso IX of León (1188–1230). When the latter in turn passed away in 1230, Ferdinand III successfully claimed the Leonese throne for himself, thereby reuniting the realms of León and Castile.

The Almohad empire was also racked by political turmoil. On the death of the caliph Yūsuf II (1213–24), a violent struggle for power erupted within the ranks of the ruling dynasty. As rival candidates for the throne jockeyed for position and recruited large numbers of Christian mercenaries into their service in support of their claims,

Almohad control over its Iberian territories rapidly dissolved. In the ensuing power vacuum, a number of local Muslim potentates hurried to take the reins of power into their own hands. One such was Muḥammad b. Hūd, who rebelled against Almohad authority in Murcia in 1228 and gradually extended his sovereignty over almost the whole of al-Andalus with the exception of Valencia. However, when Ibn Hūd was defeated by Alfonso IX of León at Alange in 1230, Badajoz and its adjoining territory were soon lost, and his authority began to crumble. Among the most prominent of the new *taifa* rulers, was Muḥammad Ibn al-Aḥmar (1237–72), who in 1237 carved out a new city-state, based upon Granada, which was to survive until the end of the fifteenth century.

Divided and vulnerable, the new *taifa* realms that arose from the ruins of the Almohad empire proved no match for the increasingly powerful and expansionist Christian kingdoms. With the enthusiastic support of the papacy, which offered renewed crusading indulgences, the Christian monarchs made spectacular territorial advances on all fronts. To the east, James I of Aragon conquered Majorca and the other Balearic Islands (1229–35), and then gradually overran the wealthy *taifa* of Valencia (1232–45); the city of Valencia itself fell in 1238. Henceforth, the kingdoms of Majorca and Valencia were to be considered separate realms within the loose dynastic union known as the Crown of Aragon. Aragonese successes in the east of the peninsula were amply matched in the west. While Alfonso IX of León advanced south into what is now Spanish Extremadura, conquering Cáceres (1227), and Mérida and Badajoz (1230), Ferdinand III of Castile moved steadily down the Guadalquivir valley, capturing Córdoba (1236), Jaén (1246) and Seville (1248). The *taifa* of Murcia was also brought under Castilian control in 1243–4. By 1249, the Portuguese, under Afonso III (1248–79), had brought their own campaigns to a close with the capture of the southernmost districts of the Algarve. Only landlocked Navarre, which in 1234 had come under the control of a vassal of the king of France, Count Thibaut of Champagne, was unable to profit from the collapse of the Almohad regime. Thereafter, Navarre would remain firmly in the French orbit – successively under the control of the counts of Champagne, the kings of France and the counts of Evreux – until its definitive incorporation into the Crown of Castile in 1512.

By the middle of the thirteenth century, with the exception of the fledgeling kingdom of Granada, which had been reduced to the status of a vassal kingdom, and a handful of minor enclaves on the Atlantic seaboard, Muslim power in the peninsula had almost been extinguished. For the Muslims, the cataclysmic collapse of Islamic power in southern Spain gave rise to a mood of soul-searching and despair, exemplified by the poet al-Rundī, who penned this moving lament for the demise of al-Andalus:

The white wells of ablution are weeping with sorrow,
As a lover does when torn from his beloved;
They weep over the remains of dwellings devoid of Muslims,
Despoiled of Islam, now peopled by Infidels!
Those mosques have been changed into churches,
Where the bells are ringing and crosses are standing . . .
What an opprobrium, when once powerful people
Have been humbled to dust by tyrants and injustice!
Yesterday they were kings in their own palaces,
Today they are slaves in the land of the Infidels!

AN EXPANDING SOCIETY

The spectacular territorial expansion of the Christian states of northern Iberia between c.1050 and 1250 was accompanied throughout by a less dramatic, but no less remarkable, movement of migration and colonization. In most areas, a desperate shortage of manpower meant that Christian lords from Portugal to Catalonia had to offer substantial inducements in order to attract settlers from the north to the newly conquered lands on the frontier with Islam. In the final decades of the eleventh century, for example, Alfonso VI of León-Castile set in train a programme of resettlement designed to bolster his authority over the lightly populated territory that lay between the Duero and the Tagus. Settlements such as Sepúlveda (founded in 1076), Ávila (1087), Segovia (c.1088) and Salamanca (c.1100) were designed not only to act as administrative centres, which would direct the process of repopulation in the vast areas they controlled, but also as strategic military bases, which would bear the brunt of any Muslim attacks and serve as a springboard for future cross-border campaigns. The massive granite walls and towers which were erected at Ávila in the 1090s, by order of Alfonso VI's son-in-law, Count Raymond of Burgundy, still stand to remind the modern visitor of that town's military origins.

Kings, bishops and nobles issued charters of liberties, which offered a variety of eye-catching incentives – including tax exemptions and immunity from prosecution for criminals on the run – with which to attract fighting men to the frontier. The conditions of settlement in these urban centres created unprecedented opportunities for social mobility. The frontier towns came to be dominated by a quasi-noble military class, the *caballeros villanos*, or 'commoner knights', whose privileged status was determined solely by their possession of a horse and military equipment, and their willingness to carry out military service on a regular basis, either by undertaking booty gathering raids into enemy territory or by participating in the campaigns of conquest that were periodically launched against al-Andalus by the king or his magnates. A similar model of colonization was implemented during the second decade of the twelfth century by Alfonso I of Aragon in some of the newly conquered settlements of the Ebro valley. In the frontier territories of Catalonia, around Tarragona, Tortosa and Lérida, the count-kings of Aragon likewise offered charters of liberties to attract settlers to those regions, but they did not experience the same degree of militarization that took place further to the west.

When the frontier advanced yet further south, to the exposed and sparsely populated territories between the Tagus and the Guadalquivir, and to the northern districts of Valencia, it proved far more difficult to attract settlers in sufficient numbers. In these regions, responsibility for defence and administration fell principally to the military orders, who were granted large *encomiendas*, or lordships, which were worked principally by Muslim farm labourers. Then, with the 'Great Reconquest' of the 1230s and 1240s, vast new areas of southern and eastern Spain were opened up for resettlement. In Majorca, and parts of Andalusia, Murcia and Valencia, urban and rural properties were shared out among those who had taken part in the conquest according to a system known as *repartimiento*. The chief beneficiaries were the nobility, the Church and the military orders, who were awarded substantial lordships in the newly conquered lands. The problem, as ever, was one of obtaining sufficient manpower to ensure the continued prosperity of the local economy. While agriculturally prosperous areas such as Seville and Córdoba initially had little difficulty in attracting colonists from northern Spain and even further afield, the acute shortage of labour in much of the rest of Andalusia and Murcia meant that large areas of fertile land were given over to pasture. This situation was exacerbated by the determination of lay and ecclesiastical landlords in central and northern

Iberia to halt the exodus of peasant families from their estates, by the fact that in some places (for example, Seville and Écija) many settlers soon opted to sell up and return to their places of origin, and by the large-scale expulsion of Muslims from Andalusia and Murcia following a major uprising in 1264–6. It was a very different story in the central and southern districts of Valencia, where Muslim farmers remained in sufficient numbers – under the authority of Christian overlords – to ensure the continued agricultural prosperity of the region. In these areas, Christian settlers, most of whom preferred to settle in the towns, would remain in a clear minority for generations to come.

The expansionism of Christian Iberia after the millennium was exemplified not only by the step-by-step conquest and colonization of Muslim-held territories, but by an equally dynamic process of 'internal expansion' which occurred well behind the front line. In the north of the peninsula, as in most areas of Western Europe after c.950, a combination of factors including population growth, climatic change, technological improvements (such as the more widespread adoption of irrigation techniques, better ploughs, water-mills and iron-edged tools) and extensive land clearance contributed to an increase in agricultural output. Fuelled in part by the flow of Muslim *parias* into the hands of the Christian élites, there was a dramatic upturn in the property market, as wealthy aristocratic families and ecclesiastical institutions eagerly sought to extend their landholdings at the expense of independent peasant proprietors. Many of the latter, mired in debt or feeling the effects of drought and famine, chose to sell off their lands in their entirety and to commend themselves to the protection of powerful local lords, who imposed a series of obligations, such as rent and labour duties, in return. In 1125, for example, Gutierre Fernández and his wife Toda Díaz ruled that the inhabitants of the Castilian village of San Cebrián de Campos near Carrión were to render two days service per month on their demesne ploughing, reaping, threshing, digging or pruning. In Catalonia, this process of seigneurialization was accelerated by the political upheaval that engulfed that region between c.1020 and 1060, as a result of which numerous peasant communities were forced into dependence by local castellans. During the second half of the twelfth century, faced with the danger that peasants might leave their farms altogether to seek better conditions in the frontier territories, lords in many districts of the north began to offer more generous landholding terms to their tenants than had once been the case. In Aragon proper and in Catalonia, by contrast, the peasant communities who inhabited the mountainous less productive land, and who were therefore more likely to seek better conditions elsewhere, were subjected to increased seigneurial burdens and impositions, the so-called six *malos usos*, the most burdensome of which was the stipulation that these peasants could not abandon their lands unless they paid a sum of money, known as the *remença*, to their lord.

Agriculture remained the bedrock of the economies of Christian and Muslim Iberia. While cereal cultivation, principally wheat, barley and rye, dominated the plains of the northern *meseta* and Aragon proper, to the south olive groves and fruit orchards abounded, while rice was cultivated in the area round Tortosa and Ampurdán, and citrus fruits were produced in the irrigated *huerta* of Valencia. One important change was a marked increase in the area of land given over to vineyards, notably in the areas of the Rioja, Navarre and Catalonia.

In the mountainous regions of the north and east, and in the lightly populated plains of the central and southern *meseta*, livestock breeding was the dominant economic activity. The advance of the frontier with Islam between 1085 and 1248, coupled with the chronic shortage of manpower and a growing demand for good-quality wool from textile manufacturers, both in the peninsula and abroad, contributed to a marked increase in pastoral activity. When they were not engaged in booty gathering raids into enemy territory, many frontiersmen devoted themselves to raising livestock, which in time of war could be safely corralled within the walls of the nearest town. Yet, stock-breeding was by no means the exclusive prerogative of the frontier towns. The lay magnates, the military orders and the bishoprics and monasteries of the Christian realms were equally important players in what became an increasingly lucrative economic activity. Associations of stockbreeders were founded in many places to protect the interests of their members. In Castile, the expansion of stock-rearing led to the creation of a larger and vastly more influential institution, known as the Royal Council of the *Mesta*, probably during the 1260s. It was the *Mesta*'s role to regulate the seasonal movement of flocks throughout the Kingdom of Castile and to arbitrate in the disputes that regularly flared up between rival livestock owners, or with local landholders, who complained of encroachment by stockowners on to their lands.

In common with most regions of Western Europe, the Christian realms of Iberia experienced a marked expansion of commercial activity and a revitalization of urban life between roughly 1000 and 1300. Symptomatic of this trend was the decline of barter and the introduction of silver coinage by Sancho Ramírez I of Aragon and Alfonso VI of León-Castile. In the north, the most important stimulus to commercial development was initially the pilgrimage to Santiago de Compostela. As the flow of pilgrims steadily increased after the millennium, colonies of foreign merchants and artisans began to set up shop at numerous points along the pilgrim-route. For example, during the second half of the eleventh century, the town of Jaca, situated at the foot of the Somport Pass across the central Pyrenees, was transformed from a relatively insignificant fortified settlement into a major conduit for commercial and pilgrim traffic between France and the peninsular realms. At Sahagún, south-east of León, a bustling mercantile centre was established with the encouragement of Alfonso VI, to which traders and craftsmen 'of many nations and strange languages', in the words of a local chronicler, were attracted. Yet, the merchants and artisans who took up residence along the pilgrim-road soon began to chafe at the seigneurial burdens that were imposed upon them by local lay and ecclesiastical lords. These tensions came to a head in 1110, when at Sahagún and other towns, 'brotherhoods' of merchants, artisans and peasants joined together in a series of revolts designed to free themselves from the authority of the great landowners. By 1117, the rebels had been forced to submit to the authority of their lords. Partly as a consequence, the commercial development of the towns of the *camino francés* appears to have slowed thereafter.

Commercial and urban growth was by no means simply a phenomenon of the pilgrimage to Compostela. Thanks to the boom in sheep farming, military-cum-stock-breeding settlements like Salamanca, Segovia and Ávila grew in importance during the twelfth and thirteenth centuries. On the northern seaboard, an expansion in sea fishing, whaling and long-distance trade enabled the ports of the Cantabrian coast (for example, Fuenterrabía, San Vicente de la Barquera and Santander) to develop rapidly during the latter half of the twelfth century and to become key players in shipping Basque iron and Castilian wool to the English and Flemish markets. By 1267, Castilian merchants had established their own commercial colony in Bruges. To the south-west, newly conquered Atlantic ports such as Lisbon, Cádiz and Seville, where Genoese merchants were to become prominent, developed into important staging-posts on the commercial routes that led from the Mediterranean to Northern Europe. Commercial exchange was further assisted by the creation of regional fairs, such as those established at Valladolid (1152), Cáceres (1229), Seville (1254) and Córdoba (1284).

It was in Catalonia, however, that the commercial expansion of Christian Iberia witnessed its greatest efflorescence. In Barcelona, increased profits from agriculture, coupled with the influx of Muslim tribute, acted as a stimulus to commercial activity during the eleventh century and transformed the city into an important hub of regional exchange. After 1140, local patrician families began to invest heavily in property, manufacturing, finance and commerce. The conquest of the Balearics and Valencia by James I of Aragon during the 1220s and 1230s, followed by that of Sicily by Peter III (1276–85) in 1282, gave new impetus to this process of commercial activity and helped Barcelona develop into a major centre of long-distance trade. Catalan merchants plied three main commercial routes: to North Africa, from where they acquired gold, ivory and slaves; to southern France, Sardinia and Sicily, which supplied large quantities of grain for the peninsular market; and to the eastern Mediterranean, where they obtained spices, cotton, perfumes and other luxury items. Aragonese exports included hides, wool and textiles, timber, lead, metalwork, paper, and foodstuffs such as olive oil, sugar, dried fruits, salt and wine.

Catalan merchants also established an important presence in the Atlantic trade, founding colonies in Seville, Lisbon and Bruges. Investors and merchants entered into commercial partnerships through short-term *commenda* contracts, whereby a merchant would undertake to sell an investor's goods overseas, or purchase merchandise on his behalf, typically in return for a quarter share of any profits. Occasionally, merchants might even join together to form a commercial company, with any profits being shared out annually among the investors. In 1257, the institution called the 'Consulate of the Sea' (*Consulat del Mar*), was founded which fulfilled the functions of a chamber of commerce, arbitrated in conflicts between merchants and developed an influential body of maritime law, the *Llibre del Consulat del Mar* (1283). Increased demand for credit led to the development of banking institutions in the fourteenth century. Although it would be misleading to suggest that Aragonese foreign policy was dictated by the Catalan merchant élite, the kings of Aragon did what they could to protect the interests of traders. In 1274, James I even lobbied Pope Innocent IV to abandon his plans for a crusade against Tunis, for fear of the damage such an expedition would cause to Aragonese commercial interests in the Maghreb.

The resurgence of commercial activity in the peninsula was accompanied by a modest expansion of industrial activity. While in much of northern and western Iberia manufacturing remained the preserve of a relatively small number of largely urban-based artisans, such as cobblers, carpenters, tailors, ironworkers and potters, who catered mainly for local markets, some of the Castilian towns that lay astride the main transhumant routes, such as Zamora, Ávila, Segovia and Soria, began to produce textiles in sufficient volume in the thirteenth century to begin exporting to neighbouring Portugal. In Catalonia and Valencia, ironwork, leather goods and textiles were also manufactured for export. One of the most important growth industries of the thirteenth century was shipbuilding, notably in the Cantabrian ports, Barcelona and Seville. A consequence of the expansion of artisan activity was the creation of guilds from the first half of the twelfth century.

THE LAND OF THREE RELIGIONS

As the Christian states expanded southwards after $c.1050$, the process of colonization was complicated by the presence of substantial communities of Muslims, Jews and Mozarabs (Christians who had been living under Muslim rule). The latter were to be found in particularly large numbers in the territory of Toledo, where they were awarded their own charter of privileges by Alfonso VI in 1101. Almoravid persecution during the first quarter of the twelfth century prompted further large-scale emigration of Mozarabs to the Christian north. In the winter of 1125–6, Alfonso I of Aragon led a daring incursion as far south as the outskirts of Granada, in the course of which large numbers of Mozarabs rallied to the king's banner and accompanied him back to the Ebro valley, where they were granted a special charter of settlement. In retaliation, the Almoravid authorities deported many of the remaining Mozarabs to Morocco, where they would remain until the collapse of the Almoravid empire in 1147.

Christian policy towards the Mudejars, that is, the Muslims who chose to remain under Christian rule, has been characterized by one historian as 'contradictory and muddled'. On the one hand, the Christian authorities regarded Mudejar workers as indispensable for the continued economic prosperity of the areas in which they dwelled and were keen for them to stay; on the other, Muslims were widely feared as potential 'fifth columnists', who might ultimately rise up against Christian rule. For James I of Aragon, 'the Moors of the

Kingdom of Valencia are all traitors and have often made us under-stand that whereas we treat them well, they are ever seeking to do us harm'. In those places where the Christians had faced armed resistance from the inhabitants, Muslims were forcibly expelled from their homes and lands. After the conquest of Majorca was completed in 1231, barely a tenth of the original Muslim population remained; in Andalusia and Murcia, a major Mudejar uprising in 1264–6 led to the ethnic cleansing of the local Muslim population. For other Muslims, the consequences of Christian conquest were graver still. When Minorca and Ibiza were brought under direct rule by Alfonso III of Aragon (1285–91) in 1287, a large proportion of the Muslim popula-tion of the islands was sold into slavery and their lands shared out among the Christian settlers.

In most cases, however, the surrender terms agreed with capitulat-ing Muslims respected the property, as well as the civil and religious rights of the conquered. Wealthy Muslims generally opted to emigrate to Granada or North Africa; those that remained were mostly small farmers or artisans of limited means. While the Christian authorities opted on security grounds to expel Mudejar citizens from major urban centres such as Toledo, Valencia and Seville, the chronic shortage of manpower meant that substantial communities of Mudejars were allowed to remain in the rural hinterland. In Valencia and Aragon, Mudejars made up at least a quarter of the population; in some districts of Navarre, notably at Tudela, the proportion was more than half. In such areas, it has sometimes been claimed, a state of *convivencia*, or harmonious co-existence, between Christian, Muslim and Jew prevailed. Muslims were considered subjects of the Crown, and they and their property enjoyed royal protection. In many areas, Mudejars enjoyed freedom of movement and the right to buy and sell. At Ávila, Cuenca and other frontier towns they were even permitted to serve in the local militia. Social interaction was extensive: Church councils in early fourteenth-century Castile complained that Jews and Muslims were attending Mass and that Mudejar minstrels were being hired to play in churches during night vigils. Linguistic evidence of social interaction is provided by the 4000 or so Arabic loan words, particu-larly terms relating to agriculture, commerce, industry and war, which were incorporated into the Romance vernaculars, particularly Castilian and Portuguese.

None the less, Mudejars were subjected to a range of discriminatory measures. In some towns, Mudejars were obliged to reside in their own *aljamas*, or ghettoes: in Murcia, Alfonso X of Castile (1252–84), the self-styled 'King of the Three Religions', even had a wall built to separate the Mudejar citizens from their Christian counterparts. In most places, Mudejars were barred from holding public office; in litigation between Christians and Muslims the latter tended to find the scales of justice weighted against them. Mudejar farmers were also liable to a far heavier range of taxes and dues than their Christian counterparts: even in Navarre, where Muslim communities enjoyed an impressive range of religious, social and economic liberties, Mudejar farmers were obliged to render up to one-quarter of their agricultural produce in tax. Although most Mudejars were allowed to trade freely with Christians, other social intercourse was discouraged: segregation of Christians, Muslims and Jews was the norm in municipal bath-houses; sexual relations between Christians and Mudejars or Jews were punishable by burning or stoning to death. Mudejar *aljamas* could also become the target of Christian popular resentment: between 1276 and 1291, for example, anti-Mudejar riots flared up in a number of towns in the region of Valencia.

The eleventh century has been described as a Golden Age for the Jews of al-Andalus. Jewish merchants were leading players in the trading networks which linked al-Andalus to the Mediterranean and beyond; Jewish literary culture enjoyed a notable renaissance; and a number of prominent Jews even came to hold positions of influence within the *taifa* states, notably Samuel b. Naghrila (d. 1056) and his son Joseph, both of whom served as chief minister to the Zīrīd rulers of Granada. However, influence on this scale could breed resentment. In 1066, anti-Jewish feeling among the Muslim populace of Granada led to the massacre of local Jews, including Joseph b. Naghrila himself. The Granada pogrom was the exception rather than the rule, but it foreshadowed the problems that lay ahead for Iberian Jewry. Under Almoravid and Almohad rule, the Jews, like the Mozarabs, were to be subjected to increased levels of persecution, as a result of which many chose to emigrate to other parts of the peninsula. By the end of the thirteenth century, Castilian tax-rolls indicate that there were some 3600 Jewish families resident in the kingdom; the figure in the territories of the Crown of Aragon was probably higher still. The Christian rulers allowed Jews free practice of their religion and they also granted them a range of social and economic privileges. Many Jews attained wealth and influence as tax collectors, diplomats, physicians, translators, financiers and merchants; others made a living as artisans and small farmers. Although Church assemblies, such as the Lateran Councils of 1179 and 1215, issued decrees designed to enforce social segregation between Christians and non-Christians, the rulers of the Iberian kingdoms proved notably reluctant to enforce them.

During the thirteenth century, the evangelization of Muslim and Jewish communities began to be promoted in some Christian circles. In 1219, a group of friars of the Franciscan Order journeyed to Seville to preach the Gospel and then crossed to Morocco, where they ultimately met martyrdom. The Dominican Ramon de Penyafort (d. 1275) founded a short-lived school of Arabic studies in Tunis in 1250, and a school of Arabic and Hebrew at Murcia in 1266 where missionaries were trained. In 1276, through the influence of the Franciscan writer and missionary Ramon Lull (d. 1315), James II (1276–1311) of Majorca founded a college to train missionaries to Islam. With royal permission, friars were allowed to preach both to Muslims and Jews, and they also took part in public disputations with Jewish and Muslim religious authorities: one such debate, between Christian and Jewish preachers, was celebrated in Barcelona in the presence of James I of Aragon in 1263. All were agreed, however, that reason not force was necessary to win over converts to Christ. Alfonso X of Castile encouraged his fellow Christians

> to convert the Moors and cause them to believe in our faith by kind words and suitable preaching, not by force or compulsion ... for Our Lord is not pleased by service that men give Him through fear, but with that which they do willingly and without any pressure.

IBERIAN POLITICS, 1250–1350

The progressive disintegration of Almohad political authority in al-Andalus between 1225 and 1248 was accompanied by the implosion of its empire in the Maghreb, as it came under attack from a number of competing Berber dynasties: the Hafsids in Tunisia; the Zayyanids based at Tlemcen; and the Merinids, who established themselves in Morocco. The latter would not only become the dominant power in North Africa for the best part of a century, but would also, like the Almoravids and Almohads before them, seek to extend their power across the Straits. Within the peninsula itself, the Nasrid emirate of Granada, founded in 1238, whose frontiers stretched roughly from

Almería to the Straits of Gibraltar, emerged as the last major stronghold of independent Muslim power. That Granada was to maintain this independence until 1492 owed less to its military strength, than to its readiness to exchange peace with Castile in return for tribute, to the political infighting which regularly convulsed the Christian north after *c*.1250, and not least to the consummate skill with which successive Nasrid rulers regularly shifted allegiance between Castile, Aragon and the Merinids in defence of their interests.

In the immediate aftermath of the fall of the Almohad empire, Castile continued to exert military pressure on the Muslim south. The armies of Alfonso X captured the tiny Muslim enclaves of Cádiz and Niebla in 1259 and 1262 respectively, while in 1260 a crusading expedition sacked the port of Salé in Morocco. Further territorial expansion was checked in 1264, however, when the Mudejar population of Andalusia and Murcia, actively supported by Muḥammad I of Granada and the Merinid emir, Abū Yūsuf Ya'qūb (1258–86), rose in rebellion. The rising was crushed, thanks in large part to the support of James I of Aragon, and was followed by the large-scale expulsion of the Mudejar population, many of whom found refuge in Granada. That the Castilian grip on the former Muslim territories of the Guadalquivir valley was still far from secure, was further demonstrated in 1275, when the Merinids, assisted by Muḥammad II of Granada (1272–1302), raided north towards Córdoba and Jaén, and routed a Christian army near Écija. The Merinids subsequently withdrew to Africa, but they retained control over the strategic ports of Algeciras and Tarifa which had been ceded to them by Muḥammad II.

The untimely death of Alfonso X's eldest son, Ferdinand de la Cerda, in the course of the campaign of 1275, was to trigger a bitter succession dispute in Castile. Alfonso X is justly celebrated as a distinguished patron of the arts, but his ambitious programme of administrative reform, his economic policies and what were widely regarded as his vainglorious claims to the crown of the Holy Roman Empire, served only to alienate the nobility, the military orders, the towns, and ultimately his own family. In 1282, Alfonso's second son, Sancho, fearing that his father intended to bequeath part of his realms to the children of Ferdinand de la Cerda, seized power and forced his father to withdraw to Seville. In a last, desperate throw of the dice, Alfonso unsuccessfully sought to regain his throne by forging an alliance with the Merinids, who besieged Córdoba and raided as far north as Madrid. On Alfonso X's death in April 1284, Sancho IV (1284–95) was crowned king of Castile. However, relations with France and Aragon were by no means cordial, because of their support for the cause of Alfonso X's grandson, Alfonso de la Cerda, who claimed the throne for himself, and matters were further complicated by the refusal of the papacy to regard Sancho's marriage to his cousin, María de Molina, as legitimate. Sancho also had to contend with renewed Merinid intervention in the south of the peninsula. In 1291, in an attempt to hinder the movement of Merinid forces across the Straits, Sancho, assisted by Muḥammad II of Granada, captured Tarifa. Prior to this, in 1291, at Monteagudo, the Castilian monarch had signed a treaty with his Aragonese counterpart, James II (1291–1327), which mapped out their future areas of expansion in North Africa, assigning Morocco to Castile.

Sancho IV's son and successor, Ferdinand IV (1295–1312), was only 9 years old when he came to the throne, as a result of which his mother, María de Molina, assumed the regency and defended her son against the rival claims of Alfonso de la Cerda. In 1296, the latter invaded Castile with Aragonese support and had himself crowned king at Jaén, but was later forced to beat a retreat. In 1301, Ferdinand's position was bolstered when the papacy finally recognised his legitimacy. Once he had come of age, Ferdinand, in alliance with James II of Aragon, renewed the military push against al-Andalus. While the Aragonese invested Almería, Castilian forces captured Gibraltar in 1309 and besieged Algeciras, prompting Muḥammad III of Granada (1302–8) to seek a new alliance with the Merinids. In the event, unrest among the Castilian magnates forced Ferdinand to raise the siege of Algeciras in 1310, while the Aragonese also withdrew from Almería without achieving their objectives.

When Ferdinand IV died in September 1312, leaving the throne to his infant son, the one-year-old Alfonso XI (1312–50), a long drawn-out struggle for the regency among the king's family erupted. It was not until Alfonso came of age, in 1325, that the authority of the monarchy was successfully restored: rebellious nobles were subdued; the king's cousin, John, was executed and another cousin, John Manuel, forced into exile; royal control over the towns was reinforced with the appointment of officials known as *corregidores*; and an important step towards legislative unification was achieved by the promulgation of Alfonso X's *Siete Partidas* in 1348. The second half of the reign was dominated by the struggle with the Merinids, who, under their emir Abū'-l-Ḥasan (1331–51), were to reinforce their authority in the Maghreb by conquering the Zayyanid kingdom of Tlemcen in 1337 and the Hafsid realm in Tunisia in 1347. In 1340, Abū'-l-Ḥasan led an expedition to the peninsula where, in alliance with Yūsuf I of Granada (1333–54), he besieged Tarifa. In response, Alfonso XI, assisted by Portuguese forces and an Aragonese fleet, as well as contingents of crusaders from Northern Europe, defeated the combined Muslim armies at the River Salado near Tarifa in October 1340. In March 1344, with the support of a substantial body of foreign volunteers, including the English earls of Derby and Salisbury, Alfonso XI tightened his control over the Straits by conquering Algeciras. Five years after that, he tried to recapture Gibraltar (which had been lost in 1333) with the aid of Aragonese forces, but the siege was abandoned after an outbreak of bubonic plague caused the death of many among the besieging army, not least that of Alfonso XI himself in March 1350. As a result of the victory at the Río Salado and the operations which ensued, Castilian control over the Straits was secured, the threat of invasion from Morocco correspondingly diminished, and Christian crusading enthusiasm began to subside. Although military operations against Granada would by no means entirely cease after 1350, the Reconquest would thereafter take a back seat to more pressing internal political concerns.

The catastrophic defeat and death of Peter II at the hands of the Albigensian crusaders in 1213 caused the almost total collapse of Aragonese influence in southern France. In 1258, by the treaty of Corbeil, James I formally renounced his title to most of his suzerain-ties in Occitania, while Louis IX of France gave up his own traditional claims to the Catalan counties; shortly afterwards, James also surren-dered his territorial rights in Provence. Thereafter, the Aragonese monarchy was to channel its energies towards reinforcing its sphere of influence in the western Mediterranean. In June 1282, James I's ambi-tious son, Peter III, responded to appeals from the Sicilian rebels who had taken up arms against their lord, Charles of Anjou, and annexed the island after a short campaign, stirring up a veritable hornets' nest in the process. Since the island was nominally a papal fief, Pope Martin IV promptly excommunicated Peter, offered the throne of Aragon to Charles of Valois, son of Philip III of France, and granted crusading indulgences to the French army that crossed the Pyrenees in June 1285 in pursuit of that claim. To add to Peter's problems, the French were backed by the king's brother, James II, who had inherited a separate kingdom of Majorca, comprising the Balearics and Roussillon, on the death of James I. In the event, the French forces

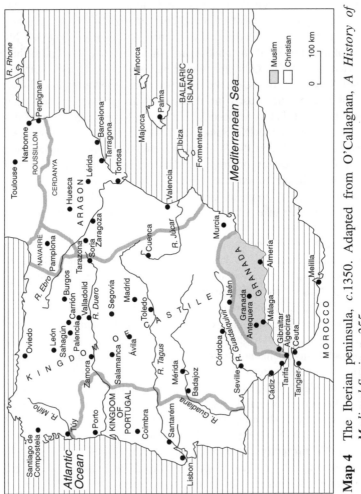

Map 4 The Iberian peninsula, c.1350. Adapted from O'Callaghan, *A History of Medieval Spain*, p. 355.

were severely hampered by poor weather and inadequate supplies and were forced to withdraw the following October. Two years later, Peter III's son, Alfonso III, defeated James II of Majorca and conquered the Balearics, as a result of which James II pledged homage and fealty to Aragon.

During the reign of Alfonso's brother and successor, James II, the Crown of Aragon was to reach a new peak of power. By the Treaty of Anagni (1295), James defused the diplomatic imbroglio with the papacy and was recognized as king of Sardinia and Corsica by Pope Boniface VIII, in return for which he agreed to restore Sicily to its former lords, the Angevins. But the latter was easier said than done. The viceroy of Sicily, James's brother, Frederick, proclaimed himself king and successfully maintained the independence of Sicily despite his brother's best efforts to reduce him. After the Sicilian war was brought to a close in 1302, Catalan influence in the Mediterranean was extended even further afield by roving groups of mercenaries, known as *almogàvers*. After enrolling in the service of the Byzantine emperor, these soldiers went on to establish duchies in Athens and Neopatria in 1311, which survived, in dependence on Sicily, until 1388. Peter IV (1336–87) was equally determined to bolster his authority over the scattered dynastic territories of the Crown of Aragon. In 1344, he definitively reincorporated the kingdom of Majorca, including the mainland lordship of Roussillon, to the Crown. In 1378, he secured effective control over Sicily by appointing his second son, Martin, as viceroy to the island, and in 1379–80, he brought the Catalan duchies in Greece under his direct authority, although they were to collapse shortly after his death. His attempts to subdue Sardinia, which remained a bone of contention between Aragon and Genoa, were less successful, however.

KINGSHIP AND GOVERNMENT

Christian society, contemporaries were fond of saying, was structured according to a hierarchical model of three orders: those that fought (the nobility), those that prayed (the clergy and monks), and those that laboured (the peasants and artisans). At the very apex of that society was the king, in whose name wars were fought and peace was negotiated, laws were passed, coins were minted and the process of colonization was directed. Yet, royal power would have withered away had it not been for the close collaboration of the great nobles of the kingdom, whose political and economic power had long since set them apart as the indispensable agents of government. For the king, the lack of a professional army meant that the military service and contingents of troops provided by his magnates were essential if he wished to wage war against his enemies. The monarch also relied upon the nobles to serve in his household, to advise him on matters of state, to serve as judges in the lawsuits that came before the court, and to conduct diplomacy on his behalf, while by a wholesale delegation of his power, he also entrusted them with large areas of the realm to administer in his name. In return for their loyal service, nobles were granted estates to hold in perpetuity, together with benefices in land, castles and money, as well as other privileges, such as immunity from taxation. Below the charmed circle of the magnates, there was a large, amorphous group of lesser nobles, known as *infanzones* or, from the twelfth century, *hidalgos*. These individuals lacked the political and economic clout of the magnates, but none the less enjoyed the social cachet and the fiscal and legal privileges conferred by noble ancestry. The same could not be said of the *caballeros villanos*, whose privileged status was determined wholly by their military function, although the line that separated such commoner-knights from those families whose noble status derived from birth became increasingly blurred with the passage of time.

Kings did not rule from a fixed seat of government. The primary and most characteristic feature of their authority was the royal itinerary, during the course of which the sovereign and his retinue journeyed around the kingdom dealing with royal business as and when it arose. In the absence of centralized administrative, legal and fiscal institutions, kings were forced to keep on the move if they were to maintain any semblance of political cohesion within their realms. They were assisted in the business of government by a small body of trusted lay and ecclesiastical magnates. Great assemblies, to which all the lay and ecclesiastical notables of the kingdom were invited, were also periodically summoned. These were ceremonial occasions, which enabled the sovereign to receive the collective fealty of the notables of his realm, but they also fulfilled consultative and judicial functions. It was at just such a 'general curia' held at León in 1109, for example, that the marriage of Queen Urraca of León-Castile and Alfonso I of Aragon was approved. By the early thirteenth century, these assemblies had developed into more formalized institutions, known as *cortes* (Catalan *corts*), to which the magnates, prelates and representatives of the towns were periodically summoned. The mass of the population – the peasantry and artisans – were denied any such representation. The primary function of the *cortes* was to give consent to the levying of new taxes, but its representatives were also allowed to present grievances to the king, seek confirmation of their privileges, and to discuss matters relating to the dynastic succession, war and diplomacy, or taxation and legislation. In Catalonia, a standing committee, called the *Diputació* or *Generalitat*, dealt with ongoing business after the *cortes* had been dissolved, and similar institutions developed in the other realms of the Aragonese confederation.

The development of parliamentary institutions during the thirteenth century was accompanied by a gradual transformation of legal structures. Influenced by the revival of Roman law, the rediscovery of Aristotelian political theory and new developments in canon law, Christian monarchs sought to bring some measure of legislative unification to kingdoms where the traditional Visigothic law-code had been supplemented or superseded by a bewildering multiplicity of territorial laws and local privileges. To this end, Alfonso X of Castile oversaw the preparation of two major codes: the 'Royal Fuero' (*Fuero Real*, c.1255), which was designed to regulate legal procedures in the towns of the kingdom; and the 'Mirror of Law' (*Espéculo de las leyes*, c.1260), which dealt with the royal administration of justice and was to form the basis of the encyclopaedic legal code, the *Siete Partidas*, which was completed in the 1260s. Nobles, who had traditionally served as justices on the royal legal tribunal, were replaced by legists trained in Roman law. These innovations reflected far more than simply a desire to standardize legal practices. By embracing the principles of Roman law, the Alfonsine law codes sought to reinforce the authority of the monarchy and emphasize the king's right to wield public authority over all his subjects, noble and non-noble alike. As the *Siete Partidas* declared:

> Kings ... are vicars of God, placed over the people to maintain them in justice and truth in temporal matters, in the same way as the emperor does in his empire. ... The king is the head of the kingdom, and just as the senses, by which all the members of the body are controlled, originate in the head, so all ought to be directed and guided by the commands which originate with the king, who is lord and head of all the people of the realm.

Alfonso X's innovations in government placed him on a collision course with the Castilian magnates, who viewed the reforms as a fundamental attack on their traditional liberties and their privileged position at the heart of government. As a result, Alfonso X had to confront a large-scale baronial rebellion against his rule in 1272, which would oblige him to abandon the programme of centralization by which he set such great store. It was a similar story in the Crown of Aragon, where James I's attempts to introduce centralizing Roman and canon law, and replace the nobles in his administration with Jews and professional jurists, provoked a major revolt in 1265–6 and led the barons of Aragon and Valencia to form a Union to defend their interests. In 1283, Peter III was forced to issue a general privilege in which he swore to respect the traditional privileges of the nobility, limit their military obligations, place restrictions on the taxes he could raise, and summon the *cortes* regularly. In 1287, Alfonso III was even threatened with deposition if he took action against any member of the Union without the consent of the Justiciar (a noble who oversaw the judicial activities of the court) and the *cortes*. The struggle between the Aragonese monarchy and the nobility would drag on until 1348, when Peter IV defeated the nobles at Epila, south-west of Zaragoza, and destroyed the Union for good. Even then, the Aragonese kings would find their power hedged about by numerous constitutional restraints, not least the unwillingness of the Aragonese, Catalan and Valencian *cortes* to grant financial aid to the king until their grievances had been addressed. In Castile, by contrast, the *cortes* proved increasingly compliant to the monarch's wishes, particularly during the fifteenth century, with the result that the Crown was able to obtain ever-higher sums in public taxation.

CULTURAL DEVELOPMENTS

The collapse of unitary political authority in al-Andalus in 1009 did not herald the cultural decadence of the region thereafter. On the contrary, the rulers of the *taifa* states sought to emulate their Umayyad predecessors by each sustaining a court of some splendour, by commissioning prestigious public building projects – such as the elegant Aljafería palace which was erected in Zaragoza by its ruler al-Muqtadir – and by exercising artistic patronage on a lavish scale. At Cuenca, for example, a school of ivory carving flourished under the patronage of the Dhu'l-Nunids of Toledo. The *taifa* courts became renowned centres of cultural excellence at which scientists, poets and other scholars were able to thrive. Among the most influential of the many writers who were active at this time of cultural flowering, were the astronomer Ibn al-Zarqiyāl (d. 1100), whose works circulated widely in Western Europe, and Ibn Ḥazm of Córdoba (d. 1064), whose voluminous writings included a celebrated disquisition on love, *The Ring of the Dove*, and a treatise on comparative religion. Some of the *taifa* rulers, notably al-Muẓaffar of Badajoz (1045–68), and al-Muʻtaḍid (1042–69) and al-Muʻtamid of Seville, were accomplished poets and scholars in their own right. During the twelfth century, the Almohad conquest of al-Andalus was to bring the region more fully into contact with Middle Eastern philosophy and science, which had largely been forbidden during the time of the Umayyad caliphate and the *taifas*. Among the most eminent of the philosophers active at this time were Ibn Tufayl (d. 1185) and Ibn Rushd (Averröes) (d. 1198), author of a series of influential commentaries on the works of Aristotle. After the disintegration of the Almohad empire in the 1220s, however, many of the leading scholars of the age sought asylum in the Maghreb or even further afield, with the result that the literary output of al-Andalus went into marked decline thereafter. The leading intellectual figure in Nasrid Granada was the poet, physician and historian Ibn al-Khaṭīb (d. 1374).

Hebrew literature and learning also flourished during the eleventh and twelfth centuries. Among the most distinguished Jewish scholars, mention should be made of the poets Solomon b. Gabirol (d. *c*.1056), best known for the influential philosophical work *The Fountain of Life*, Moses b. Ezra (d. 1138) and Judah Halevi (d. 1141). A number of Jewish scholars explored the relationship between Judaism and Aristotelian philosophy, by far the most celebrated of whom was Moses Maimonides (d. 1204), who was forced into exile by Almohad persecution and ended his days in Egypt. Jews also played a prominent part in the translation of Arabic works into Latin and Castilian under the patronage of Alfonso X of Castile (see below).

Prior to the thirteenth century, literary culture in the Christian north remained largely the preserve of a small ecclesiastical élite and Latin the dominant language of learning. Historical writing, which was to find its most impressive expression in the ambitious 'general histories' penned by Archbishop Rodrigo Jiménez of Toledo (d. 1247) and Bishop Lucas of Túy (d. *c*.1249), enjoyed a particular surge in popularity. Yet, while

Latin was to remain an important vehicle for literary expression throughout the later Middle Ages, vernacular texts began to proliferate from the thirteenth century onwards. Works of epic verse, of which the Castilian *Cantar del mio Cid* (*c*.1207) is the most celebrated example, and lyric poetry, sung in Provençal, Galician-Portuguese and Castilian, enjoyed widespread popularity. Under the patronage of Alfonso X of Castile, the range of works produced in the vernacular expanded dramatically, including as it did two monumental works of history – the 'General History' (*General Estoria*) and the 'History of Spain' (*Estoria de Espanna*) – and the 'Canticles of Saint Mary' (*Cantigas de Santa María*), a collection of 400 songs in praise of the Virgin composed in Galician-Portuguese. Alfonso's contemporary, James I of Aragon, was responsible for an autobiographical account of his reign in Catalan; other major writers in Catalan included the historians Bernat Desclot (d. 1288) and Ramon Muntaner (d. 1336), the physician Arnau de Vilanova (d. 1311) and, not least, the indefatigable Ramon Lull, who was reputedly the author of as many as 250 works in Catalan, Latin and Arabic in the fields of comparative religion, philosophy and poetry. During the fourteenth and fifteenth centuries, authors began to explore new literary genres. The 'Book of Good Love' (*El Libro de Buen Amor*), by the Archpriest of Hita, Juan Ruiz (d. *c*.1351) poked fun at the loose morals and corruption of the clergy; chivalric tales, such as the Catalan works *Tirant lo Blanch* and *Curial and Guelfa*, enjoyed particular popularity.

It has often been said that the late medieval peninsula constituted a 'cultural bridge' between Islam and Western Christendom. With the fall of Toledo in 1085 and the advance southwards of the frontier thereafter, cultural contacts between Christians and Muslims intensified. Mudejar styles of architecture and decoration, characterized by the use of brick, plaster and wood rather than stone, were embraced in many areas of the Christian realms. One of the most striking examples is the Chapel of La Asunción, erected in the royal nunnery of Las Huelgas in Burgos at the end of the twelfth century, which was strongly influenced by Almohad architectural styles and was almost certainly built by Muslim craftsmen. Conversely, some of the frescoes which adorn the ceiling of the Sala de los Reyes in the elegant palace-complex of the Alhambra in Granada – much of which was erected under Nasrid patronage during the fourteenth century – may have been executed by Christian artists.

Acculturation was also manifested in the extensive translation of

Arabic works, mostly philosophical and scientific texts, into Latin and the vernacular. 'It befits us to imitate the Arabs especially', commented one of the earliest translators, Hugo of Santalla (*fl*. 1145), 'for they are as it were our teachers and precursors in this art'. From the first half of the twelfth century, translators were active in Barcelona, Tarazona and Tudela, but the most important centre of study was established in Toledo, where a group of Iberian and foreign scholars, including Domingo González, archdeacon of Segovia, the Italian scholar Gerard of Cremona, the converted Jew Avendaut and John of Seville, collaborated in an ambitious programme of translation. It was thanks to the efforts of translators like these that the works of Ancient Greek thinkers, such as Aristotle, Euclid and Ptolemy, as well as those of Arabic and Jewish scholars, began to circulate widely in the Latin West. Alfonso X of Castile commissioned the translation into Castilian of a number of Arabic scientific and philosophical works, as well as treatises on more esoteric matters, such as magic and chess.

Christian Iberia was also becoming increasingly exposed to European cultural and intellectual trends. In particular, the thirteenth century saw the foundation of the first universities in the peninsula. The schools which were founded at Palencia by Alfonso VIII of Castile *c*.1200 did not prosper; those at Salamanca, which were granted royal privileges by Alfonso IX of León in 1218, were later to become one of the most distinguished centres of learning in Christendom. Other universities were established at Lisbon (1290), which later relocated to Coimbra (1308), Lérida (1300), Valladolid (1346) and Huesca (1354). The university curriculum consisted principally of law, philosophy, rhetoric, logic, grammar and medicine. Alfonso X even proposed to establish a centre of learning in Seville, where Arabic and Latin might be taught, but the project does not appear to have got beyond the drawing board.

CRISIS AND RECOVERY

During the fourteenth century, the economic expansion which had been such a notable feature of the Iberian peninsula since the millennium, was interrupted. The effects of warfare and periodic outbreaks of famine, such as those which affected Catalonia in 1333 and 1347, were exacerbated by the spread of disease. Between 1348 and 1350, an epidemic of bubonic plague – better known as the Black Death – swept across Western Europe. Within the peninsula, its effects were particularly pronounced in the territories of the Crown of Aragon: Peter IV estimated that around a third of his subjects died as a consequence of the epidemic; in Valencia and Zaragoza, the mortality rate reached 50 per cent; at the Cistercian abbey of Poblet near Tarragona, two abbots, 59 choir-monks and 30 lay brothers perished from the plague in 1348 alone.

The social and economic consequences of the plague were widely felt: a severe shortage of manpower forced landlords to reduce rents by up to two-thirds; agricultural land was abandoned and villages deserted; prices rose sharply; and royal revenues declined, with the result that taxes had to be raised in order to meet the shortfall in income. As the rural economy declined, lay and ecclesiastical lords tried to recoup their losses by increasing the seigneurial burdens on the work-force. As a result, outbreaks of unrest among agricultural workers and artisans became commonplace. In the towns of the Castilian *meseta*, *hermandades*, or brotherhoods, were established to defend communities against the excesses of the nobility and to curb local brigandage. In Catalonia, demographic decline, compounded by growing financial insecurity and increasingly fierce commercial competition from the Castilians and Genoese, led to the decline of the once buoyant Catalan trading empire. Between *c.*1350 and 1450 the volume of trade that passed through Barcelona fell five-fold.

The economic trend was by no means uniformly downward. Castilian sheep rearing, less heavily reliant on manpower, expanded dramatically during the fourteenth and fifteenth centuries, in response to growing foreign demand for quality merino wool, particularly from cloth manufacturers in Flanders and Italy. At the beginning of the fourteenth century, there were an estimated half a million sheep in Castile; by 1480 the figure had grown to some 5 million. Supervised by the increasingly influential *Mesta*, transhumant flocks circulated along three major migration routes called *cañadas*: one stretched from León south to Badajoz; another from the central Duero valley to the valleys of the Alcudia and the Guadalquivir; and another from the hill area around Cuenca down to Murcia and the Upper Guadalquivir. In the summer, these flocks grazed in the north before moving down to the pasture lands of La Mancha, Extremadura and Andalusia in September. The wool trade brought great prosperity to the nobility, military orders and high clergy, who owned the majority of the flocks, and to transit centres such as Burgos, through which the bulk of Castilian raw wool passed prior to shipping from the Cantabrian ports.

Another symptom of the social crisis which gripped the peninsula in the fourteenth century was a marked rise in Christian hostility towards the Jews. Crude anti-Semitic propaganda, claiming that Jews had ritually murdered Christian children or caused the Black Death, circulated widely, particularly during the Castilian civil wars of the 1360s, and Jewish *aljamas* became the target of violent attacks. In the summer of 1391, up to 4000 Jews were reportedly massacred in Seville, followed by similar pogroms in towns throughout Andalusia, and as far afield as León, Burgos, Valencia, Barcelona, Jaca, Majorca and Perpignan. Many thousands of Jews only saved themselves by converting to Christianity and became known as *conversos*. Mudejar communities were also subjected to increased Christian hostility, although without the large-scale loss of life experienced by the Jews.

The political history of the peninsula in the fourteenth and fifteenth centuries was marked by regular dynastic crises and civil wars. In the kingdom of Granada, internal divisions within the Nasrid ruling house were such that the emirate changed hands on no fewer than ten occasions between 1417 and 1450. Between 1450 and 1460, Navarre was similarly convulsed by civil war, between the aristocratic supporters of John, prince of Aragon, and those of his son, Charles, prince of Viana. In the Crown of Aragon, the failure of Peter IV's second son, Martin I (1395–1410), to produce a legitimate heir and his attempts to enthrone his illegitimate grandson, Frederick, provoked a grave political crisis, as four rival candidates staked their own claim to the crown. Eventually, in June 1412, a commission of nine representatives, nominated by the *cortes* of Aragon, Catalonia and Valencia, convened at Caspe and designated a member of the Castilian Trastámara house, Ferdinand of Antequera, as king. Under Ferdinand I (1412–16), and his sons Alfonso V (1416–58) and John II (1458–79), the consolidation of Aragonese power in the western Mediterranean would remain a primordial concern. Alfonso V tightened his control over Sicily and Sardinia, and in 1442–3 he conquered the kingdom of Naples, which thereafter was to become the seat of his government. On Alfonso's death in 1458, Naples passed to his illegitimate son, Ferdinand, while the rest of the Aragonese confederation was bequeathed to the latter's half-brother, John II. John inherited a difficult situation. In Catalonia, rural and urban unrest was endemic and the king's attempts to resolve the plight of the peasantry, or to achieve some measure of municipal reform, provoked a rebellion against his authority in the 1460s. Social unrest was at its most intense in Barcelona, where faction-fighting between the patrician élite (the *Biga*) and a party of traders and artisans (the *Busca*), dragged on until 1472.

In Castile, the reign of Peter I (1350–69) was to be dominated by that king's bitter struggle for the throne with the illegitimate sons of Alfonso XI and Leonor de Guzmán. Peter's ruthless conduct towards his family, which later won him the epithet 'the Cruel', and his supposed favouritism towards the Jews, alienated many among the secular and ecclesiastical magnates, who offered their support to his half-brother Henry Trastámara. Peter IV of Aragon, who engaged in a prolonged yet fruitless war with Castile between 1357 and 1367, offered his support to the pretender and, to complicate matters further, England and France, then engaged in the Hundred Years War, also became embroiled. With the backing of the French and Aragonese, who provided the funds to recruit a large army of mercenaries, Henry was proclaimed king in 1366, only to be driven out the following year by Peter I, who had allied himself with the English and Navarrese. The civil war dragged on until 1369, when Peter was defeated at Montiel and murdered by his half-brother, who would rule thereafter as Henry II (1369–79).

Despite its victory in the Castilian civil war, the position of the Trastámara dynasty remained precarious. John of Gaunt, Duke of Lancaster, who had married Peter I's daughter and heir, Constanza, in 1371, was determined to press his own claim to the Castilian throne. When a war for the Portuguese succession broke out in 1383, between Henry II's son, John I of Castile (1379–90), and the Master of the Military Order of Avis, who was shortly to be proclaimed John I of Portugal (1385–1433), English forces intervened on the side of the latter, who inflicted a humiliating defeat on the Castilians at Aljubarrota (1385). The following year, Lancaster invaded Galicia and concluded an alliance with the Portuguese, which was cemented by the marriage of the duke's daughter, Philippa, to John I of Portugal in 1387. However, a joint Anglo-Portuguese invasion of Castile proved a military fiasco and prompted Lancaster to conclude a negotiated settlement with John I at Bayonne in 1388: the duke and his wife renounced their claim to the Castilian throne in return for a sizeable cash payment and annual pension, and the marriage of their daughter, Catherine, to the future Henry III (1390–1406). The following year, the truces of Leulingham and Monção brought French and English intervention in peninsular politics to an end.

One of the most striking developments of the second half of the fourteenth century was the expansion of Castilian naval power. During the 1370s and 1380s, in alliance with the French, Castilian war-fleets launched regular raiding expeditions against the south coast of England, while at the same time increasing numbers of traders, many of them Basques, began to ply the sea-routes that linked the Atlantic and the Mediterranean. Castile's burgeoning commercial interests in the Bay of Biscay and Flanders brought her into conflict with the merchants of the Hanseatic League, a struggle that was resolved in Castile's favour by the 1440s; to the south, meanwhile, in the still largely uncharted waters of the eastern Atlantic, Alfonso XI of Castile laid claim to the Canary Islands in 1345. However, it was not until the 1390s that the colonization of the Canaries got under way and the archipelago was not to be finally subjugated until the 1470s. Yet, Castile was not the only power committed to maritime expansion in the eastern Atlantic. After the conquest of Ceuta in July 1415, Portuguese fleets established a presence on the Azores, Madeira and the Cape Verdes, and began to explore along the west coast of Africa, setting up trading forts (*feitorias*), from which they bartered with the local peoples for gold, ivory and slaves. By the 1460s, the Portuguese had advanced as far south as the Gulf of Guinea and in 1483, Diogo Cão reached the mouth of the Congo. Intense rivalry between Portuguese and Castilian commercial interests was to provide the background and impetus to the subsequent discovery of America in 1492.

The Trastamaran 'revolution' saw the nobility of Castile attain a new peak of power and influence, as Henry II and his successors, John I and Henry III, showered titles, offices, privileges and lordships upon their supporters. The latter constituted a 'new nobility' drawn largely from the ranks of the *hidalgos*, who would come to dominate the political, social and economic life of the kingdom for generations to come. These magnates had the wherewithal to raise their own private armies, they appropriated royal revenues and they stoutly resisted any attempt by the Castilian monarchy to undermine their privileges or power. During the minority of John II (1406–54), the regency was held by the young king's mother, Catherine of Lancaster, and his uncle Ferdinand of Antequera. Once John II came of age, he was happy to delegate power to his court favourite, Álvaro de Luna, whose origins among the lesser nobility, his perceived venality and rumoured homosexuality, and above all his attempts to centralize and strengthen royal power, won him the implacable hostility of the great nobles, not least that of the sons of Ferdinand of Antequera. Although driven into exile in 1427, and again in 1438, Luna recovered his pre-eminent position in Castile, until 1453, when a new aristocratic conspiracy, hatched by the king's second wife, Isabella of Portugal, led to his fall from power and execution.

The reign of John II's son, Henry IV (1454–74), was dominated by the question of the succession. Although Henry regarded his daughter Joanna, born of his second wife Joanna of Portugal in 1462, as his rightful heir, it was widely rumoured that Henry was both impotent and a homosexual, and that Joanna of Castile was in fact illegitimate. The king's supposed favouritism towards Jews and Mudejars compounded his unpopularity. When, in 1465, Henry refused to accept a programme of constitutional reform that had been tabled by the Castilian nobles, the latter deposed the king in effigy, at the so-called 'Farce of Ávila', and proclaimed his half-brother, Alfonso, king in his stead. In the event, Henry's position was to be temporarily bolstered by the defeat of the rebels in 1467 and by the death of the Prince Alfonso the following year. However, the controversy over Joanna's legitimacy did not disappear and many nobles switched their support to Henry's half-sister, Isabella, whom the king formally recognized as his legitimate heir in 1468. The accession of Isabella to the throne of Castile in 1474, followed by that of her consort, Ferdinand, to that of Aragon five years later, which brought together the separate branches of the Trastámara line into dynastic union, was to herald a new age in the history of the peninsula.

3

The Universal Monarchy, 1474–1700

In the short space of barely a century, between 1479 and 1580, the Hispanic realms were to experience an extraordinary change in their fortunes. The two peninsular heavyweights, the kingdoms of Castile and Aragon, were joined together in dynastic union in 1479, an event which, in the eyes of traditionalists, marked the birth of the modern Spanish state, and peninsular unity was forged for the first time since the Visigothic era with the annexation of Granada (1492), Navarre (1512) and Portugal (1580). During this same period, Spain acquired – by conquest and settlement – a vast American empire and also had a substantial European one thrust upon her after the accession of the Habsburg Charles I to the Spanish throne in 1516. For a few decades, Spain became not only the arbiter of political affairs in Europe, but the most powerful monarchy on the planet: this was the first empire of which it could truly be said that the sun never set.

But Spain was not to enjoy her pre-eminent position for long. Spanish political hegemony in Europe was soon to be challenged by a resurgent France and the emerging Protestant states of England and Holland. In the seventeenth century, Spain's determination to defend her 'reputation' at all costs embroiled her in a series of ruinous wars which placed an enormous strain on her financial resources and led ultimately to the loss of her European empire.

THE CATHOLIC MONARCHS

When later generations tried to explain the reasons for Spain's remarkable rise to global pre-eminence in the sixteenth century, they invariably looked back to the reigns of Isabella I of Castile (1474–1504) and her consort Ferdinand II of Aragon (1479–1516) as the catalyst. The achievements of the Catholic Monarchs (*Reyes Católicos*), as the rulers were dubbed by Pope Alexander VI in 1496, were manifold and far reaching: decades of civil conflict were brought to an end and the authority of the monarchy restored; the eternal rivals Castile and Aragon were joined together in dynastic union; the Reconquest was brought to a triumphant conclusion with the conquest of Muslim Granada in 1492, and a strategic presence was established in North Africa; the supremacy of the Catholic Church in the peninsula was reinforced; and the foundations of Spain's European and New World empires were laid. Contemporaries, both at home and abroad, were acutely aware that a remarkable transformation had taken place. In his celebrated political treatise *The Prince* (1513), Niccòlo Machiavelli described Ferdinand of Aragon as 'almost a new prince, because he has been transformed from a weak king into the most famous and glorious king in Christendom'.

Yet, when Isabella had proclaimed herself queen of Castile on the death of her half-brother Henry IV, in December 1474, the omens for her reign could scarcely have been bleaker. Although Isabella could count upon the active support of her husband Ferdinand, heir to the throne of Aragon, whom she had married in 1469, as well as that of many of the leading lay and ecclesiastical magnates of Castile, she had to engage in a lengthy military and diplomatic struggle with her niece and rival for the throne, the 11-year-old Joanna, nicknamed '*la Beltraneja*', because she was allegedly the illegitimate offspring of Henry IV's queen, Joanna of Portugal, and the court favourite Beltrán de la Cueva. The Infanta Joanna had the enthusiastic backing of her uncle, Afonso V of Portugal (1438–81), whom she subsequently married in May 1475, as well as that of a section of the Castilian nobility (the most powerful of whom was Diego López Pacheco, marquis of Villena), the archbishop of Toledo, and a number of the major towns, including Burgos, Salamanca and Zamora. The regions of Andalusia, Extremadura and Galicia also came out in support of Joanna, with the result that more than half of the kingdom lay in rebel hands. The future of Castile seemed to hang in the balance. If Joanna's supporters had prevailed, the political map of the new Hispania would have been very different: Castile's fortunes would have been inextricably tied to those of Portugal.

However, Joanna's cause received a set-back after Ferdinand of

Aragon defeated the Portuguese at Toro near Zamora in March 1476. An invasion of the Basque region by Louis XI of France, who feared the consequences that an alliance between Castile and Aragon might bring, was also repulsed. In January 1479, Castile and Aragon were brought together in dynastic union when Ferdinand succeeded to the throne of Aragon on the death of his father, John II. Hostilities with Portugal were finally brought to a close in September 1479, when peace terms were agreed at Alcaçovas. Portugal evacuated the territories it had occupied and recognized Isabella to be the legitimate queen of Castile; the unfortunate Joanna was confined to a nunnery in Portugal; Isabella and Ferdinand's daughter, also called Isabella, was betrothed to be married to Afonso, heir apparent to the Portuguese throne; and Castile renounced any claims to the Portuguese territories in Africa and in the Atlantic region west of Cape Bojador, with the exception of the Canaries which remained in Castilian hands.

A NEW MONARCHY?

Ferdinand and Isabella have sometimes been characterized as 'new monarchs' who, in common with their contemporaries Henry VII of England and Louis XI of France, were supposedly committed to the creation of a unified and centralized state under their authority. There is little to commend such a view. For all its symbolic value, the dynastic union of Castile and Aragon changed relatively little. Royal government under the Catholic Monarchs remained resolutely traditional in its institutions and outlook. True, Ferdinand and Isabella were careful to project to the world an impression of close political partnership: all governmental decisions were made in their joint names; they pursued a common foreign policy; their heads appeared together on the coins they minted; and they sought religious uniformity throughout their disparate realms as a means to bind the loyalties of their subjects together. Yet, while contemporaries would thereafter routinely refer to Ferdinand and Isabella as the rulers of 'Spain', the monarchs themselves did not do so. Just as Isabella was regarded as the 'queen proprietress' of Castile, so Ferdinand was considered the sole legitimate ruler of Aragon. The administrative, political and legal unification of Castile and Aragon was never even mooted, let alone attempted. The Crown of Aragon was to remain a loose confederation of states – Aragon proper, Catalonia, Valencia, Majorca, Sardinia and Sicily – each with its own legislature, laws, currency and system of taxation. Customs barriers between Castile and Aragon remained in place. The only measure of economic unification introduced was the decree of 1497 which laid down that the gold coins of Castile, Valencia and Catalonia were to have equal value.

'Now we are all brothers', the municipal authorities in Barcelona wrote to their counterparts in Seville in 1479. From the very beginning, however, the 'union' of Castile and Aragon was not a partnership of equals. Castile boasted a territory three times that of the combined realms of the Crown of Aragon, and possessed approximately five times the population; its economy, based in large part upon the thriving wool trade, was by far the more dynamic of the two. The Granada campaigns and the subsequent conquest and colonization of the New World were to be almost exclusively Castilian undertakings and Castilians would come to dominate the administrative apparatus of empire. Foreign policy, which sought above all to contain French influence and dominate the western and central Mediterranean, may have been conditioned in part by traditional Aragonese strategic interests, but it was Castile that was charged with the execution of that policy and Castile which reaped many of the benefits. King Ferdinand himself came to devote far more of his energies to Castilian affairs than to those of his patrimony: during his 37 years on the throne, he spent three in Catalonia, fewer than three in Aragon proper, and only six months in Valencia. In his absence, his realms were each governed by a *Llochtinent*, or viceroy, appointed by the Crown. In 1494, Ferdinand established a permanent Council of Aragon, an advisory body which accompanied the king on his travels and kept him appraised of the situation in his dynastic territories. The preponderance of Castile and the political marginalization of Aragon were to stir up resentments in the east of the peninsula which would not be easily overcome.

The government of Castile under Isabella and Ferdinand had far more to do with the vigorous reassertion of royal authority than with the centralization of power. In the aftermath of the war of succession, those aristocratic rebels against the Crown who had not already been won over by the promise of an amnesty were gradually brought to heel. The wealthy and powerful military orders, which had become such a tool of aristocratic ambition during the civil wars of the reign of Henry IV, were successively brought under royal control. The *hermandades*, or municipal peace-keeping forces, were revived at the *cortes* of Madrigal in April 1476 and placed under the overall control of a central *junta*, or council. For the next 20 years, the *Santa Hermandad*, as this organization was known, was to act as the mainstay of royal authority in Castile, patrolling rural districts and meting out summary justice on rebels and criminals alike. The *Santa Hermandad* was also an important source of money and troops for the Crown. The militias raised by the body, which by 1490 numbered some 10,000 infantry, were to play an important part in the campaigns to conquer the emirate of Granada; in 1498, however, in response to protests from the towns at the cost of maintaining this fledgeling royal standing army, the Catholic Monarchs restored the *Santa Hermandad* to its original peace-keeping role. Royal authority over the towns was restored by the appointment of *corregidores*, or civil governors, an office first instituted in the fourteenth century. By 1479 there were 44 *corregidores* in post throughout Castile.

The reassertion of royal authority in Castile was assisted by the series of administrative reforms promulgated at the *cortes* of Toledo in 1480. The principal organ of government, the Royal Council (*Consejo Real*), later to be known simply as the Council of Castile, was reorganized. The Castilian magnates, who had formerly dominated the council, were excluded from its deliberations and their place was taken by university-educated jurists (*letrados*), most of whom were drawn from the ranks of the lesser nobility. To this body were added the Council of the Inquisition (1483) and the Council of the Military Orders (1495). As a result of the move towards conciliar administration, the political influence of the *cortes*, which was no longer attended by the clergy and nobility, waned dramatically and its powers to grant subsidies became steadily less significant as the Crown was able to draw on other revenue streams, such as custom duties, the imposts levied on cattle-ranching and sheep-raising, the *alcabala* (a 10 per cent sales tax), and the sums raised by the *Santa Hermandad*. As a result, Isabella was to summon the *cortes* on only nine occasions during her reign, and not at all between 1480 and 1498. Judicial administration, which hitherto had been itinerant, was reformed and two supreme courts of appeal, known as the *Audiencia y Chancillería*, were established in Valladolid and, from 1505, Granada. Finally, the 'Act of Resumption' provided that all Crown properties and rents that had been alienated or usurped since 1464 were to return to royal control. By measures such as these, the Catholic Monarchs successfully constrained the political strength of the Castilian nobility, although the social and economic predominance of the magnates remained intact.

While the restoration of royal authority in Castile was accompanied by a marked tendency towards authoritarianism, in Aragon Ferdinand sought to restore order and stability to the region by promising to uphold the traditional laws, liberties and institutions of each of the constituent realms. No attempt was made to reform the contractual constitutional system which placed strict limits on the ability of the monarch to promulgate new laws, recruit soldiers or raise taxes without the agreement of the local legislatures, a decision which would have important implications for the Spanish monarchy in the future. However, Ferdinand's prolonged absences from his dynastic realms made it difficult for him to impose his authority over the independent-minded nobility. In Aragon proper, for example, his attempts to restore public order by introducing the *Santa Hermandad* were vigorously resisted and private wars remained endemic. Ferdinand's most conspicuous success was to bring peace to the Catalan countryside by issuing the 'Sentence of Guadalupe' in April 1486, which gave the *remença* peasants effective ownership of their own land by freeing them from seigneurial jurisdiction and abolishing the 'six evil customs' which had traditionally been exacted by their lords.

THE RECONQUEST COMPLETED

For most of the fifteenth century, the conquest of the Muslim emirate of Granada had ceased to be a pressing objective for the embattled and otherwise preoccupied Castilian kings. Low-intensity cross-border conflict had remained endemic, and towns and castles along the frontier had occasionally changed hands, but there had been no major territorial gains for either side. In any case, the large sums of tribute which had been regularly paid by the Nasrids into the coffers of the Castilian monarchs had represented a major disincentive to destroy the emirate. For Ferdinand and Isabella, however, a renewal of hostilities with Granada was by no means an unattractive prospect, in that it offered an opportunity to harness the restless energies of the Castilian nobility and instil in their subjects a common sense of loyalty to the monarchy. The *casus belli* was provided by the Muslim attack on the frontier town of Zahara in December 1481. In retaliation, Christian forces captured Alhama the following February and undertook preparations for a major campaign. Whether the outright conquest of Granada was being mooted at this stage is uncertain, but, in the event, the fall of

Alhama proved to be the prelude to a grinding 10-year-long war of attrition. Troops were provided by the Castilian nobles, the towns and the *Santa Hermandad*, and contingents of foreign (largely Swiss) mercenaries were also recruited. Spiritual indulgences were offered by the papacy and volunteers from across Europe travelled to Spain to take part in the crusade. One such was the Englishman Edward Woodville, who played a prominent part in the capture of Loja in May 1486. To help defray the expenses of the campaign, in 1485 Pope Innocent VIII granted Ferdinand and Isabella one-tenth of the revenues of the Spanish Church: by this, and other papal grants, an estimated 800 million gold maravedís entered the royal treasury between 1484 and 1492. To these sums, the *Santa Hermandad* contributed a further 300 million maravedís between 1482 and 1490.

The Christians were helped in their enterprise by the internecine struggles that convulsed the Nasrid ruling house. When the reigning amir, Abū 'l-Ḥasan (1464–85), was ousted from Granada by his son 'Abd Allāh – enthroned as Muḥammad XII (1482–92), but known to the Christians as Boabdil – in July 1482, the former retreated to Málaga and civil war erupted. Boabdil was defeated and captured by Christian forces at Lucena in 1483 and only allowed to go free once he had sworn an oath of vassalage to Isabella and Ferdinand. In 1485, Abū'l-Ḥasan abdicated in favour of his brother Muḥammad b. Sa'd, known as al-Zaghal (the Valiant) who, as Muḥammad XIII (1485–87), pursued the power struggle with Boabdil. While civil war continued between the rival factions, the Christian forces, who enjoyed overwhelming superiority in financial and military resources, including an increasingly significant artillery capability, neutralized the principal Muslim strongpoints one by one: Ronda fell in 1485; Málaga in 1487; and al-Zaghal surrendered Guadix and the port of Almería in 1489. Finally, the city of Granada itself was subjected to siege in April 1491 and the following November the terms of its surrender were agreed. In January 1492, Ferdinand and Isabella entered the city in triumph. Boabdil was awarded a lordship in the Alpujarras mountains to the south, but the following year agreed to cross to Morocco in return for financial compensation. Some 200,000 Muslims are estimated to have emigrated to North Africa in the aftermath of the conquest; those that remained were guaranteed their property, laws, customs and religion, as well as their own judges and officials. The fall of Granada, the last foothold of Muslim power in mainland Western Europe, was greeted with jubilation. It was, one observer declared, 'the most signal and blessed day there has ever been in Spain'.

THE ADVANCE OF EMPIRE

The conquest of Granada and the destruction of Islamic power in the peninsula did not mean that the Reconquest tradition and the flame of crusade were also extinguished. In her last will and testament of 1504, Queen Isabella urged her successors 'to devote themselves unremittingly to the conquest of Africa and to the war for the faith against the Moors'. King Ferdinand is even said to have to have toyed with the idea of undertaking a crusade as far afield as Egypt or Jerusalem. 'For the king', wrote the historian Peter Martyr in 1510, 'the conquest of Africa constitutes an obsession.' Similar aspirations had regularly been articulated since the twelfth century, but by the time of the fall of Granada the determination to curb the activities of Berber pirates who operated along the Spanish coastline and, further afield, to counter the rising power of the Ottoman Turks in the Mediterranean had made such intervention a pressing objective. In pursuit of this policy, Castilian forces occupied a number of strongpoints along the north coast of Africa: Melilla (1497), Mers el-Kebir (1505), Peñón de Vélez (1508), Oran (1509) and Bougie, Tripoli and Algiers (1510–11). However, the all-out conquest of the Maghreb does not appear to have been seriously considered at this stage.

Increasingly, Ferdinand's attention was drawn towards his other chief rival for supremacy in the western Mediterranean, France. In 1493, a longstanding territorial dispute was resolved when the provinces of Cerdanya and Roussillon, which had been occupied by the French since 1462, were restored to Aragonese sovereignty. However, conflict between the two powers flared up again when Charles VIII of France invaded Italy in 1494 and overran Naples the following year. Seeing the Crown of Aragon's own traditional interests in the region to be at stake, Ferdinand orchestrated an intricate diplomatic alliance against the French, known as the 'Holy League' (comprising Spain, the Holy Roman Empire, England, Milan and Venice), and dispatched a task force of mostly Castilian troops to Italy under the leadership of Gonzalo Fernández de Córdoba, later nicknamed 'the Great Captain'. The latter organized the Spanish infantry into highly disciplined, mobile regiments called *tercios*, each about 3000 strong, which, armed with pikes, short swords and firearms, proved more than a match for the heavily armoured French cavalry and Swiss pikemen. The French were soon dislodged from Naples and a new king, Ferrante II, was installed on the throne. In 1503, Córdoba defeated joint Franco-Swiss armies at Cerignola and Garigliano, as a consequence of which Ferdinand brought Naples under his direct rule and consolidated his authority in the central Mediterranean.

Military operations were backed up by a series of skilful diplomatic initiatives designed to isolate the French in Europe. Dynastic links were forged with England (through the marriage of the Monarchs' daughter Catherine of Aragon to Arthur, heir to the English throne and then, on his death, to his brother Henry VIII); with Portugal (through the marriage of Isabella's daughter and namesake to Afonso, heir to John II (1481–95), and then to the latter's successor Manuel I (1495–1521), who later married another daughter of Ferdinand and Isabella, María); and with the Holy Roman Empire (through the marriage of their son John with Margaret, daughter of the Emperor Maximilian, and that of their daughter Joanna to Philip the Fair, archduke of Austria). Spanish interests abroad were further cultivated by a network of diplomatic agents and resident ambassadors, notably in Rome, Venice, London and Brussels.

In April 1492, still buoyed by their victory at Granada, Ferdinand and Isabella agreed to sponsor a project of exploration that had been presented to them by an ambitious Geonese merchant-mariner named Christopher Columbus (d. 1506). Columbus's main objective was to obtain direct access to the lucrative markets of Asia by sailing west across the Atlantic, but he also presented his expedition as an opportunity to acquire new territories for the Spanish Crown and to convert the inhabitants of Asia to Christianity, thereby opening up a second front in the struggle against Islam. Columbus's earlier attempts to seek backing for his expedition at the Portuguese, French, English and Spanish courts had all been rebuffed: his scientific calculations, which hugely underestimated the true distance between Europe and Asia, were regarded as suspect; his belief that his expedition was guided by divine Providence aroused scepticism; and his personal demands were judged excessive. In any case, the Portuguese, the pioneers in maritime exploration, were already too committed to their own exploration of the African coastline: in 1488, Bartholomew Dias rounded the Cape of Good Hope for the first time and opened up the sea route to India.

In the same month, Ferdinand and Isabella granted Columbus the sponsorship he craved. In addition to receiving financial backing, Columbus was awarded noble status and appointed to the hereditary offices of admiral, viceroy and governor of any lands he might discover, as well as a 10 per cent share of any profits. On 3 August

1492, Columbus departed from Palos near Huelva with three ships and a crew of 88 men. Replenishing supplies in the Canaries, the tiny flotilla sailed westwards and on 12 October reached the Bahamas. From there, the fleet briefly reconnoitred the coastal waters around Cuba and Hispaniola (modern Haiti and the Dominican Republic) before heading back to Spain. In the enthusiastic report Columbus sent to the Catholic Monarchs, he played up the economic potential of the islands in gold, spices and slaves. Ferdinand and Isabella duly pledged support for a further expedition to the Indies and sought papal confirmation of their claims to the newly discovered territories. In April–May 1493, Pope Alexander VI decreed that Spain was to enjoy sovereignty over all the lands discovered or to be discovered west of an imaginary line drawn north–south 100 leagues west of the Cape Verde islands; the following year, in response to Portuguese protests that the papal ruling threatened their own interests in the southern Atlantic, the Treaty of Tordesillas moved the demarcation line a further 270 leagues westwards, an unwitting consequence of which was later to bring Brazil under Portuguese rule. The papal ruling also committed the Spanish Crown to the evangelization of the indigenous peoples of the Indies.

In September 1493, Columbus led a substantial expedition of 17 ships and 1200 men to Hispaniola with the objective of founding a permanent trading post, from where he planned to trade with the wealthy emporia of Asia. However, the experiment failed. Apart from some gold and slaves, the fabulous wealth that Columbus had promised failed to materialize, while the colony he had established in the north of the island suffered from disease and debilitating shortages of food and water, as a result of which many of the settlers rebelled against Columbus's authority. During his third expedition to America (1498–1500), when he reached Trinidad and explored the coast of mainland South America, the commercial objectives of Columbus's original proposal were abandoned and full-scale colonization was attempted on Hispaniola. Lands were distributed among the settlers and Indian communities were required to labour for the Spaniards in the fields and mines. By now, however, Columbus had become discredited at court and in 1500 he was arrested and sent back to Spain in chains. Although Columbus was soon released and undertook a fourth and final expedition to the Indies (1502–4), during the course of which he explored the coastal regions of Honduras down to the Panama isthmus, he never recovered the functions of governor and viceroy in the Indies and died, rich but disillusioned, in 1506.

Henceforth, the American colonies were to be ruled directly by the Crown of Castile; all trade with the Indies was to be channelled through Seville and supervised by the Casa de la Contratación (founded 1503). Although contemporaries would continue to refer to the hemisphere as 'the Indies', it soon became clear that the territories Columbus had discovered in the Caribbean belonged not to Asia at all, but to an entirely different and hitherto unknown land-mass, soon to be dubbed 'America', after the Florentine navigator Amerigo Vespucci. In 1519–22, a Spanish expedition crossed the Pacific Ocean and after a long and punishing journey – during the course of which its leader, the Portuguese Ferdinand Magellan, and most of the crew died – circumnavigated the globe for the first time, demonstrating how far the Spaniards still lay from their original goal.

THE QUEST FOR RELIGIOUS UNITY

The reigns of Isabella and Ferdinand saw the monarchy tighten its grip over the immensely powerful Spanish Church. Bishops, many of whom had considerable military resources at their disposal and had played a leading role in the political in-fighting of the preceding decades, were required to surrender their fortresses to the Crown. The monarchs also engaged in a determined struggle with the papacy to secure the right to appoint their own candidates to bishoprics. In 1486, Innocent VIII granted them the *patronato*, or right of royal patronage, over all future ecclesiastical appointments in the kingdom of Granada, and this right was extended to the American colonies in 1508. The royal right to present candidates to bishoprics throughout Spain was eventually granted in 1523. The papacy also allowed the Monarchs to tap into the revenues of the Church, by granting them in perpetuity the *tercias reales* (one-third of the tithe) in 1494, and substantial other sums of money with which to fund the crusading campaigns in Granada and North Africa.

Yet, royal policy towards the Church was not conditioned uniquely by questions of power and wealth. Under the guidance of her confessor, Hernando de Talavera (1428–1507), and his successor, the zealous Francisco Jiménez de Cisneros (1436–1517), archbishop of Toledo, Queen Isabella sponsored a series of reformist measures designed to improve the moral and intellectual standards of the clergy, root out clerical abuses, such as absenteeism, simony and concubinage, and enforce stricter discipline among religious orders. In 1508, Cisneros founded the University of Alcalá de Henares near Madrid, which aimed to improve standards of education among the clergy. By and large, however, the results of these initiatives were disappointing. The reforms aroused considerable resistance in some cathedral chapters, which regarded them as an attack on their autonomy, and many monasteries went unreformed.

Isabella and Ferdinand were particularly determined to protect their kingdoms from heresy. As we have seen, relations between the Christian and Jewish communities had come increasingly under strain from the late fourteenth century onwards. Faced by the threat of violence and subjected to increased missionary pressure by the Church, large numbers of Jews in Castile and Aragon had converted to Christianity. However, the readiness with which many of these *conversos*, or *marranos* (pigs) as they were also cruelly dubbed, had found influential positions in the secular and ecclesiastical hierarchy of the kingdom aroused suspicion and jealousy among 'Old Christians', many of whom cast doubt on the sincerity of the *conversos*' Christian belief.

It was in response to a mounting wave of popular hostility towards the *conversos*, that an Inquisition was set up by Ferdinand and Isabella in 1478. A papal Inquisition had first been established in the Crown of Aragon at the beginning of the thirteenth century, at the height of the Albigensian crusade, but thereafter had remained inactive; a similar initiative had been mooted by Henry IV of Castile but never implemented. The primary purpose of the New Inquisition was to root out heretical beliefs and practices from among the *converso* population. However, its responsibilities also included the suppression of witchcraft, superstition and immorality (for example, homosexuality and bigamy), as well as the censorship of books. As a result of its investigations, suspected heretics were required to appear before a tribunal of inquisitors at an elaborate ceremony called an *auto de fe*, or 'act of faith', where punishments (which might include confiscation of property, exile, imprisonment or execution) were confirmed. The impact of the Inquisition was uneven. According to one account, some 700 Judaizing *conversos* were burnt in Seville alone between 1480 and 1488, and another 5000 punished; in Catalonia, most *conversos* fled the region before the Inquisition could even begin its investigations.

As anti-Semitism reached a new crescendo, many official bodies (including religious orders, cathedral chapters and university colleges) adopted statutes of *limpieza de sangre*, or 'purity of blood', which debarred anyone of Muslim or Jewish descent from holding public office. At the same time, concern that the presence of large numbers of practising Jews in the peninsula was preventing the complete assimilation of the *conversos* into the Christian fold meant that the former also became the target of discriminatory measures, such as the requirement to wear distinctive dress (1476) and that Jewish and Mudejar (Muslim) *aljamas* be walled off from Christian quarters (1480). Finally, on 31 March 1492, a royal edict was passed which declared that all Jews in Castile and Aragon were either to convert to Christianity or face expulsion. As a result of this draconian measure, at least 50,000 Jews from Castile and Aragon are estimated to have fled the kingdom: the majority departed for Portugal and then, when similar anti-Jewish measures were enforced there in 1497, to North Africa, Italy and the eastern Mediterranean.

The policy of the Catholic Monarchs towards its Mudejar subjects was initially tolerant and conciliatory. In the aftermath of the conquest of Granada, the first archbishop of the city, Hernando de Talavera, sought to win converts to Christianity by gentle persuasion and encouraged the use of Arabic during Mass as a means to speed the process. However, Talavera's gradualist policy was brusquely overturned in 1499 by Archbishop Cisneros, who embarked upon a programme of forcible conversion. Cisneros, and the equally zealous Queen Isabella, regarded Spain's religious heterodoxy as both an affront to the Christian faith and a threat to the authority of the Crown. This hard-line policy provoked a Mudejar rebellion in Granada in 1499 and in the Alpujarras mountains to the south the following year. The rebellions were soon crushed and Cisneros and Queen Isabella ruled that the terms of surrender that had been agreed at the time of the fall of Granada were null and void. Further mass conversions ensued and in February 1502 the queen issued an edict requiring all Mudejars in Castile who would not convert to Christianity to leave the country, although in the event few chose the road to exile. These policies were accompanied by a series of measures designed to eradicate the distinctive cultural traditions of the Mudejars: Arabic books and manuscripts were burned; traditional dress was banned; and bath-houses were outlawed. In Aragon, however, where Mudejar estate workers enjoyed the protection of their Christian landlords, similarly draconian measures were not introduced until 1526. The repudiation of the capitulation terms of 1492, the policy of mass conversion and the sustained attack on the cultural identity of the Moriscos, as the converted Mudejars were pejoratively to be known, marked the final rejection of the pluralistic tradition in Castile. This policy of intolerance stored up problems which would return to haunt the Spanish Crown in the future.

THE HABSBURG SUCCESSION

The fragility of the dynastic union of Castile and Aragon was graphically demonstrated by the events that followed the death of Queen Isabella in November 1504. Under the terms of the queen's will, her daughter Joanna was named as her successor to the throne of Castile. However, the will stipulated that if Joanna proved unfitting to rule – a clear reference to the new queen's rapidly deteriorating mental health – her father, Ferdinand of Aragon, was to hold the regency of Castile until his grandson Charles, the firstborn of Joanna and the Archduke Philip, came of age. Isabella viewed with deep misgivings the fact that by these arrangements the kingdom of Castile would pass from the Trastámara dynasty to the House of Habsburg, and to a grandson who was, as she put it, 'of another nation and another tongue'. But the death of her son, Prince John, in 1497, and of her grandson Michael, born to Princess Isabella and King Manuel I of Portugal, two years after that, had left the queen with little room for manoeuvre. When Joanna and her consort Philip arrived in Castile to take up the throne in 1506, the dynastic union of Castile and Aragon appeared to have been sundered for good. Ferdinand returned to his dominions in Aragon and the following year married a niece of Louis XII of France, Germaine de Foix. However, when Philip died prematurely in September 1506 and his widow Joanna lapsed into apparent insanity and was confined in the castle of Tordesillas (where she was to remain until her death in 1554), Ferdinand was invited to return to Castile to rule as regent.

For the last nine years of his life, Ferdinand governed as sole ruler of Castile and Aragon. Domestic policy in Castile was largely entrusted to Cardinal Cisneros, while Ferdinand retained a particularly close interest in foreign policy matters. It was his concern for the welfare of his Amerindian subjects in the New World colonies, for example, that led to the promulgation of the Laws of Burgos in 1512. That same year, he took advantage of a dispute over the succession to the throne of Navarre to bring that kingdom under his authority; three years later, Navarre was formally joined to the Crown of Castile, although it retained its traditional institutions and laws.

On Ferdinand's death in January 1516, the crowns of Castile and Aragon passed to his 16-year-old grandson Charles I (1516–56), who had already inherited Flanders, the Franche Comté and the Habsburg territories in Germany and Central Europe from his late father. Even before the young king could travel to Spain, a group of nobles, fearful of the prospect of Castile falling under foreign domination, plotted to offer the throne to Charles's Spanish-born brother Ferdinand. However, the conspiracy was defused by the ever-vigilant Cisneros, who also had to quell an uprising in Navarre in 1517, and Ferdinand was sent away to Flanders where he could no longer be the focus of aristocratic plotting. But misgivings about the Habsburg succession persisted and Charles's conduct on arrival in Spain in 1517 served only to deepen this anxiety. Born in Ghent and raised at the Burgundian court of the Emperor Maximilian I, Charles knew no Castilian, nor anything of peninsular affairs, and surrounded himself with a large Flemish entourage whose members he showered with offices, titles and wealth. Fears that Castile might be reduced to little more than a satellite state within the vast Habsburg empire were heightened by the king's election as Charles V, Holy Roman Emperor, in succession to his grandfather Maximilian in June 1519. Writing shortly after his election to the imperial dignity, his Chancellor Mercurino de Gattinara assured Charles that 'you are on the path to a universal monarchy, you will unite Christendom under one yoke'. When Charles travelled to Germany the following year, having secured the promise of funds from the disgruntled Castilian *cortes* for the second time in three years, and having left the reins of government in the hands of his fellow country-man and former tutor, Adrian of Utrecht, discontent boiled over into outright rebellion.

The revolt of the *comuneros* of 1520–1 had its origins in an alliance of some 13 towns of northern Castile which joined together in a *Junta Santa*, or Holy League, in protest at what they saw as the high-handed government of the realm by an absentee monarch and his foreign cronies who were thought to be bleeding the country dry. Chief among the rebels' demands were that Charles return to Spain immediately, that the appointment of foreigners to high office cease forthwith, and that excessive demands for taxation be curbed. At the very heart of the *comunero* movement, however, lay the fundamental belief that the *Junta* was defending the traditional political rights of the Castilian municipalities and the nobles, which were seen to have been eroded since the time of the accession of the Catholic Monarchs, and that, ultimately, the rights of the community were superior to those of the monarchy. As one *comunero* cleric put it, 'When princes are tyrants, then communities must govern'. Initially, the *comuneros* were able to attract support from a wide spectrum of society: nobles, clergymen and peasants joined together in common cause; royal *corregidores* were expelled and municipal government was entrusted to local communes; and Adrian of Utrecht and the other members of the Council of Castile were forced to flee Valladolid, the administrative centre of the kingdom.

However, the rebellion soon began to run out of steam. Outside of northern Castile support for the rebellion was largely tepid or non-existent and attempts by the rebels to win the support of Queen Joanna in Tordesillas came to nothing. Moreover, although sections of the Castilian nobility had been broadly sympathetic to the rebels' cause in the early stages of the rebellion, they soon became alienated, as popular protest degenerated into mob violence in the towns and anti-seigneurial risings in the countryside, prompting the nobles to seek a rapprochement with the Crown. The defeat of the *comuneros* by a royalist army at Villalar near Tordesillas in April 1521, and the summary execution of the leaders, Juan de Padilla, Juan Bravo and Francisco Maldonado, marked the beginning of the end for the movement.

A simultaneous popular uprising in Valencia and Majorca by members of the urban *agermanats*, or brotherhoods, which had been prompted principally by deteriorating social and economic conditions, notably a bitter antipathy towards the feudal landlords and the local Mudejars, rather than by any overt political grievances, was also crushed. By the time Charles V returned to Spain in November 1522, accompanied by a sizeable army of German mercenaries, the country had been pacified and royal authority restored.

CHARLES V AND THE DEFENCE OF EMPIRE

The defeat of the *comunero* and *agermanat* rebellions ensured not only that the Habsburg succession would be firmly established in Castile and Aragon, but that henceforth Spain's destiny would be to play a leading role in sustaining the world-wide Empire of Charles V. Just as the *comuneros* had warned, the emperor's peripatetic style of government and his extensive imperial commitments beyond Spain's shores meant that he was to be absent from the peninsula for much of his reign – including a 14-year-long stretch between 1543 and 1556 – and that Spain's national interests were to be subordinated to wider questions of dynastic security and prestige. This did not mean that Spain herself was relegated to the margins: Spaniards came to exercise considerable influence in the imperial hierarchy, and the emperor regarded Spain, and Castile in particular, as a vital source of money and soldiers with which to fulfil his imperial duties. In defence of the Habsburg dynasty, the *tercios* of Castile were soon to become known and feared on battlefields throughout Europe.

During Charles's prolonged absences from the peninsula, the government of the Spanish realms was delegated to his wife, Empress Isabella of Portugal (d. 1539), and later to their son Philip (born 1527). In practice, however, most day-to-day policy decisions were left to the emperor's chief advisers, notably the influential Secretary of State, Francisco de los Cobos (d. 1547). No attempt was ever made to bind the diverse Habsburg territories under one overarching administrative system, nor was fiscal and institutional unity imposed upon the diverse realms that made up the Spanish monarchy. In Castile itself, the conciliar system of government was further expanded and refined by the addition of a Council of War (1522) and a Council of State (1526), both of which were advisory bodies, as well as a Council of Finance (1523) and a Council of the Indies (1524). Under Cobos's direction, the bureaucracy of state was also expanded. The *cortes* of Castile and Aragon were regularly summoned, but were viewed by the Crown largely as a mechanism to secure funding for the emperor's military ventures rather than to act as consultative bodies.

Imperial policy under Charles V was driven by a steadfast determination to safeguard the interests of the Habsburg dynasty and to defend the 'unity of Christendom' against internal and external foes alike. The struggle with his arch-rivals for European hegemony, the Valois kings of France, dominated the emperor's strategic thinking throughout most of his reign, with the lands of the Burgundian inheritance and Italy remaining the main bones of contention between the rival powers. Charles was particularly keen to bring the duchy of Milan, which controlled the main lines of communication that ran from his dominions in southern Italy to Flanders and Germany, under his authority; for its part, the French Crown was determined to prevent its complete encirclement by the Habsburg Empire. When Francis I of France invaded Milan in 1523 and again in 1524, Charles promptly counter-attacked, and in February 1525 Francis was defeated and captured at Pavia. Pope Clement VII, in alliance with England, France and the Italian principalities, then joined forces against the emperor, whose unpaid mutinous troops won notoriety by sacking Rome in 1527. By the terms of the Treaty of Cambrai in 1529, Charles acquired the duchy of Milan and, with it, effective control over the entire Italian peninsula; in return, he renounced his own claims to the French territories of Burgundy, Provence and Languedoc.

Peace with France enabled Charles to devote more resources to confronting the rising tide of Ottoman power in Central Europe and the Mediterranean. The failure of the Turks to take Vienna in 1529 and the capture of Tunis by an imperial expeditionary force in 1535 appeared to suggest that the Ottoman advance had been halted. But renewed hostilities with France, which had no qualms about seeking a strategic alliance with the Turks in 1536, and a deteriorating political situation in northern Europe, led the emperor to leave the crusade against Islam on hold, with the result that Christian power in the Mediterranean was gradually eroded. An expedition against Algiers failed in 1541, and Tripoli, Peñón de Vélez and Bougie were lost to the Ottomans in quick succession between 1551 and 1555.

Spaniards themselves considered Charles V's European campaigns to be of only marginal benefit to themselves. In 1527, the Castilian *cortes* went so far as to refuse point-blank to underwrite the costs of the emperor's campaigns against the Ottomans in Hungary. Yet, as Charles's imperial commitments expanded, the emperor looked increasingly to Spain to bear the financial burden of empire. While the constitutional restrictions on the amount of tax that could be levied meant that the Crown of Aragon yielded only limited amounts of money to the emperor, Castile, the Spanish Church and the American colonies constituted major sources of revenue. Income from America, in particular, assumed increasing importance as Spanish interests in the New World expanded dramatically during the 1520s and 1530s. The Crown was entitled to the *quinto*, the one-fifth tax levied on all American bullion and precious stones, as well as the various taxes and custom duties levied in the colonies. Bullion receipts from the New World averaged 324,000 ducats per year between 1536 and 1540, and rose to 871,000 per year between 1551 and 1555; overall, the government was in receipt of some 11.9 million ducats between 1516 and

1560. Yet, even these prodigious sums were not enough to bridge the budgetary deficit that grew up during Charles's reign, with the result that he was forced to borrow heavily at exorbitant rates of interest from German and Italian bankers. By 1556, 68 per cent of state income in Castile was given over to the repayment of annuities, known as *juros*, which had been issued by the Crown.

The final years of the reign of Charles V were to be overshadowed by the struggle with the Protestant reform movement in Northern Europe. Under the leadership of a former Augustinian monk, Martin Luther, the Reformation openly challenged the authority of the universal Catholic Church. Acutely aware of what he regarded as his God-given responsibility to defend the unity of faith in his dominions, Charles responded vigorously to the challenge. Like Queen Isabella before him, the emperor regarded heresy not simply as an attack on the unity of Christendom, but on the political unity of his dominions. Within Spain itself, the Inquisition acted energetically to prevent Lutheranism from taking root: Lutheran books were banned; the mystical religious grouping known as the *alumbrados*, or 'enlightened ones', which had called into question certain aspects of the Catholic faith, was suppressed; and supporters of the ideas of the Dutch theologian and philosopher Desiderius Erasmus, who had campaigned for the reform of clerical abuses, were denounced as closet Lutherans.

In Germany, however, the emperor's attempts to stamp out heresy were frustrated. In 1521, at the Diet of Worms, he declared Luther to be under the ban of the Empire, but, when this failed to have the desired effect, as Luther found powerful protectors among the German princes, Charles sought to broker an agreement between the reformers and the papacy at the Council of Trent in 1545. When negotiations foundered, Charles went on the offensive. He defeated the Protestant princes at Mühlberg in 1547, but renewed attempts to secure a compromise between Catholics and Protestants in Germany proved in vain. By the Peace of Augsburg (1555), the emperor recognized that the German princes were to be free to choose the religion they pleased. The following year, crushed by failure, Charles V abdicated in Brussels and divided the empire between his brother, Ferdinand I of Austria, who became Holy Roman Emperor, and his son, Philip II (1556–98), who inherited the Hispanic realms and their American colonies, the Italian territories of Sicily, Sardinia and Milan (the kingdom of Naples had already been granted to Philip at the time of his marriage to Mary Tudor of England in 1554), and the Burgundian lands of the Franche Comté and the Netherlands. Mentally exhausted, Charles retired to the monastery of Yuste in Extremadura, where he died in September 1558.

SPAIN AND THE NEW WORLD

Writing in the 1550s, the historian Francisco López de Gómara described Columbus's 'discovery' of America to be 'the greatest event since the creation of the world'. Yet, for 25 years after Columbus first set foot in the New World, the vast profits that he had confidently promised to his royal sponsors remained elusive. In the frenzied search for gold on Hispaniola, the native political structure was broken up, lands were seized and Indian communities that were not sold into outright slavery were allocated to lords (*encomenderos*), who, in return for Indian labour in the fields and mines, were theoretically required to look after the physical and spiritual welfare of their vassals. A combination of social and economic dislocation, maltreatment, malnutrition and, above all, the impact of European epidemic diseases, such as measles, typhus and smallpox, to which the natives had no immunity, caused the indigenous population to plummet. By 1514, only 22,726 Indians remained, the gold deposits were largely exhausted (over 30 tons had been shipped back to Spain), and the settlers were forced to turn to commercial farming (notably sugar cultivation) to keep the colonial economy afloat. In the desperate search for new sources of labour and precious metals, small groups of Spanish conquistadors fanned out across the Caribbean: Puerto Rico, the Bahamas and Cuba were settled with similarly catastrophic results; in 1510, Vasco Núñez de Balboa established a settlement at Darién in the Panama isthmus and, three years later, reached the Pacific coast.

In 1519, the exploration of mainland America began in earnest. In August of that year, an ambitious *hidalgo* named Hernán Cortés set sail from Cuba at the head of a small expeditionary force comprising some 600 men, 32 horse and a handful of cannon. Landing on the coast of what is now Mexico, Cortés began the march inland that would culminate two years later in the conquest of Tenochtitlán, capital of the wealthy and powerful Aztec empire. Cortés's spectacular success was matched by Francisco Pizarro, who in 1531, at the head of an even smaller army of 180 men and 27 horse, advanced from Panama into Andean South America and overthrew the mighty Inca empire in less than two years, acquiring a huge booty in gold and silver in the process.

How were so very few Spaniards able to overthrow the Amerindian civilizations? Superior military technology undoubtedly played a part: Spanish steel weapons and armour were more than a match for Indian obsidian-tipped arrows and spears; horses (hitherto unknown in the New World) proved invaluable in pitched battles, though less so in urban warfare or in hilly terrain; and, for all their technical limitations, arquebuses and cannons helped to disrupt enemy battle formations. More important still was the Spaniards' ability to exploit local political divisions. Hernán Cortés recruited an estimated 200,000 native troops from among the subject peoples of the Aztecs, such as the Cempoalans and Tlaxcalans, with which to prosecute his campaign against Tenochtitlán, while Pizarro astutely allied himself with one of the competing factions for the Inca throne. Native resistance was further weakened by the impact of European epidemic diseases and by fatal indecision among the indigenous ruling élites. Finally, we must take into account the character of the conquistadors themselves. The majority of the estimated 150,000 Spaniards who crossed to the New World between 1493 and 1550 hailed from the impoverished regions of Andalusia, Extremadura and southern Castile. Most were young single men aged between 14 and 30; a quarter were of *hidalgo* stock, many of them impoverished *segundones*, or younger sons, who were denied any prospect of an inheritance at home by the system of entail; the rest were mostly labourers, artisans, traders and soldiers of limited means. Imbued with the militant Catholicism of the Reconquest and inspired by the tales of chivalry then much in vogue, what all these determined and supremely self-confident men had in common was a burning sense of loyalty, to Crown and Church, and an unquenchable thirst to acquire wealth, status and power. As Bernal Díaz del Castillo, one of Cortés's loyal foot-soldiers, candidly confessed: 'We came here to serve God and His Majesty, and also to get rich.'

The extraordinary achievements of Cortés and Pizarro spurred other would-be conquistadors to range far and wide across the Americas in search of similar riches. In 1539, Hernando de Soto reached Florida and explored inland as far as the Mississipi; and in 1540–2 Francisco Vázquez Coronado, lured by rumours of a wealthy civilization known as the seven cities of Cibola, penetrated the territory that now comprises the American states of Arizona, New Mexico, Texas, Oklahoma and Kansas. In South America, numerous expeditions set out in search of El Dorado, a kingdom rumoured to be rich in gold. In the course of one of these expeditions, Francisco de Orellana became the first European to navigate along the Amazon (1539–41). By the 1540s, the pace of conquest began to slow down. The mythical realms of El Dorado and Cibola remained elusive, but the main sources of wealth – in terms of agricultural land, precious metals and manpower – had been located. The deserts, rainforests and pampas that covered much of the rest of the American continent held little attraction for the Spaniards, while the stiff resistance the conquistadors encountered, for example from the redoubtable Araucanians in southern Chile, acted as a powerful disincentive to undertake further territorial expansion.

Spanish authority over its New World colonies was enforced through a network of towns which were founded in the aftermath of conquest. Some, like Mexico City and Cuzco, were founded upon existing indigenous settlements; others, like Vera Cruz (1519), Quito (1534), Bogotá (1536) and Santiago de Chile (1542), were new foundations. Churches were built, the infrastructure of ecclesiastical government was established and Spanish missionaries arrived to carry out their own 'spiritual conquest' of the native peoples. Indigenous political structures were gradually dismantled and traditional economic life was transformed through the creation of *encomiendas* (lordships) and the introduction of European crops (wheat, vines and olives) and animals (horses, sheep, pigs and cows). In return, New World plants (notably tomatoes, maize, beans and potatoes) were gradually incorporated into the diet of Europeans. The greatest impact of all, however, was demographic. Just as had occurred in the Caribbean, the combined impact of war, disease and famine caused the indigenous population to decline rapidly: according to one estimate, the native population of central Mexico fell from about 25.2 million in 1518 to 2.65 million in 1568. Rotational labour drafts, known as the *repartimiento* in Mexico and the *mita* in Peru, were implemented in an attempt to meet the shortage of manpower, but from the end of the sixteenth century free-wage labour was gradually introduced as settlers turned to agriculture and livestock raising as a commercial venture.

The plight of the Indians gave rise to a wide-ranging debate during the first half of the sixteenth century. Spanish churchmen, who saw an opportunity to establish perfect Christian communities unsullied by the corruption of the Old World, denounced the mistreatment of the Indians and demanded the suppression of the *encomienda* and an end to slavery. 'Are these Indians not men? Do they not have rational souls? Are you not obliged to love them as you love yourselves?', asked the Dominican Antonio de Montesinos in a sermon he delivered to the settlers of Hispaniola in 1511. The conquistador turned Dominican friar Bartolomé de Las Casas devoted most of his career to campaigning on the Indians' behalf and published a number of incendiary works, which denounced Spanish cruelty in the New World. Las Casas's views were countered by the scholar Juan Ginés de Sepúlveda who drew on the Aristotelian doctrine of natural slavery to argue that the Indians were naturally inferior to the Spaniards and deserved to be subjected.

By and large, the Spanish Crown was sympathetic to the arguments expressed by the pro-Indian lobby. Quite apart from its humanitarian concerns, the Crown was anxious to prevent the emergence of an entrenched colonial aristocracy, which might ultimately undermine royal authority in the colonies. As a result, steps were taken to undermine the economic importance of the *encomienda*: slavery was gradually suppressed; *encomenderos* lost the right to demand forced labour; and the *encomiendas* themselves were gradually transferred to royal control. For all that, the Crown was acutely aware that if it allowed the native peoples to be freed from economic domination by the Spanish settlers, as Las Casas and others demanded, the colonies would face bankruptcy and the Crown would lose a major source of its revenue. Ultimately, therefore, the material interests of Crown and settlers remained closely intertwined.

PHILIP II: THE APOGEE OF SPANISH POWER

At the time of his succession in 1556, Philip II was already an experienced ruler in his own right, having held responsibility for the government of the Spanish realms on his father's behalf at various times since 1543, and having acted as 'King Consort' to Queen Mary Tudor of England after their marriage in 1554. From the very outset, Spain was the centre of gravity of Philip's realms and once he returned from the Netherlands in 1559, he never ventured outside the peninsula again. Unlike his outgoing and energetic father, Philip was renowned for his reserved manner and his sedentary and bureaucratic style of government. In 1561, he chose Madrid, close to the geographical centre of the peninsula, as his permanent capital city, and two years later he began the construction of the vast, sombre palace of El Escorial, on the southern slopes of the Guadarrama mountains, 48 kilometres to the northwest. As well as a royal residence and pantheon, El Escorial was a

Jeronimite monastery and a centre of learning; it also became the nerve centre of government. Ensconced in his cramped office at El Escorial during the months of spring and summer, for upwards of nine hours a day, Philip kept careful track of affairs of state, paying meticulous attention to detail, delegating as little as possible, and trusting few. The result was that the king was swamped with paperwork and decision making could prove a grindingly slow process. 'Decisions are taken so slowly that even a cripple could keep up with them', grumbled the king's personal secretary Gonzalo Pérez.

To contemporaries, Philip II's power and the resources at his disposal appeared overwhelming; yet, to consider him an 'absolute' monarch is probably wide of the mark. Keen though Philip was that the royal writ be respected and obeyed throughout his realms, in practice the king's authority over his far-flung dominions was hedged about by numerous constraints. The various territories that made up the Spanish Monarchy, as well as the still-powerful Church and nobility, watched jealously over their privileges and liberties. Rebellions against the monarchy broke out in the Alpujarras in 1568, in the Netherlands in 1572, and in Aragon in 1591. Within Castile, the powerhouse of empire, where the centralization of royal power was most marked, the king relied heavily on the co-operation of the nobility, the bishops and the towns to impose his will. Even the once compliant Castilian *cortes* tried to resist as best it could the king's attempts to impose new taxes and voiced concerns about the direction of imperial policy. Equally striking, in 1590, when the king's former secretary, Antonio Pérez – who had been implicated in the murder of Juan de Escobedo, secretary to the king's half-brother Don John of Austria – escaped from prison in Madrid and took refuge in Aragon, Philip's attempts to bring Pérez to book were thwarted.

Like his father before him, Philip's main objective as king was to protect his realms against attack and to safeguard the religious unity of Christendom against heretics and infidels alike. During the early part of his reign, the king devoted much of his attention to the Mediterranean, where Ottoman fleets and Barbary corsairs continued to challenge Spanish naval supremacy. An expeditionary force, under the leadership of the Duke of Medinaceli and Admiral Andrea Doria, was dispatched to capture Tripoli in 1560, but was routed by a Turkish fleet at Djerba and 10,000 troops were forced to surrender. Thereafter, Philip sought to curb the Islamic threat by building up his naval strength in the Mediterranean and by reinforcing key strongpoints such

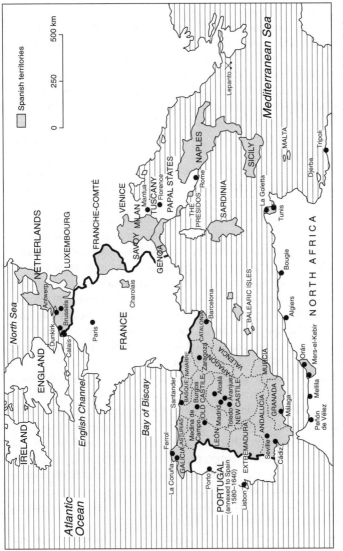

Map 5 The Spanish Empire in Europe at the succession of Philip II (1556). Adapted from Geoffrey Woodward, *Philip II* (Longman, 1992), p. viii.

as Malta, where a besieging Ottoman army was repelled in 1565. Five years later, at Lepanto off the coast of Greece, the combined naval forces of the Christian Holy League – a coalition comprising Spain, Venice and the Papacy – led by Don John of Austria, inflicted a crushing defeat on an Ottoman fleet. The victory at Lepanto was greeted with jubilation, both in Spain and in much of Europe, but it did not mark the destruction of Islamic naval power. Tunis, conquered by Don John in 1573, was lost to the Ottomans the following year. Thereafter, however, the intensity of the military struggle between the two powers began to diminish, as Philip sought to channel his military resources towards the suppression of the Protestant rebellion in the Netherlands, and his counterpart, the Ottoman sultan Murad III, became preoccupied by unrest on his Persian frontier, and in August 1580 the two monarchs signed a truce.

Philip II's most conspicuous success was the dynastic union of the Spanish and Portuguese Crowns in 1580. Philip had a good claim to the Portuguese throne through his mother, Isabella, daughter of Manuel I of Portugal. The death of the incumbent on the Portuguese throne, King Sebastian I (1557–78), while engaged on an ill-fated crusade to Morocco, followed by that of his successor the elderly Cardinal-King Henry two years later, allowed Philip to press his own claim to the throne. The prospect of a dynastic alliance with Spain was welcomed by the Portuguese ecclesiastical establishment, by members of the intellectual élite, many of whom had already forged strong links with their counterparts in Castile, and by the merchant community of Lisbon, mindful of the commercial advantages that the union might bring. For once, Philip did not procrastinate. By August 1580, Spanish forces had pacified the whole of Portugal and her overseas colonies in the Azores, West Africa, the Spice Islands and Brazil were soon brought under Philip's authority. Taking up residence in Lisbon, where he remained until February 1583, the king governed with tact: no attempt was made to suppress the institutions or laws of the Portuguese, let alone their language, coinage or customs; the members of the Council of Portugal were drawn exclusively from the Portuguese administrative élite; and after the death of the king's first viceroy, the Habsburg Archduke Albert of Austria, in 1593, the post was reserved for members of the Portuguese nobility.

During the half-century that followed the forcible conversion and mass baptism of the Spanish Muslims of Granada in 1502, little attempt was made to assimilate the 'Moriscos' into Christian society.

However, tensions between the Moriscos and the Christian authorities began to mount steadily after 1550. Although these Moriscos, some 400,000 in number, represented barely 6 per cent of the total Spanish population, their numbers were heavily concentrated in Aragon, Valencia and Granada, where they were viewed with mistrust by the authorities, who regarded them as potential fifth-columnists who might lend active support to any future invasion of the peninsula by the Turks, and by the Inquisition and the Church authorities, who suspected that Islamic practices were still rife among them. The grievances harboured by the Moriscos of Granada were both economic and religious. The local silk industry, which was the economic mainstay of the region, had experienced a deep recession as a result of government policies: exports had been banned, swingeing tax increases imposed and the profitability of Granadan silk eroded by the importation of raw silk from neighbouring Murcia. Between 1559 and 1568, the authorities also forcibly appropriated some 100,000 hectares of land from Morisco landowners unable to demonstrate proof of ownership. Parallel to this process, the Moriscos were subjected to a series of vexatious measures designed to accelerate their assimilation into Christian society: the use of the Arabic language was prohibited; traditional customs, culture and dress were suppressed; Morisco houses were subjected to regular inspection; and Morisco children were required to be brought up away from parental control. In December 1568, a Morisco rebellion erupted with ferocity in the region of the Alpujarras. Royal troops under the command of Don John of Austria, waged a bitter and bloody campaign against the insurgents, but the insurrection was not finally quelled until 1571, by which time some 60,000 lives had been lost. Fearing further unrest, the government forcibly deported over 100,000 Granadan Moriscos to Andalusia, Extremadura and Castile, with the result that the population of the province of Granada fell by over a quarter.

In 1566, Philip II famously observed to Pope Pius V that 'rather than suffer the least damage to religion and the service of God, I would lose all my states and a hundred lives, if I had them, for I do not propose nor desire to be the ruler of heretics'. As attempts to negotiate a compromise between Catholics and Lutherans foundered during the 1540s, the hierarchy of the Roman Catholic Church, meeting at the Council of Trent in 1545–7, 1551–2 and 1562–3, began to map out a strategy of reform, which simultaneously sought to curb the clerical abuses which had given rise to the Reformation movement in the first place and to conduct a vigorous counter-offensive against the proponents of heresy. Philip II was a willing champion of this 'Counter Reformation'. Within Spain itself, the Inquisition remained watchful: between 1556 and 1562 a number of Protestant cells in Seville, Valladolid and other towns were suppressed. In the Netherlands, however, Philip's readiness to ride roughshod over the Dutch Estates-General in order to raise further funds and his determination to enforce religious orthodoxy provoked a rebellion against Spanish authority in 1566. The king responded by dispatching the Duke of Alba to the Netherlands, at the head of a large Spanish army, with the task of suppressing the rebels. But Alba's hard-line policy towards the Dutch, which led to the execution of over 1000 of the rebels including two of the ringleaders, the counts of Egmont and Horn, and his imposition of sales and property taxes to fund his military expenses, only exacerbated matters. In 1572, under the leadership of William Prince of Orange, another military revolt erupted and seven northern provinces seceded from Spanish rule. For the next three decades, Philip's policy towards the rebel provinces was to fluctuate regularly, as attempts at negotiation alternated with concerted assaults on rebel positions. In 1576, Spain's reputation was besmirched when mutinous troops sacked Antwerp and massacred more than 7000 of its inhabitants. After 1578, however, under the able leadership of Alexander Farnese, Duke of Parma, Spanish authority was gradually restored over the mainly Catholic southern Netherlands. Yet, the Protestant northern provinces remained defiant and Philip's refusal to countenance any sort of religious compromise ensured that a political settlement with the rebels was impossible. By the 1590s, it was becoming increasingly clear to the government in Madrid that the Dutch war had reached stalemate.

One of Philip's immediate objectives on his succession to the throne was to bring the simmering hostilities between Spain and France to an end. Spanish victories at St Quentin in northern France in 1557, and at Gravelines the following year, had the desired effect of bringing the French to the negotiating table. By the treaty of Câteau-Cambrésis of 1559, the French renounced their longstanding claims in Italy, but retained the port of Calais which had been captured from the English the previous year; the peace was sealed by Philip's marriage to Elizabeth of Valois, daughter of Henry II of France. Thereafter, Philip's ongoing preoccupations in the Mediterranean and the Netherlands meant that he would seek to avoid confrontation with his French neighbour. When the Wars of Religion between Catholics and Protestant Huguenots erupted in France in the 1560s, Philip was happy to stand on the sidelines until, fearful that the Huguenot Henry of Navarre might become king, he joined forces with the Catholic Holy League led by the duke of Guise in 1585. In 1590, Spanish armies, in league with their Catholic French allies, invaded France in an attempt to oust Henry of Navarre, who had ascended to the French throne, but became bogged down in heavy fighting. Even when Henry converted to Catholicism in 1593 and won over the bulk of the population to his cause, Philip kept up the military pressure and drove France to seek an alliance with the Netherlands and England in 1596. Two years later, hostilities between France and Spain were brought to an end by the treaty of Vervins, without major gain for either side.

After the death of his second wife Mary Tudor and the accession of her sister, the Protestant Elizabeth I, to the English throne in 1558, Philip's policy towards England was initially restrained, fearing that if Elizabeth were toppled by the Catholic pretender to the English throne, Mary Queen of Scots, it would result in an Anglo-French alliance to the detriment of Spanish power. During the 1580s, however, Anglo-Spanish relations began to deteriorate sharply. While Philip offered support to Catholic conspiracies against Elizabeth in 1583 and 1586, she demonstrated her backing for the Protestant Dutch rebels and allowed English privateers, such as John Hawkins and Francis Drake, to plunder Spanish treasure fleets and the Caribbean colonies. Elizabeth's decision to send an expeditionary force under the command of the earl of Leicester to shore up the Dutch rebellion in 1585, followed by the execution of Mary Queen of Scots two years later, finally prompted Philip to declare war.

The Spanish Armada, which set sail from Lisbon in May 1588 with 130 warships and 19,000 men, under the leadership of the Duke of Medina Sidonia, formed part of an ambitious strategy to undertake an amphibious invasion of England. Yet, Philip does not appear to have believed that the all-out conquest of England was a realistic objective. Instead, his military show of strength was probably designed to ensure English neutrality in the Dutch war, compensation for Spanish shipping losses suffered and freedom of religious expression for English Catholics. If successful, the king believed, it would be possible to crush the Dutch rebellion once and for all. However, outmanoeuvred and outgunned by the English forces as it made its way up the English Channel, the Armada was unable to rendezvous with the Duke of Parma, who stood ready with another invasion army, and was forced into the North Sea. Harried by English warships and decimated by storms and shipwrecks, the much depleted Armada was forced to circumnavigate the north of the British Isles before returning to Spain. The failure of the Armada did not mark the collapse of Spanish naval power, as has sometimes been claimed, but it was a blow to Spanish prestige and it encouraged Spain's enemies to redouble their attacks. La Coruña, Lisbon and the Azores were raided by English fleets in 1589, Cádiz was sacked by the earl of Essex in 1596, and private expeditions against Spanish shipping proliferated. For all that, Philip sanctioned further expeditions to England in 1596 and 1597, only to be thwarted again by adverse weather conditions.

THE 'BLACK LEGEND'

The meteoric rise of Spain to great power status during the course of the sixteenth century was as unwelcome to Spain's neighbours as it was unexpected. Resentment at Spain's political and military hegemony was compounded by the ideological divisions engendered by the Reformation and Counter-Reformation. Philip II's efforts to uphold Catholic unity in Europe, exemplified by his uncompromising policy towards the Dutch, English and French Protestants, contributed to a rising fear and hatred of Spain across Europe. The Protestant states, in particular, orchestrated a virulent propaganda campaign, in which Philip was portrayed as a ruthless tyrant bent on world domination and Spain was caricatured as a hotbed of fanaticism, obscurantism and unparalleled cruelty. The death of his son, the mentally unstable Charles, who, it was claimed, was poisoned at his father's behest in 1568, was held up to the world as an example of Philip's cold-hearted brutality. This 'Black Legend' spread rapidly abroad, fuelled by best-selling polemical works such as Las Casas's accounts of Spanish atrocities in the Indies and William of Orange's *Apologia* (1581), which highlighted Spanish abuses of human rights during the course of the Netherlands war. Philip himself refrained from entering the propaganda war, with the result that the highly negative and one-sided view peddled by the king's enemies persisted in many historiographical accounts until relatively recently.

THE STRAINS OF EMPIRE

Spain under Philip II attained an unprecedented position of power and prestige. Yet, the cost of administering and sustaining the far-flung empire was crippling. During the 1570s and 1580s, Spain's burgeoning commitments in the Mediterranean and Northern Europe made necessary a massive increase in military spending. A programme of naval rearmament was put in train and the army grew rapidly in size, until by 1587 an estimated 100,000 men were under arms. At the beginning of the reign, annual military expenditure in Castile stood somewhat below 2 million ducats; by 1598 the figure had reached about 10 million ducats and the state was in debt to the tune of 85 million ducats. The Armada of 1588 alone cost about 10 million ducats.

With the military budget threatening to escalate out of control, the government did what it could to meet its commitments. State revenues from all sources rose by an impressive 180 per cent – from 3.1 million ducats to 8.7 million – between 1556 and 1577, and by a further 48 per cent to 12.9 million ducats between 1577 and 1598. In part, this was achieved thanks to efficiencies in the collection of ordinary taxes, such as the *alcabala* sales tax and customs duties, to increases in 'extraordinary' taxes payable by laity and clergy (such as the *millones* tax imposed on the sale of oil, vinegar, wine and meat), and to a range of fund-raising initiatives, such as the sale of public offices and patents of nobility (*hidalguía*), and the disposal of communal waste lands (*baldíos*). Through tithes and a variety of other clerical impositions, such as the *cruzada* (levied to fund the crusades against the Turks) and the *excusado* (levied on church property), revenues from the Church increased steadily, so that, by the 1590s, the Spanish Church was providing more than one-fifth of the government's annual revenue. Most important of all, government income from the *quinto* and from the other taxes and customs duties levied in the colonies soared during the reign of Philip II, from 372,350 ducats in 1556 to 5.7 million in 1595. In total, over 64.5 million ducats in gold and silver were received by the government from the American colonies during the reign. Yet, despite the unprecedented revenues that Philip enjoyed from Castile and the Indies, his territories in Aragon, Italy and the Netherlands yielded only limited subsidies to the Crown and the king's attempts to increase taxation from these sources were largely unsuccessful. Like his father before him, Philip was forced to raise huge loans from bankers in Genoa, Antwerp and Augsburg to cover the shortfall in income, and on no fewer than three occasions – in 1557, 1575 and 1596 – he declared a state of bankruptcy in an attempt to restructure his debt repayments. As the reign progressed, the proportion of state revenue put aside for the payment of *juros*, or state annuities payable for loans to the Crown, mushroomed: in 1557 the state *juro* debt stood at 36 million ducats; by 1598 it had reached 85 million. However, Philip's steadfast refusal to cut back on his military commitments meant that the debt crisis was never solved. It would be left to his successors to pick up the bill.

PHILIP III AND THE *PAX HISPANICA*

'God who has given me so many kingdoms, has denied me a son capable of ruling them' was Philip II's own damning judgement on the abilities of his son and successor, Philip III (1598–1621). The new king lacked the appetite for hard work that had characterized his conscientious, introverted father, preferring to devote his energies to an extravagant round of hunting and partying. During his reign the court resumed a peripatetic existence, spending up to nine months away from Madrid at a time, although more often than not the reasons for its movements were recreational or religious rather than political. In 1601, the seat of government was transferred from Madrid to Valladolid, where it remained until 1606, when Philip was persuaded to return to Madrid on payment of 250,000 ducats by the town council. The ministerial team which had served Philip II was dismantled, with the exception of Juan de Idiáquez, who retained an influential role in government until his death in 1614. The new king was happy to delegate responsibility for affairs of state to his ministers, with the result that traditional political institutions which had withered under Philip II's rule enjoyed a new lease of life: the conciliar system was revitalized and the bureaucracy substantially expanded; the *cortes* came to enjoy increased influence over the Crown's finances; the aristocracy, whose political influence had waned under Philip II, returned to the fore; and the influence of royal secretaries diminished at the expense of ministers. Among the latter, by far the most influential was Francisco Gómez de Sandoval y Rojas, duke of Lerma (d. 1625). Lerma did particularly well out of office. He amassed an estimated personal fortune of over 3 million ducats, promoted his family and friends to positions of power in the state and ecclesiastical hierarchy, and sold public offices to the highest bidder. Philip III's reliance upon a chief minister, known as a *valido* or *privado*, rather than upon a team of royal secretaries, set the trend for seventeenth-century government. The power of the *valido* resided in his close friendship with the king, to whom he controlled access, and his control of the patronage system by which he built up a network of supporters in government.

Given the grave financial situation that Philip III had inherited, and conscious of a widespread war-weariness which had begun to permeate Spanish society, Lerma's immediate priority on coming to power was to reduce Spain's military commitments abroad. The death of Elizabeth I in 1603 and the accession of James VI of Scotland to the English throne permitted the signing of an Anglo-Spanish peace accord the following year. In the Netherlands, the Army of Flanders under the leadership of Ambrosio de Spinola captured Ostend in 1604 and led a major offensive against the Dutch rebels in 1605–6. However, the campaign ground to a halt when, not for the first time, lack of funds led the troops to mutiny and prompted the Spanish and Dutch to enter peace negotiations: in 1609, a 12-year truce was signed at Antwerp. Meanwhile, a network of ambassadors and diplomats strove to consolidate Spain's influence abroad. A dynastic alliance with France was sealed in 1615, when Philip's daughter, Anne, married the young Louis XIII, and Prince Philip wed the latter's sister, Elizabeth.

It may have been partly in an attempt to stem internal criticism of Lerma's 'peace policy' in Northern Europe that he and his fellow ministers decided to readdress the problem of the Moriscos. Ever since the rebellion of the Alpujarras of 1568–71, the situation of the Moriscos had remained at the forefront of political debate in Spain. In 1582, the complete expulsion of the Moriscos had been mooted, only to be dropped in the face of opposition from some Valencian nobles, who relied heavily on Morisco manpower and feared the economic consequences of such a measure. The Church authorities, however, in particular the archbishop of Valencia, Juan de Ribera, remained determined to uphold Christian orthodoxy in the peninsula and deplored the reluctance of many Moriscos to renounce the beliefs and traditions of Islam; they also viewed with alarm the steady growth in the Morisco population at a time when the Christian population was falling. Popular support for the expulsion was also vociferous.

In January 1608, the intensive lobbying bore fruit when the Council of State approved the expulsion of the Moriscos of Valencia; the decree received royal assent in April of the following year and was subsequently extended to other regions of Spain. The Valencian nobles were won over by promises that they would be compensated with the property that their Morisco vassals left behind. According to one estimate, some 117,000 Moriscos were expelled from Valencia in 1609, to be followed by a further 150,000 from Aragon and Castile between 1610 and 1614. The majority of the emigrants found asylum in North Africa; others travelled to France, and from there to Italy, Salonika and Istanbul; yet others perished resisting expulsion or on the journey into exile. A separate edict ordered that Morisco children aged five or under remain in Spain: a total of 1832 Morisco children were reportedly sent from Valencia to Castile to serve in the households of the clergy and nobility. By and large, the expulsion was greeted with popular enthusiasm, but in some areas the economic consequences were grave. In Valencia, where Moriscos had accounted for almost a third of the population, and in Aragon, agricultural production and tax returns slumped.

Lerma's pre-eminent position as *valido* to Philip III was gradually eroded. His policy of 'disengagement' from Northern Europe was viewed in some quarters as dishonourable, while his venality and his blatant manipulation of patronage led to widespread resentment. To compound matters, as government expenditure continued to outstrip income and the state remained saddled by massive *juro* debt, Lerma presided over a steady deterioration in state finances, compounded by his decision to mint debased *vellón* coinage (made of copper rather than of silver and copper mixture), which stoked up inflationary pressures in the economy.

After Lerma was finally removed from office in 1618, the dominant figure in government was Baltasar de Zúñiga, who argued that the time had come for Spain to reassert her power in Europe. In 1619, some 17,000 Spanish troops were sent to help the Emperor Ferdinand II of Austria put down a rebellion which had broken out in Bohemia the previous year; and in 1620 Spanish forces overran the Alsace and the Rhine Palatinate. These campaigns marked the beginning of Spain's involvement in a long, complex European power struggle known to historians as the Thirty Years War. Meanwhile, pressure was growing for a resumption of hostilities with the Dutch provinces, notably from the Portuguese, who had watched with a mounting sense of alarm as the Dutch had begun to threaten their traditional commercial interests in West Africa, India, Indonesia and Brazil, and from within Spain itself, where there was a widespread feeling that the Dutch had profited from the 12-year truce to undermine Spain's own economic ties with the New World. When the truce of Antwerp expired in 1621, neither the Spanish nor the Dutch were in any mood to return to the negotiating table.

PHILIP IV AND OLIVARES: THE DEFENCE OF REPUTATION

On the accession of Philip IV (1621–65), the direction of government policy was dominated by Zúñiga and then, after his death in 1622, by his nephew and protegé Gaspar de Guzmán, count of Olivares (from 1625, duke of San Lúcar la Mayor). One of the immediate priorities of the new regime was to conduct a thorough-going purge of Lerma's network of cronies and relations who had held power hitherto. The notoriously corrupt Rodrigo Calderón was beheaded in 1621; the dukes of Osma and Uceda were imprisoned; and Lerma himself only escaped imprisonment by virtue of his rank of cardinal, but was required to disburse large sums of money to the Treasury in return. A special commission, the *Junta Grande de Reformación*, drew up a number proposals for reform, including curbs on court expenditure, a programme of fiscal reorganization (notably the replacement of the *millones* levy and the *alcabala* by a single tax) and the abolition of many municipal offices. The reforms also sought to improve society's morals: brothels and theatres were to be closed, and censorship of books was to be intensified. However, the proposals aroused considerable opposition and in the event few were implemented.

Within months of the death of Philip III in March 1621, hostilities with the Dutch provinces had resumed and Spain's military intervention in support of Habsburg Austria had intensified. From a Spanish perspective, these military operations were wholly defensive in intent: above all else, Zúñiga and Olivares sought to show support for the Habsburg cause, protect the Catholic faith and uphold Spain's power and reputation abroad. Spain's rivals, however, were alarmed by what they perceived as a new phase of imperialist expansion and in 1625 England and France joined the Dutch Provinces, Venice and Savoy in declaring war on Spain. In the short term, Spain acquitted herself creditably. In 1625, Breda was recaptured from the Dutch, a feat of arms later immortalized in Velázquez's famous painting *The Lances*; the port of Bahía in Brazil, which had been occupied by the Dutch the previous year, was retaken; and an English attack on Cádiz was driven off. 'We have had all Europe against us, but we have not been defeated', Philip IV could proudly announce to the Castilian *cortes*. Thereafter, however, Spain suffered a number of humiliating military reverses: in Italy, attempts to block the French claimant to the duchy of Mantua ended in costly failure (1628–31); the war in the Netherlands continued to prove a ruinous drain on money and men, and Breda was lost again in 1637; France, which had earlier agreed peace terms in 1626, re-entered the fray in 1635; and four years later Spanish naval power suffered a crushing defeat at Dutch hands at the Battle of the Downs. On the other side of the Atlantic, the Spanish silver fleet was captured by the Dutch off Cuba in 1628, and a combined Hispano-Portuguese fleet, which had tried and failed to retake Pernambuco in Brazil, was defeated by the Dutch in 1640. On more than one occasion, Olivares was presented with a chance to secure an honourable peace, but his inability to compromise and his determination to uphold Spain's reputation at all costs meant that these opportunities were spurned.

Olivares had long been aware that if Spain was to meet her burgeoning military commitments abroad, then state revenues had to rise. By 1627, the situation had reached the point that a state of bankruptcy was declared and Olivares was forced to negotiate new loans from Portuguese *converso* bankers in order to keep the government afloat. The problem was not only that silver remittances from American treasure shipments were no longer sufficient to meet the shortfall in income, but that the fiscal burden on Castile was proving dangerously unsustainable. 'It is only reasonable', wrote Pedro Fernández de Navarrete in 1626, 'that the burdens should be distributed in proper proportion . . . It is quite unreasonable that the head [Castile] should be weakened while the other members, which are very rich and populous, should simply stand by and look on while it has to bear all these heavy charges.' The Union of Arms, published by Olivares in 1626, was designed to solve the problem of finance once and for all by bringing about the military and fiscal integration of the Spanish monarchy. It envisaged the creation of a standing army some 140,000 strong, to which all the constituent parts of the monarchy would contribute men and money in proportion to their size and resources. Yet, while Naples, Sicily and Flanders, as well as the American colonies, proved amenable to the proposals, Olivares's plans met with intense hostility in the east of the peninsula: the *cortes* of Aragon and Valencia were willing to contribute only small sums of money, while the Catalans refused to co-operate at all, alleging that the measures amounted to an infringement of their own traditional *fueros*. As a result, it was to an exhausted Castile that Olivares had to turn in 1631–2, and again in 1635–6, in order to secure the funds he needed to keep Spain on a war footing. When Olivares again tried to impose the Union of Arms on Catalonia in 1639 and authorized the billeting of Castilian troops on Catalan soil to forestall any future French invasion, it provoked a rebellion against the Spanish monarchy the following year. In 1641, the Catalans swore allegiance to Louis XIII of France, who speedily sent an army to bolster their cause. The revolt of the Catalans was followed by a similar insurrection in Portugal, where discontent stemmed not only from Olivares's increasing fiscal demands, but from the inability of the Crown to protect the Portuguese colonies from Dutch attack. By that stage, Spanish forces were severely over-stretched and finances were at breaking point. 'I am induced to think', wrote Sir Arthur Hopton, the English ambassador in Madrid, in 1641, 'that the greatness of this monarchy is near to an end.'

The Catalan and Portuguese revolts certainly spelled the end for Olivares, who was forced from office in January 1643. The following May, the French inflicted a crushing defeat on an invading Spanish army at Rocroi. In 1647–8, Naples and Sicily, suffering the consequences of poor harvests and rising taxation, rose in rebellion. State debt had reached a point that the monarchy again declared bankruptcy in 1647. To make matters worse, plague ravaged southern Spain in 1647–52. By this stage, it had become clear to Philip IV and his new chief minister, Olivares's nephew Luis Méndez de Haro, that peace was a prerequisite if the monarchy was to preserve its power and prestige intact. By the Treaty of Munster of 1648, Spain formally recognized what it had for decades sought to deny: the independence of the United Provinces of Holland. The treaty left the southern provinces of the Netherlands in Spanish hands, but condemned its chief commercial centre, Antwerp, to economic ruin by allowing Holland to blockade the River Scheldt.

During the decade that followed, Spain's fortunes see-sawed. The outbreak of civil war in France in 1648–53 allowed the recovery of Catalonia in 1652, as well as a number of strongpoints in Flanders. From 1655, however, Spain found itself at war with the English Commonwealth. In that year, English forces captured Jamaica, and in

1658 a joint Anglo-French force defeated the Army of Flanders at the battle of the Dunes, as a result of which Spain lost control of a number of strategic points, including Dunkirk and Gravelines. The Spanish Monarchy had demonstrated extraordinary resilience during the preceding 35 years, but its finances were once again at rock-bottom: treasure fleets had been destroyed by the English in 1656 and 1657, and an outbreak of plague in Naples had caused major loss of life, with the result that tax revenues had plummeted. In November 1659, the Peace of the Pyrenees brought to an end 24 years of bitter conflict between France and Spain: Spain agreed to relinquish Cerdanya, Roussillon and most of Artois to France, as well as a few strongpoints in Flanders; in return, Spanish sovereignty over Catalonia, the Spanish Netherlands, Franche Comté and her Italian territories was confirmed. The peace accord was sealed with the marriage of Philip's daughter, María Teresa, to Louis XIV of France. Peace with France and England (in 1660) at last allowed Philip and Haro to devote their attention to the Portuguese revolt, but defeats at Elvas (1659), Ameixal (1663) and Vilaviçiosa (1665) put paid to any hopes that the peninsula might be reunited under Spanish rule. In 1668, desperate to reduce its military commitments, almost at any price, Spain formally recognized the independence of Portugal.

SOCIAL AND ECONOMIC DEVELOPMENTS

In common with most regions of Western Europe, Spain experienced a period of pronounced demographic growth during the sixteenth century. Reliable statistics are hard to come by, but it is estimated that the population of Spain as a whole rose from about 4.7 million inhabitants in 1534 to about 7 million in 1591. Andalusia, and in particular the towns of the fertile valley of the Guadalquivir, experienced markedly rapid growth, thanks in large part to the booming trade with the Indies: Seville, the hub of American commerce and administration, saw its population increase by 136 per cent during the period 1530–88.

Population growth, both in the peninsula and in the American colonies, led to increased demand for food, higher prices and a marked rise in agricultural output. The increase in production was achieved largely by extending the area of cultivation, rather than by adopting better techniques to raise yields. None the less, adverse climatic conditions, the poverty of much of the soil and backward agricultural methods meant that output could not always keep up with demand: the spectre of famine was never far away and grain regularly had to be imported from Sicily and Northern Europe to make good the shortfall in supply. Stock-farming was also an important mainstay of the rural economy and Castile remained the chief supplier of raw wool to the looms of England and Flanders.

Population growth, agricultural expansion and the arrival of increasing amounts of American bullion from the 1530s onwards acted as a stimulus to industrial activity. Centres of cloth manufacture, notably in Segovia, Toledo, Barcelona and Valencia, enjoyed a significant rise in output during the first half of the sixteenth century. Other sectors to experience growth during this period included silk production in Granada and Murcia, leather working in Toledo, Seville and Burgos, iron mining in Vizcaya, and shipbuilding in the ports of Cantabria and Vizcaya. One of the most notable consequences of Spain's 'economic boom' was a marked rise in inflation. Between 1511 and 1559 the price of wheat in Andalusia rose by 109 per cent, oil by 197 per cent and wine by 655 per cent. During the sixteenth century as a whole prices quadrupled.

In the short term, the 'price revolution' meant increased profits for producers, manufacturers and merchants alike. The principal beneficiaries of this expansionary process were the aristocracy and the Church, who held the lion's share of productive land in the country. Although the political power of the aristocracy had been steadily eroded since the time of the Catholic Monarchs, its dominant economic position had never been seriously challenged and many nobles continued to enjoy seigneurial jurisdiction over large swathes of territory. Aristocracy is an elastic term, in that its membership ranged from powerful and wealthy grandees, whose number was limited by Charles V to just 20, to impoverished *hidalgos* who were ten-a-penny in the north of Spain. What set these nobles apart from the rest of society was the right to partial immunity from taxation and a shared belief in the essential honour of their status.

Merchants were the other great beneficiaries of the 'price revolution'. Simón Ruiz, who built up an extensive network of trading interests from his base at Medina del Campo, was but one among a number of wealthy and influential Castilian merchants who prospered at this time of economic expansion. By and large, however, the Spanish middle class remained small in comparison with those in other Western European countries. Manual work and commerce were so widely despised in a society obsessed with the values of the military aristocracy, that it was by no means uncommon for merchants, or their descendants, to sell up their business interests altogether, invest the proceeds in land, loans and state bonds, and snap up the patents of nobility that were regularly sold off by the Crown, in order to join the ranks of the landowning nobility. Besides, if at the beginning of the sixteenth century Castilian merchants and financiers were still signifi-cant players in the Hispanic commercial world, after 1550 they were increasingly displaced by foreign (especially Genoese) entrepreneurs. The principal victims of the price revolution were peasant farmers and urban workers. As wages failed to keep pace with rising prices, taxes and rents, living standards for the mass of the population steadily dete-riorated and the gap between rich and poor widened. Real wages fell by about 20 per cent during the first half the sixteenth century, and then fell by a further 12 per cent to 1600.

The process of demographic and economic expansion appears to have slowed to a halt by about 1580. Thereafter, the impact of epidemic disease (bubonic plague, smallpox, diphtheria), famine and malnutrition caused Spain's population to fall sharply. The epidemics of 1596–1602 and 1647–52, for example, together accounted for over one million lives. Subsistence crises (in particular those of 1605–7, 1615–16, 1630–1, 1647) caused widespread famine and lowered resis-tance to disease; and the expulsion of over a quarter of a million Moriscos between 1609 and 1614 further accelerated the process of depopulation. Spain was also haemorrhaging large numbers of men and women overseas: in Galicia alone, 68,000 men were recruited to fight abroad between 1621 and 1659, while an estimated 250,000 Spaniards migrated to America in the period 1506–1600 and a further 200,000 during the first half of the seventeenth century. With the exception of the capital, Madrid, which continued to grow rapidly during the seventeenth century, most Spanish towns experienced a fall in population: that of Seville, the greatest city in the peninsula, fell from 125,000 to 75,000 during this time. In rural areas, many villages shrank or were abandoned altogether: nearly half the villages of the kingdom of Valencia were reportedly deserted in 1638, largely as a consequence of the Morisco exodus.

Unsurprisingly, Spain's demographic crisis had a profound impact on economic activity. Weakening demand and lower yields caused a slump in agricultural output, while the number of sheep declined after 1550 as rising prices made Spanish wool uncompetitive abroad. What profits were still to be made from the countryside were concentrated in the hands of a small élite of secular and ecclesiastical landlords. For most peasant farmers, it was a struggle simply to survive and many were forced by rising debts and the weight of taxation to leave the land altogether. While some found employment as paid agricultural wage-labourers (*jornaleros*), many others joined the swelling ranks of paupers and vagrants who congregated in the towns in search of charitable handouts; in some areas, such as Catalonia, many of the rural dispossessed turned to brigandage in order to make ends meet. At the same time, Spanish industry was also contracting. The agrarian crisis meant that consumer demand diminished at the same time as rising inflation and heavy taxation were making Spanish goods deeply uncompetitive abroad. The once flourishing textile industry of Segovia, which in 1580 could boast upwards of 600 looms, had only 159 looms in operation by 1691. It was a similar story in the Vizcayan shipyards, where rising costs of materials and labour led to falling orders during the last two decades of the sixteenth century. Despite the spectacular increase in American treasure shipments to Spain after about 1550, the bulk of the profits were appropriated by foreign merchants and financiers who used the bullion to import manufactured goods from elsewhere in Europe, rather than to provide capital for investment in local industries, with the result that Spain began to suffer a widening balance of payments deficit. Most of the bullion that flowed into the royal coffers was likewise exported to fund Spain's expanding overseas commitments, or else to keep up with loan repayments with foreign bankers. At the same time, the volume and value of American trade was in decline, partly because the Spanish colonies were becoming increasingly self-sufficient and partly because foreign competitors (chiefly the English, French and Dutch) had succeeded in penetrating the American markets.

By the beginning of the seventeenth century, the sense that Spain was caught up in a downward spiral of decline was deeply ingrained. Writing in 1600, Martín González de Cellorigo famously complained: 'Our republic has come to be an extreme contrast of rich and poor, and there is no means of adjusting them one to another. Our condition is one in which we have rich who loll at ease, or poor who beg, and we lack people of the middling sort, whom neither wealth nor poverty prevent from pursuing the rightful kind of business enjoined by natural law.' Cellorigo was but one among a number of so-called *arbitristas* active between about 1580 and 1620, who tried to make sense of

Spain's deepening economic, social and political crisis, and offered suggestions (*arbitrios*) for reform. While many among them high-lighted the weaknesses of Spain's agricultural and manufacturing sectors, others, such as Diego de Saavedra Fajardo, called into question Spain's 'imperial destiny' under Habsburg rule and went so far as to call for a complete withdrawal from the Netherlands and America. After about 1660, however, the first green shoots of recovery were to be seen. Spain's population gradually began to rise, despite the serious impact of famine and disease between 1676 and 1686, although Spain would not make good its losses until the middle of the eighteenth century. The rural economy also began to recover, as agricultural output increased and exports of raw wool rose, although there was no corresponding expansion of manufacturing until monetary devaluation in 1680 provided the necessary stability to help restore business confidence and encourage investment in industry.

CULTURAL TRENDS

Spain's rise to empire during the sixteenth century and its political and economic travails during the seventeenth were accompanied by an unprecedented flowering of cultural creativity. During the reign of the Catholic Monarchs, the influence of the cultural currents of the Italian Renaissance led to a growing appreciation of classical learning and humanist thought. There was a revival of the study of classical languages and Latin learning became a badge of status and refinement among the upper classes. Among the most illustrious of the Spanish scholars of this period was Antonio Nebrija (d. 1522), whose Castilian grammar of 1492, the first to be compiled in any modern European vernacular, was designed in part to underline the supremacy of Castilian in the peninsula. During the reign of Charles V, Spain's exposure to Renaissance humanism became more pronounced, notably through the writings of Erasmus, but it remained a minority interest and died a death during the 1530s, as humanist ideas became increasingly associated with Lutheran heresy. After 1550, Castilian literature entered a remarkable 'Golden Age' of creativity which was to last for over a century. Despite Philip II's decrees of 1558–9, which imposed strict censorship on foreign works and prohibited education abroad, Spain's imperial connections ensured that she remained receptive to the cultural trends developing beyond the Pyrenees.

Among the most notable products of this explosion of cultural creativity, were 'picaresque' novels (which dealt with the subject of social delinquents), such as the anonymous *Lazarillo de Tormes* (1554), Mateo Alemán's *Guzmán de Alfarache* (1599–1602) and Francisco de Quevedo's *Buscón* (1626), and poetry of diverse genres, such as the mystical writings of Santa Teresa de Avila (d. 1582), St John of the Cross (d. 1591) and Fray Luis de León (d. 1591). Spanish theatre, exemplified by the prolific output of Lope de Vega (d. 1635), Tirso de Molina (d. 1648) and Calderón de la Barca (d. 1681), enjoyed a reputation that spread well beyond her frontiers. By far the most celebrated product of this Golden Age, however, was Miguel de Cervantes's peerless *Don Quijote de la Mancha* (published in two parts in 1605 and 1615), which remains one of the greatest novels of European literature. Many of these works were read and translated abroad. Beyond the sphere of literary creation, the period saw the publication of a number of important treatises in the fields of medicine (particularly at the University of Valencia), navigation and engineering.

As the Spanish empire and the bureaucracy of state expanded during the sixteenth century, there was a corresponding increase in demand for university-trained *letrados*. As a result, no fewer than 22 new universities were founded in Spain during the sixteenth century and a further five in the American colonies. By the late sixteenth century it is estimated that there were over 20,000 male students in Castile; women were excluded from the educational system. Among the most influential institutions, was the University of Alcalá de Henares, which became the foremost centre of theological study in the peninsula. It was at Alcalá that the Polyglot Bible, an edition of the Bible in its four languages, was begun under Cardinal Cisneros's supervision and finally published in 1522. New schools were also founded in many towns. Among the most influential, were those established by the Jesuit Order, which was founded in Spain by St Ignatius Loyola in 1540. The rise in levels of literacy went hand in hand with a marked increase in the availability of printed books. Between 1470 and 1501, over 800 titles were published in Spain, and a further 1300 titles between 1501 and 1520. Among the most popular titles were the masterpiece *La Celestina* (1499) by Ferdinand de Rojas (d. 1541) and works of chivalric fiction such as *Amadis of Gaul* (1508). None the less, written culture remained a minority interest and illiteracy was widespread, particularly in the countryside. Of the 150 men who accompanied the conquistador Pedro de Valdivia on his campaign in Chile in 1540, only 33 could read and write. For the illiterate masses, orally transmitted ballads and folk-tales continued to be popular.

   The economic boom between around 1480 and 1570, and the influx of bullion from the Indies, encouraged kings, nobles, merchants and clerics to invest large sums of money in ambitious building programmes of various kinds and in the decorative arts. Lavish private residences were erected, such as the royal palaces of El Escorial and El Buen Retiro, constructed for Philip II and Philip IV respectively, and the residence built in Guadalajara for the duque de Infantado; at the same time, a number of cathedrals, such as those of Granada, Segovia and Seville, were either erected or completed. Wealthy patrons acted as enthusiastic patrons of the visual arts: among the most illustrious of the many painters who found fame and fortune in sixteenth- and seventeenth-century Spain were El Greco, 'the Greek', Domenico Theotocopoulos (d. 1614), Diego de Velázquez (d. 1660), Bartolomé Esteban Murillo (d. 1682) and Francisco de Zurbarán (d. 1664). The Spanish élite were also enthusiastic connoisseurs and collectors of books and paintings: the marquis of Leganés had assembled a collection of some 1333 paintings by the time of his death in 1655.

THE LAST OF THE HABSBURGS

When the 4-year-old Charles II (1665–1700) acceded to the Spanish throne on the death of his father Philip IV in 1665, the reins of government were entrusted to the late king's widow, Mariana of Austria, in collaboration with a five-man regency council. The latter was soon sidelined by the queen's Austrian confessor, Father Nithard, but neither he nor any of the other mediocrities who subsequently wielded power at court – such as Ferdinand de Valenzuela and the king's half-brother, Joseph John of Austria – were able to provide the intelligent and decisive leadership the Spanish monarchy so badly needed. With memories of Olivares's ill-starred 'Union of Arms' still fresh in the minds of many, there was little likelihood that the desperately needed overhaul of Spain's administrative systems was going to be attempted, with the result that the governing class lapsed into inertia. Charles himself came of age in 1675, but he was weak in body and mind, and proved unequal to the task of government.

   On the domestic front, there were the first signs of demographic and economic recovery, particularly in the regions of the periphery, but any lingering hopes that Spain might once again exercise political hegemony in Europe quickly evaporated. As government debts continued to mount and tax revenues fell, state finances could no longer sustain the high levels of military spending that had been the norm under Olivares. And this at a time when Spain's arch-rival, France, under the increasingly ambitious Louis XIV, was expanding its military capability to unprecedented levels and subjecting Spanish positions in Flanders and elsewhere to relentless pressure. The Peace of Nijmegen, which brought Franco-Spanish hostilities to an end in 1678, required Spain to cede to France the Franche Comté and some 15 towns in Flanders; in 1684, Luxembourg and the county of Flanders were also relinquished. By the end of the decade, Spain was barely able to fund military operations beyond its own frontiers and the once mighty armies of Flanders and Milan had dwindled into insignificance. When war with France broke out again in 1689, Spain had to rely chiefly upon manpower supplied by its Dutch and Austrian allies to defend its territories in the Netherlands and Italy. In 1697, Spanish power reached a new nadir when French troops invaded Catalonia and captured Barcelona. By the Peace of Rijswijk of that year, Spain ceded half of the island of Hispaniola to the French, but recovered Catalonia, Luxembourg and Flanders.

The final years of the reign of Charles II were to be dominated by the question of the royal succession. The king's failure to father an heir by either of his two wives – Maria Luisa of Orléans and Mariana of Neuburg – gave rise to a period of intense diplomatic manoeuvring, as Spain's rivals collected like vultures 'to prey on the corpse of the Monarchy', as one historian has put it. Three candidates presented themselves: Prince Joseph Ferdinand of Bavaria, the Archduke Charles of Austria and Louis XIV's grandson, Philip, duke of Anjou. In 1698, the other European powers, fearing the consequences if the Spanish inheritance were to be allowed to pass intact into the hands of one royal house, agreed that the dominions of the Spanish monarchy should be partitioned among the three candidates. Charles II, however, was determined that the empire should avoid dismemberment and named Joseph Ferdinand as sole heir to the Spanish monarchy. When the latter died unexpectedly in 1699, the Bourbon Philip of Anjou was named as Charles's heir apparent. Yet, far from preserving the Habsburg inheritance, the establishment of the Bourbon dynasty in Spain was to give rise to a general European conflict, which was soon to tear Spain and her empire apart.

4

· · · · · · · ·

The Enlightened Despots,
1700–1833

The eighteenth century in Spain was a period of continuity and change. On the one hand, the process of demographic and economic expansion which had already got under way during the final decades of the previous century became more pronounced. On the other, the Bourbon monarchy which established itself in the peninsula in 1700 implemented a number of significant reforms which were designed to enhance the power and resources of the state, safeguard its still vast colonial empire, and restore Spain's international standing. This expansionary process, which reached its peak between 1740 and 1790, was brought to an abrupt halt by the French Revolutionary Wars and the ascendancy of Napoleon Bonaparte, which not only inflicted untold destruction and suffering upon the peninsula, but also led to the loss of most of the Spanish empire shortly afterwards.

THE WAR OF THE SPANISH SUCCESSION

The death of the childless Charles II in November 1700 brought Habsburg rule in Spain to an end. Under the terms of his will, Charles left the kingdom of Spain, its European possessions and its overseas empire to a prince of the Bourbon royal house, the 17-year-old Philip, duke of Anjou, whose grandfather was Louis XIV of France and whose grandmother, María Teresa, was the daughter of Philip IV of Spain. The alliance of the French and Spanish royal dynasties was greeted with enthusiasm in Spanish diplomatic circles, appearing to offer as it did a means for Spain to maintain her territory, power and status intact. 'There are now no Pyrenees', declared Louis XIV, 'two

134

nations that have for so long been rivals will in future be a single people; the lasting peace between them will assure the tranquillity of Europe'. However, the Habsburg House of Austria had an equally strong claim to the Spanish succession. The emperor Leopold I was the son of another of Philip IV's daughters, Margarita Teresa, and although he and his eldest son Joseph had already relinquished their claims to the Spanish throne, his second son, Archduke Charles, was in no mood to let such a rich inheritance slip through his fingers. Elsewhere in Europe, the Bourbon succession aroused considerable alarm. Unconvinced by the stipulation in Charles II's will that 'this Crown and that of France shall ever remain sundered', and fearful that a Franco-Spanish alliance would threaten their own vital political and economic interests, the maritime powers, England and the United Provinces of the Netherlands, took up arms on behalf of the House of Austria. In May 1702, the Grand Alliance of the Hague, comprising Austria, England and the Netherlands, declared war on France and Spain; the following year, Portugal, enticed by the promise of territorial acquisitions both in the peninsula and in the Americas, joined the war on the side of the Alliance.

The War of the Spanish Succession, although nominally fought over the Spanish throne, embroiled the participants in a major European conflict, whose effects were felt as far afield as America, and in which global interests in trade and the colonies were often as important as political and dynastic concerns. From a purely Spanish perspective, the conflict was both a civil war and a desperate struggle to avoid dismemberment by hostile foreign powers. The irony was that while the notoriously xenophobic Castilians came out in support of a Frenchman, now styled Philip V (1700–46), the subjects of the Crown of Aragon, for whom the experience of Habsburg rule had proved far from happy, mostly rallied to the cause of the Austrian archduke. In Catalonia, where support for the Allies was at its strongest, the rebellion against the Bourbons, though enthusiastically supported by the populace, was directed by the ruling merchant élite of Barcelona, whose overriding aim was not outright independence, but the defence of regional autonomy against Bourbon centralization and direct access to the lucrative markets of the American colonies. In Valencia, and to a slightly lesser extent Aragon, political unrest largely took the form of violent social protest by peasant vassals who chafed at seigneurial domination.

To begin with, Philip V's position within Spain remained secure. His subjects initially proved loyal, although they viewed with misgivings the sizeable French entourage which accompanied their new monarch, and in the American colonies the change of dynasty was accepted with equal equanimity. But with her own military strength now but a pale shadow of its former self – at the beginning of the war the Spanish army could barely muster 13,000 infantry and 5000 cavalry – Spain was forced to rely principally on French military muscle to defend what remained of its European empire. Spain's chronic lack of naval power was painfully illustrated as early as 1702, when an Anglo-Dutch squadron attacked Cádiz and on its return to base destroyed the Spanish treasure fleet and its French escort which had put into Vigo. The war in the peninsula began in earnest in the spring of 1704 following the arrival of Archduke Charles, now proclaimed Charles III, in Portugal; in August the Allies captured Gibraltar. The following year, Valencia and Catalonia came out in support of Charles, who established his court in Barcelona. 1706 represented a veritable *annus horribilis* for the Bourbon cause: on the wider European stage, the duke of Marlborough's victory at Ramillies signalled the loss of the Spanish Netherlands; the Austrian victory at Turin forced the French to withdraw from northern Italy; within the peninsula itself, Majorca and Aragon declared their support for Charles, as did some sections of the Castilian aristocracy, while the Allies entered Madrid and forced Philip V to retreat north to Burgos. However, backed by the enthusiastic efforts of the clergy, who pronounced the war against the Allies to be a holy crusade, the king rallied support within Castile and, with renewed French supplies of manpower, money and *matériel*, launched a vigorous counter-attack. Madrid was soon restored to Philip's control and in April 1707 Bourbon forces led by the Marshal duke of Berwick won an important victory at Almansa near Albacete, as a result of which they were able to regain control of Valencia and Aragon. Beyond the Pyrenees, however, the tide of the war had turned decisively against the Bourbons. By 1709, when Pope Clement XI formally recognized Archduke Charles as the rightful king of Spain, Louis XIV of France seemed about to accept the Allies' demands that Philip V abdicate the Spanish throne and the French army withdraw from Spain for good.

When the Bourbon succession had first been mooted in 1700, Louis XIV's instructions to his grandson had been clear: 'Be a good Spaniard; that is your first duty; but remember that you were born French in order to preserve unity between both nations; this is the way to make them both happy and to preserve the peace of Europe.' French influence in Spain in the succeeding years had been maintained and reinforced not only by the French military, but by a civilian army of diplomats, bureaucrats and courtiers. These included the French ambassador Michel-Jean Amelot, who became the driving force in reforming the Spanish administration between 1705 and 1709; the financier Jean Orry, who in 1702 was charged with the Herculean task of restoring Spain's ailing finances to good health; and the Princess des Ursins, who wielded considerable influence at the court of Philip V. But when Amelot tried to push through a French-sponsored peace plan in 1709, Philip stood his ground: 'The crown of Spain, which God has placed on my head, I will maintain as long as a drop of blood flows in my veins . . . I will never quit Spain while I have a spark of life.' But in 1709 Spain was in no position to go it alone, a fact that became all the more apparent when the Allies reoccupied Zaragoza and Madrid in August–September 1710, prompting Louis XIV to send fresh armies to the peninsula to the prop up the Bourbon cause. By the beginning of 1711, however, it was time for the war-weary Allies themselves to take stock of their war aims. Defeat at Villaviciosa (Guadalajara) the previous December had rendered the likelihood of outright victory in the peninsula more remote than ever. Then, in April 1711, Emperor Joseph I of Austria died, leaving the throne to his brother Archduke Charles. The English and Dutch, for whom the prospect of the union of the Austrian and Spanish Empires was equally unappealing, speedily opened negotiations with the Bourbons at Utrecht in January 1712 and concluded them a little over a year later. Abandoned to their fate by the Allies, the Catalans fought desperately on, but in September 1714 Barcelona finally surrendered to a joint Franco-Spanish army after a two-month long siege.

The Treaties of Utrecht (April 1713) and Rastatt (March 1714) marked the formal end of the War of the Spanish Succession. In so far as Philip V was recognized as the legitimate king of Spain (in return for his abandonment of any claim to the French throne), the partition of Spain had been avoided, and the Spanish American empire had been preserved intact, the Bourbons had achieved most of their primary war aims. However, Emperor Charles was amply recompensed with the Spanish territories in the Netherlands and Italy (Milan, Tuscany, Sardinia and Naples), while Sicily passed to the ruler of Savoy. The British also hung on to their principal war gains – the rock of Gibraltar and the island of Minorca (captured in 1708) – and won important trading concessions in the Spanish Indies, namely the exclusive right to transport African slaves to the Spanish empire for a period of 30 years and to send an annual shipment of 500 tons of merchandise to the Indies. Utrecht was clearly a humiliation for Spain, in that it marked the end of her Burgundian-Habsburg empire and allowed the English a precious toe-hold in the peninsula, as well as important trading rights. But, by the same token, the loss of her European territories at last freed Spain from a debilitating drain upon her financial resources and gave her the chance to redirect her energies towards the American colonies. In this respect, at least, Utrecht represented an opportunity as much as a setback.

THE GOVERNMENT OF PHILIP V (1700–46)

Philip V and his ministers would seek to govern Spain according to French principles of statecraft: centralization, rationalization and modernization were to be their watchwords. In the short term, the main objective for the Bourbon regime was to enhance the authority of the Crown and mobilize the resources of the state for war. The former was achieved partly by carrying out a fundamental reorganization of the administration of state along French lines: the *despacho*, or cabinet council, became the chief decision-making body in the realm and the influence of the former Habsburg councils of state, which had customarily been the preserve of the aristocracy, was sharply reduced. Only the Council of Castile, with responsibility for home affairs, retained any significant measure of influence. Executive power was transferred to a series of secretariats, or ministries, responsible for state, war, justice and ecclesiastical affairs, Navy and the Indies, and finance, while policy direction was entrusted to a new bureaucratic élite, recruited from the ranks of the lesser nobility, rather than to the grandees of longstanding. The *cortes*, now modified to incorporate representatives from the entire Spanish kingdom, ceased to play any meaningful political role and met only three times during the eighteenth century.

The defeat of the rebellious eastern realms was viewed by Philip V and his ministers as an opportunity both to exact retribution and carry out the political rationalization of the state by which they set such great store. In June 1707, the king issued a stern edict, known as the *Nueva Planta*, or New Plan, which, 'on account of the rebellion which they have raised, thus breaking the oath of allegiance they swore to me as their lawful king and lord', swept away all the privileges and liberties which the inhabitants of Aragon and Valencia had hitherto enjoyed. The regional councils and *cortes* were abolished; local officials were replaced by Castilian *corregidores*; the traditional *fueros* were superseded by Castilian law; and Castilian-style high courts were established. In Catalonia, a similar edict imposing Castilian control was enacted in January 1716. Riding roughshod over the clause in the Treaty of Utrecht which had stated that the Catalans were to be offered a pardon and their 'ancient rights and estates fully restored to them', the government introduced a raft of institutional changes which suppressed the autonomous powers of the region. Castilian replaced Catalan in the local administration and courts; Catalan universities were abolished and were replaced by a new, pro-Bourbon, university at Cervera; and Castilian law was introduced, although it did not entirely supersede Catalan civil law. Plans to introduce compulsory military service were shelved in the face of furious protests. By contrast, in the Basque region and in Navarre, which had proved stoutly loyal to the Bourbon cause, the local *fueros* and courts were preserved. In a further attempt to bind the eastern realms more closely to the rest of Spain, the first steps towards fiscal unification were taken with the introduction of a single comprehensive tax on property and income in Aragon (1714), Valencia (1716) and Catalonia (1717). The administrative reforms marked the end of an era. At the stroke of a pen, the autonomy of the eastern kingdoms had been erased and in their place was a Spanish monarchy that was stronger, more centralized and, in theory at least, more united than ever before; in this respect, the *Nueva Planta* may be said to have marked the birth of Spain as a modern state.

Once the War of the Spanish Succession was over, however, the impetus for reform slackened to a snail's pace. In part this may be attributed to the personal failings of Philip V, who was easily manipulated by the dominant court figure, the Princess des Ursins, until her dismissal in 1714, and then by his second wife, the Italian Isabella Farnese. Philip was prone to regular bouts of mental illness, the most prolonged of which occurred in 1732–3, when the king refused even to see his ministers or sign any official documents. In January 1724, the king suddenly abdicated in favour of his son Louis, only to resume the throne the following September on the death of the latter from smallpox. Philip's irrational behaviour and his progressive disengagement from government left a political vacuum which was filled by a succession of foreign advisers, such as the Italian Cardinal Alberoni, who dominated the government between 1714 and 1719, and the unscrupulous Dutchman Ripperdá, who self-interestedly wielded power between 1724 and 1726. Thereafter, Spanish ministers came to the fore, notably José Patiño, who implemented the *Nueva Planta* in Catalonia and later held the posts of secretary of the Indies and navy, finance, war and, finally, from 1733, secretary of state.

If, as the king's ministers intended, Spain was to become a powerful state once more and was to be able to defend her American empire against her colonial rivals, she needed an army and navy to match her ambition. To this end, during the first half-century of Bourbon rule well over 50 per cent of the Crown's total annual income was regularly designated towards the military budget. A modern standing army, some 70,000 strong, based upon the French system of regiments was established. An ambitious programme of naval expansion was also put in train under the direction of Patiño: dockyards and naval bases were either rebuilt or, as in the case of Ferrol in Galicia, constructed from scratch; Spain's first naval academy was established; and a programme of shipbuilding was begun. Although Patiño's best efforts were frequently undermined by a lack of resources and the competing demands of the army, the court and the state bureaucracy, by the time of his death Spain could boast a fleet of 34 major warships, 9 frigates and 16 smaller ships.

Despite the best intentions of Philip V's ministers, Spanish foreign policy remained firmly orientated towards Europe. Egged on by Isabella Farnese, Philip V's overriding strategic objective was to recover Spain's former influence in Italy and to carve out a kingdom for the couple's son, Charles. To this end, Spanish forces invaded Sardinia in 1717 and attacked Sicily, only to be thwarted when France, Britain, the United Provinces and Austria formed the Quadruple Alliance (1718) against them. Forced to the negotiating table, Spain renounced her territorial gains by the Treaty of Cambrai (1724). However, on the outbreak of the War of the Polish Succession (1733–8), Spanish forces conquered Naples and Sicily from Austria in 1734 and installed Charles as king of the Two Sicilies. Thereafter, colonial rivalry with Britain, prompted by disagreements over Gibraltar and Minorca, and over large-scale British smuggling in the Caribbean, dominated Spanish attention. A brief, yet fruitless, war in 1727–8, was followed by another much longer and far more debilitating conflict in 1739, the so-called 'War of Jenkins' Ear', which dragged on until 1748 without major gain for either side.

For all the achievements of the first half-century of Bourbon rule, Spain's overall position was not without weakness. Fiscal reforms had successfully boosted government income from some 120.3 million reales in 1703 to 360 million in 1745, and the tax burden was far more equitably balanced between Castile and the rest of the kingdom than before, but taxation receipts struggled to keep pace with state spending. Quite apart from having to fund an ambitious and costly foreign policy, and meet the competing claims upon revenues by the burgeoning state bureaucracy and the newly professionalized army and navy, there was the problem of funding a royal court that was far more lavish than it had ever been under the Habsburgs. Inspired by the grandeur of Versailles, Philip V devoted vast sums of public money towards building sumptuous new palaces for himself in Madrid and La Granja de San Ildefonso near Segovia, and to extending the existing palace at Aranjuez. In 1731, the English ambassador, Benjamin Keene, calculated that from an annual revenue of 19 million pesos, the royal family spent about 7 million, the army 8.7 million, and the navy and bureaucracy accounted for the rest. By the time of Philip V's death in 1746, the state was still spending well beyond its means. The immediate priority of the new regime, therefore, would be to provide the resources that Spain urgently needed if she were once again to return to a position of greatness.

FERDINAND VI (1746–59)

Like his father before him, Ferdinand VI, the only surviving son of Philip V's first marriage to María Luisa of Savoy, was an emotionally unstable individual. Ill prepared for the task of government, the new king preferred to devote most of his energies and resources towards the upkeep of a lavish court, at which musical virtuosi, such as the composer Domenico Scarlatti and the celebrated Neapolitan *castrato* singer Farinelli, were fêted, and elaborate entertainments, such as the spectacular water-borne festivities that were held regularly on the Tagus at Aranjuez, were organized. None the less, in spite of the king rather than because of him, the reign of Ferdinand VI marked an important stage in Spain's recovery after the War of Spanish Succession. A combination of strong ministerial leadership, international peace and steadily increasing state revenues would enable the first administration of Ferdinand VI to look to the long term, strengthen the country's infrastructure, and begin to close the yawning technological gap that had opened up between Spain and her rivals. Two ministers came to dominate the new regime: Zenón de Somodevilla, marquis of La Ensenada, who from 1743 held several of the key ministries of government, including war, finance, navy and the Indies, as well as the secretaryship of state and the post of superintendent of revenues; and José de Carvajal, who from 1746 occupied the posts of secretary of state, governor of the council of the Indies and president of the *junta* of commerce. The two men were often at loggerheads with one another over key policy issues: in foreign affairs Ensenada favoured an alliance with France as a counterweight to British naval supremacy, while Carvajal, related on his mother's side to an English aristocratic family, preferred an accommodation with British interests; in the economic sphere, Ensenada gave priority to Spain's trade with the Indies, while Carvajal set greatest store by the promotion of national industry by the state.

For all their differences, both in terms of policy and personality, Ensenada and Carvajal were agreed that in the short term the overriding priority for the government was to build up the financial resources and military strength of the state. It was fanciful to suppose that Spain would be able to confront France or Britain on equal terms, but rather, as Ensenada himself put it in 1752, that Spain 'will be respected and no longer subject to the will of these two powers'. International peace was a prerequisite if these objectives were to be achieved. Hostilities with Britain were brought to an end by the Treaty of Aix-la-Chapelle of 18 October 1748; then, when a new conflagration, the Seven Years War, broke out in 1756 between France and Austria on the one hand, and Britain and Prussia on the other, Spain initially chose to maintain a prudent position of neutrality.

Ensenada sought to enhance the resources of government by implementing a wide-ranging programme of financial reform. Central to his plans was his proposal to introduce a single tax on income, the *catastro*, which, for the very first time, would be levied on all subjects, noble and non-noble alike, according to their ability to pay. To this end, between 1750 and 1754 a detailed survey of property and income was carried out throughout Castile by newly appointed royal officials called intendants, who had wide-ranging powers over justice, finance, military affairs and other general administration. However, faced by the voluble resistance of the nobility and clergy, who viewed the proposed tax as a challenge to the established social order, the legislation was shelved.

Other financial reforms met with rather more success: the administration of provincial taxation was brought under direct state control; stricter controls were placed on American trade and private treasure returns; and the creation of the *Giro Real* ensured that foreign exchange transactions were managed by the state. As a result of these efficiencies in tax collection, by the time of the death of Ferdinand VI in 1759 state revenues enjoyed an unprecedented surplus of 300 million reales.

The principal beneficiary of Ensenada's fiscal prudence was – as he had always intended – the Spanish Navy. By 1753, about one-fifth of total state expenditure was dedicated to its marine arm. The dockyards of Cádiz, Cartagena and Ferrol were rebuilt, steps were taken to make Spain self-sufficient in timber and naval stores, and engineers such as Jorge Juan, who visited England in 1749–50, were sent abroad to study the latest shipbuilding techniques and recruit the designers and craftsmen who would build the new generation of Spanish fighting ships. By 1754, Spain had 45 major warships and 19 frigates, a force substantial enough to arouse considerable anxiety in British government circles. Indeed, it was the British ambassador in Madrid, Keene, who engineered the conspiracy that led to the removal of Ensenada from office by the duke of Huéscar and the anglophile Ricardo Wall in the summer of 1754. Ensenada's fall from power was accompanied by a purge of many of his fellow reformers in government. The new regime shared little of the vision and drive that had characterized Ensenada; indeed, it appears to have lacked a coherent policy of any kind. Many of the innovations that had been introduced in the fields of taxation and commerce were allowed to lapse and, just as Keene had anticipated, the naval budget was drastically pruned. In 1758, moreover, the state was gripped by paralysis when the unstable Ferdinand VI, mourning the death of his queen, Barbara of Braganza, lapsed into complete madness. It was not until Ferdinand died in August 1759, and his half-brother Charles came to the throne, that the task of government could begin anew.

CHARLES III (1759–88)

Charles III was already an experienced ruler by the time he ascended the Spanish throne in 1759 and his credentials as a reformer were impressive. As king of Naples and Sicily since 1734, he had already grappled, with some degree of success, with problems all too similar to those he was to encounter in Spain: a system of government and taxation that remained inefficient and unequitable; a nobility and clergy whose power and privilege represented a challenge to the authority of the monarchy; and a moribund economy in urgent need of revitalization. What is more, under his patronage, Naples had become a thriving centre of culture and learning. Contemporaries were impressed by his energy and by the close interest he paid to the affairs of government, for which he found time despite his daily hunting expeditions. After a series of undistinguished rulers, Charles appeared to be the dynamic monarch Spain needed – the enlightened despot *par excellence* – if fundamental reform were truly to be brought about.

Charles recruited to his first administration an able team of ministers, the most influential of whom were the Italians Leopoldo di Grigorio, marquis of Squillace, who had served in the king's government in Italy, and who served in Spain as minister of finance from 1759 and minister of war from 1763, and the marquis of Grimaldi, appointed minister of state in 1763. They were actively supported by a group of Spanish bureaucrats, many of whom were university-trained lawyers, known as *manteistas* or *golillas*, who were of *hidalgo* stock but lacked the wealth or connections of their rivals for power, the *colegiales*, an élite group of university graduates drawn from the higher ranks of the aristocracy, who had hitherto dominated the hierarchy of the government, the judiciary and the Church. Typical of the new breed of minister were Pedro Rodríguez de Campomanes and José Moñino, later count of Floridablanca, who were to stand at the forefront of reforming policy during the reign of Charles III. The new ministerial team was under no illusions of the scale of the task that faced them: 'How much reform have we needed in Spain: so much that although we have tried, we have not known where to begin', one minister, Manuel de Roda, candidly admitted. The arrival of Charles III in Spain was soon followed by a raft of reformist initiatives designed to boost royal revenues further and enhance royal authority. For example, Ensenada's income tax plans were dusted down in 1760 and a committee set up to study its implementation; two years later, Campomanes launched a determined drive to recover seigneurial rights and properties which had previously been alienated by the Crown.

The Bourbon monarchs showed themselves particularly determined to subordinate the wealthy and powerful Spanish Church to their authority and to keep papal interference to a minimum. After a protracted campaign that had been begun by Philip V, a concordat of 1753 had conceded to the Spanish Crown the *real patronato universal*, which confirmed the Crown's right of presentation of both the episcopate and most of the secular clergy. Under Charles III, royal control over the Church was tightened further: the collection of the ecclesiastical tax known as the *excusado* was brought under government control (1761); it was decreed that royal permission had to be granted before papal documents could be published in the kingdom (1762); and ecclesiastical institutions were barred from acquiring further property (1765). Steps were also taken to bring the Inquisition more fully under royal control, although no attempt was made to curb its powers. By the second half of the eighteenth century, the volume of cases being tried annually by the Inquisition had slowed to a trickle, but the tribunal remained active and vigilant. In 1776, the intendant of Seville, Pablo de Olavide, a prominent royal official who was responsible for a number of reformist initiatives in Andalusia, was arrested as a suspected heretic and sentenced to eight years imprisonment.

One of Charles III's earliest foreign policy initiatives was to abandon the prudent policy of neutrality which had brought such benefits to Spain under Ensenada and Carvajal, and to enter the Seven Years War on the side of France. On paper the policy had much to commend it. The third Family Compact of August 1761, which sealed the military alliance, sought to combine Spain and France's respective military strengths into a potent fighting force capable of challenging British naval power. But when Spain finally entered the war in 1762, the tide of the war had already turned decisively in Britain's favour, France was on the brink of defeat and there was little that Spain could do to alter the overall pattern of events. The subsequent Peace of Paris of February 1763 required Spain to surrender Florida and all the Spanish territories in North America east of the Mississippi, as well as commercial rights in the Honduras, to Britain. However, she recovered Havana and Manila, which had been lost to the British during the brief hostilities, and acquired Louisiana from France by way of compensation for her losses.

Military defeat was followed by domestic upheaval. In March 1766, a popular uprising broke out in Madrid. For four days anarchy reigned in the capital, Squillace's house was sacked by the mob and Charles III was forced to flee to Aranjuez. The unrest was followed by disturbances in over 60 other Spanish cities and towns, although only a few, such as Zaragoza, experienced the same level of violence as Madrid.

Whether the Madrid uprising was a spontaneous outbreak of civil unrest, brought about by food shortages (the harvest of 1765 had been disastrous and the price of bread had soared) and resentment against the tax increases introduced by Squillace to finance the recent war with Britain, or whether the riots were instigated or at any rate manipulated by a prominent clique of nobles and clerics who resented being marginalized from power by foreigners and parvenus, and saw the reform programme as a threat to their own wealth and position, has been much debated. In the event, the riots of 1766 changed little: Squillace himself was promptly dismissed, but there was otherwise little alteration of policy or personnel. The count of Aranda, appointed president of the Council of Castile, was charged with restoring order in Madrid, while in the provinces food riots were put down and new security measures, including the appointment of *alcaldes de barrio* to oversee the policing of urban districts, were implemented.

Its authority restored, the government set about finding the culprits for the disturbances of 1766 and suspicion soon rested on the Jesuit Order. To a government so committed to the principles of absolutist monarchy, the international organization of the Jesuit Order, its exceptional wealth, its quasi-independent activities in the American colonies (in Paraguay the Order held nearly 100,000 Guaraní Indians under its protection), its influential role in education, and its close ties to the aristocracy and to the papacy (to which it owed a vow of obedience), all added to the suspicion that the Jesuits were not only an obstacle to reform, but a threat to public order and the authority of the Crown. A government document compiled the following year condemned the 'spirit of fanaticism and sedition, false doctrine and intolerable pride' of the Order, which was identified as 'an open faction which disturbed the state with interests directly opposed to the public welfare'. In February 1767, a royal edict was published which expelled the Jesuits from Spain and its territories overseas, and expropriated Jesuit properties. Jesuit university chairs were abolished and attempts were made to bring the universities more closely under government control and encourage reform of university curricula. Public reaction in Spain was muted and the response of the clergy, many of whom resented the power and influence that the Jesuits had enjoyed, was hardly more vociferous; six years later, the Company of Jesus was abolished altogether by Pope Clement XIV.

With the dismissal of Squillace, Charles III sought to strengthen his administration and give it a clearer Spanish identity. Within the new regime, the count of Aranda stood out both in terms of his breeding and his political outlook. Aranda was a soldier aristocrat of the old school, valued by the king more for his ability to maintain order in the country and inspire the confidence of the aristocracy than for his commitment towards enlightened reform. Although not opposed to reform for its own sake, Aranda distrusted the centralizing policies of his colleagues, which in his view rode roughshod over regional traditions and liberties; he also resented the prominent position in government enjoyed by outsiders like Grimaldi and by *golilla* bureaucrats like Campomanes and Moñino. Aranda and his supporters believed in the need to rein in the absolutist tendencies of Charles III. The count and his supporters harked back to the more consensual model of government, which had served Spain in the heyday of Habsburg rule, in which the aristocracy of the realm had acted as a moderating influence on royal powers, and in which the liberties of the regions had been understood and respected by the central government. As president of the Council of Castile between 1766 and 1773, Aranda came to head the so-called Aragonese Party, an informal faction of aristocrats, clerics and military men who sought to restrain the increasingly centralist and bureaucratic nature of the Bourbon state. Aranda himself trod a careful line, ready to cross swords with *golilla* ministers, but unwilling to champion some of the extreme reactionary views articulated by many of his supporters. Even when Aranda was effectively sidelined from politics after his appointment as ambassador to France in April 1773, the Aragonese Party did not disappear and tensions within government between the rival factions, *colegiales* and *golillas*, continued until the appointment of Floridablanca as secretary of state in February 1777. The ascendancy of Floridablanca ensured that the Bourbon political project, with its commitment towards centralization, modernization and reform was not to be derailed. Floridablanca, left to his own devices by the king, who himself took progressively less interest in the affairs of state, met regularly with his fellow ministers to discuss matters in depth and co-ordinate policy. Each minister was closely assisted by a staff of professional officials, the so-called *covachuelas*, whose task it was to ensure the smooth running of their departments, while provincial intendants kept the central government appraised of social and economic developments in their regions.

Military reform was a central preoccupation of government under Charles III, just as it had been under Philip V and Ferdinand VI. Chastened by Spain's defeat in the Seven Years War, Charles instigated a thorough overhaul of the country's fighting capability. Whereas Ensenada had looked to British expertise when he sought to expand Spain's naval capacity in the middle of the century, Charles and his ministers looked to Prussia to provide the military know-how that would bring about the modernization of the Spanish Army. By 1761, the regular army numbered approximately 60,000 men; military academies were established at Ávila and Segovia to drill recruits in the latest military tactics; and heavy arms factories at Barcelona, Santander and Seville saw to it that the army remained well-supplied with field guns. At the same time, naval construction (based principally in Ferrol and Havana) continued apace, although Spain now relied upon France rather than England to provide it with the necessary technical expertise: by 1783, the Spanish Navy possessed 67 ships of line and 32 frigates, making it the second largest navy in Europe after the British. None the less, Spain's ability to mount and sustain major campaigns was fatally undermined by the lack of an efficient supply system, by a surfeit of officers (in 1796 there were still 132 generals) and by problems of recruitment, which forced the government to rely on volunteers and foreigners to keep the army up to strength: by end of the reign there were as many as eight foreign regiments. Likewise, despite the important role played by the Spanish Navy in defending Spain's colonial interests and her transatlantic commerce, the poor standard of naval officers meant that in wartime it rarely performed with credit, preferring wherever possible to stay in port.

Spanish military expansion during the 1760s and 1770s was matched by a more belligerent foreign policy. Despite her defeat by Britain, Spain continued to cultivate the Franco-Spanish alliance and when hostilities with the British flared up again in 1779 Spain managed to acquit herself far more creditably. The root of the new conflict was the outbreak of the War of American Independence of 1775. Any misgivings that Charles and his ministers harboured that the colonial rebellion might lead to a similar outbreak of secessionist unrest in Spain's own American colonies, was outweighed by the recognition that the American war offered an opportunity to reverse the losses of the Paris treaty of 1763. In an attempt to square the circle, the Spanish government lent logistical support to the North American rebels, without ever recognizing the independence of the American states; at the same time, a direct attack was launched on British positions in Central America, which culminated in the capture of the Pensacola coastal strip in Florida in May 1781. This strategy was accompanied by a concerted assault on British positions in Europe: a joint Franco-Spanish expedition made preparations to invade England itself in 1779, only to fall victim to disease among the troops; Gibraltar was the object of a lengthy but fruitless siege between 1779 and 1782; and the island of Minorca was recaptured in 1782 after 74 years of British rule. The ensuing Peace of Versailles (September 1783) saw Florida and Minorca return to Spanish rule, although the British were awarded commercial rights in the Honduras.

By the time of the death of Charles III in December 1788, Spain's credentials as an imperial power appeared to have been fully restored. Spanish military power had been revived and the empire had expanded with the acquisition of Florida and Louisiana, while at home Minorca (though not Gibraltar) had been recaptured. On the domestic front, the grandees had been tamed as a political force, the Spanish Church lay more firmly under government control than ever before, and the peninsular and colonial economies were displaying impressive signs of growth. Steps had also been taken to promote a sense of Spanish patriotic feeling, with the creation of a national anthem (1770) and flag (1785). On the negative side, the state was once more running into debt. Thanks to Ensenada's prudent housekeeping, Charles III had inherited a substantial financial surplus, but the spiralling military budget and the wars of 1762–3 and 1779–83 soon wiped out this 'peace dividend'. From 1779, by which time all attempts to revive Ensenada's *catastro* had been abandoned in the face of fierce protests, the government attempted to bridge the growing gap between income (about 450 million reales) and expenditure (over 700 million) by issuing royal bonds known as *vales reales*. However, this financial expedient left a legacy of debt which would come to haunt the new regime in years to come.

CHARLES IV AND THE CRISIS OF THE *ANCIEN RÉGIME*

When Charles IV (1788–1808) succeeded to the throne, the new king gave every impression that he would continue the policies that his father had championed. However, the outbreak of the French Revolution in 1789 was to shatter these assumptions. Fearful that Spain and the Bourbon monarchy might succumb to the same revolutionary ideas that had infected France, the king's chief minister, Floridablanca, imposed a rigorous *cordon sanitaire* designed to halt the entry of French revolutionary literature into the country: customs controls were tightened; the Spanish press was subjected to heavy censorship; and the Inquisition, enjoying an Indian summer, drew up lists of prohibited materials and led a drive against the chief proponents of now suspect enlightened ideas, both within government and higher education. Victims of the purge included Campomanes, who was dismissed from the presidency of the Council of Castile in 1791. Ironically, however, Floridablanca's intransigent policy towards France was seen by Charles IV to be detrimental to his cousin Louis XVI's efforts to reach a constitutional settlement with the new French regime, and in February 1792 the chief minister was dismissed. Floridablanca's successor, his long-time political adversary the count of Aranda, sought to sustain Louis XVI's position by pursuing a more moderate policy towards the revolutionary regime in France, but with little success. When the French king was ousted from the throne in August 1792 and a Republic declared, Aranda's political reputation collapsed around him and he too was dismissed the following November.

The appointment of the charismatic Manuel Godoy to the post of secretary of state in 1792 marked the first attempt by Charles IV to place his own stamp on government. The 25-year-old Godoy, who hailed from an Extremaduran noble family, enjoyed no firm political following or social base, nor had he risen from within the *golilla* ranks of the state bureaucracy. Needless to say, many of Godoy's contemporaries harboured deep misgivings about his suitability for the post. Quite apart from his complete lack of any political or administrative experience, there was a question mark over his morals: Godoy was a renowned womanizer and it was even rumoured that the king's wife, Queen María Luisa, had taken him as her lover. Almost immediately, Godoy was plunged into a major political crisis. In January 1793, Louis XVI was executed. For a regime to which the principle of absolutist monarchy was all, the elimination of the French royal house was an outrage that could not be tolerated and Spain speedily sought a military alliance with Britain against its former ally. In March, France declared war.

But Spain and Britain, after decades of war and political tensions, proved uncomfortable bedfellows. The Spanish government mistrusted British intentions and was determined to maintain its fleet – the guarantee of its imperial status – intact at any cost, with the result that the Spanish Navy stayed in port for most of the war, to the considerable exasperation of the British commanders. In 1794–5, the French launched major offensives in Catalonia and the Basque provinces and overran large swathes of territory, including Roussillon, Gerona and San Sebastián. The fall of Vitoria to the French in July 1795 prompted the Madrid government to seek terms. By the Peace of Basle (July 1795) Spain recovered all the territories that had been occupied in the peninsula, but agreed to surrender the colony of Santo Domingo to France. The peace was greeted with enthusiasm and relief in Spain: Godoy was awarded the grandiose title of 'Prince of Peace' (*Príncipe de la Paz*) by Charles IV in recognition of his negotiating efforts. The following year, at San Ildefonso, Spain signed a new treaty with the French Republic and declared war on Britain. Unlike the Family Pacts of old, however, the Treaty of San Ildefonso was not a partnership of equals. Spain was reduced to little more than a French satellite and condemned to a long and ruinous war which was to destroy once and for all any pretensions she still harboured to great power status. British seapower proved overwhelming: in February 1797, the Spanish fleet suffered a major defeat at British hands at Cape Saint Vincent and on the other side of the Atlantic, Trinidad was lost. Meanwhile, a British naval blockade cut Spain off from her colonies. While 171 ships made the voyage from America to Cádiz in 1796, only 9 ships made the same journey in 1797. Spain was plunged into economic recession and state revenues slumped. By 1798, state finances were in the red to the tune of 800 million reales.

Inevitably, these military disasters weakened Godoy's position at home. His rapid rise to power, his venality and his readiness to appoint members of his own family to prominent positions in government had aroused considerable resentment among hard-core traditionalists and enlightened reformists alike. In March 1798, under pressure from France, which was unhappy at what it perceived as his efforts to undermine the Franco-Spanish alliance, Godoy was forced from power. Two years later, however, as political tensions began to mount between conservatives and those progressives, known as liberals, who were disillusioned with the progress of reform, Godoy was returned to office by Charles IV.

War with Britain was finally brought to an end by the Peace of Amiens (March 1802). While Spain was required to hand over Trinidad to Britain, her own gains from the war – the insignificant Portuguese border town of Olivenza, which had been captured during the 'War of the Oranges' in 1801 – were risible. For the next two years,

Spain enjoyed neutrality of a sort, but she remained bound to France, to the point that she was required to purchase her neutrality by paying a substantial monthly subsidy. When hostilities with Britain flared up again in 1804, the British blockade on Spanish shipping resumed and in October 1805 a joint Franco-Spanish naval force was comprehensively defeated by Nelson near Cape Trafalgar in south-west Spain. Military disaster was accompanied by a mounting social and economic crisis at home. Epidemics of yellow fever (1800) and cholera (1804) caused major loss of life in several Andalusian towns, while a series of poor harvests, in particular those of 1803–4, forced up wheat prices and left starvation, malnutrition and disease in their wake. The subsistence crises prompted peasant uprisings in Galicia (1798), Valencia (1801) and Bilbao (1804), and bread riots in Segovia (1802) and Madrid (1808). Catalonia and Valencia, which were already suffering the consequences of a slump in demand for their textiles in the colonies, were further hit by the renewed British naval blockade which brought transatlantic trade to a virtual standstill. With tax revenues unable to keep pace with spending, and with colonial income at an all-time low, state finances were in free-fall. The government sought to bridge the gap by massive state borrowing and by authorizing the expropriation of some Church properties (1798), but no attempt was made to tax the privileged aristocracy.

Political tensions came to a head in 1807–8. Godoy's pre-eminent position came under sustained attack from a new 'Aragonese party' of aristocrats, army officers and conservative clerics. The traditionalists sought and found a willing patron in the heir to the throne, Ferdinand, Prince of Asturias, who bitterly resented the high esteem with which Godoy was held by the king and queen, and even feared that he was to be excluded from the succession. In 1807, Ferdinand wrote secretly to Emperor Napoleon of France requesting 'paternal protection' from him and permission to marry into his family. Likewise, Godoy looked to Napoleon to bolster his precarious position and ensure his future. For his part, Napoleon, whose objective was to bring British commerce to its knees by excluding it from continental ports, laid plans to bring Portugal (a staunch ally of Britain) within his sphere of influence. The Treaty of Fontainebleau (October 1807) provided for the partition of Portugal and its overseas colonies between Spain, France and Godoy himself, who was to be allotted an independent principality in the Algarve. Portugal was soon overrun by French and Spanish forces, whereupon Napoleon decided that the time had come to intervene directly in the dynastic disputes of the Bourbons. In early 1808, Madrid and other major centres were occupied by French garrisons and Charles's court withdrew to Aranjuez. It was in Aranjuez, on the night of 17 March 1808, that a mob of soldiers and peasants, egged on by Prince Ferdinand's supporters and the members of the Council of Castile who were party to the conspiracy, rioted. The 'Tumult of Aranjuez' was an aristocratic and clerical *coup* masquerading as a popular revolt. It spelled the end for Godoy, who was imprisoned, and also for Charles IV, who abdicated two days afterwards in favour of his son Ferdinand. The accession of Ferdinand VII (1808–33), was greeted with jubilation throughout Spain, seeming to offer as it did the prospect of national renewal. However, celebrations were short-lived. Napoleon, by now tiring of the faction-fighting at the Spanish court, had resolved to convert Spain into a satellite state and summoned Charles and Ferdinand to meet him at Bayonne. In May 1808, both father and son were obliged to abdicate in favour of the emperor, who in turn offered the throne to his brother, Joseph Bonaparte, who was proclaimed Joseph I of Spain.

SOCIETY AND ECONOMY IN BOURBON SPAIN

The eighteenth century in Spain witnessed a period of significant demographic and economic growth. Thanks in large part to the fact that Spain remained free from major epidemics of bubonic plague, her population increased by about 40 per cent, from around 7.6 million inhabitants in 1717 to 10.5 million in 1797, and more than doubled in more prosperous coastal regions such as Valencia and Catalonia, which enjoyed the most pronounced economic expansion. Even so, infant mortality throughout Spain remained high, at 25 per cent, and epidemic diseases (yellow fever, cholera, smallpox, typhus) and periodic food shortages combined at regular intervals (for example, in 1763–5, 1786–7 and 1803–5) to increase the death rate: at the end of the century life expectancy remained at about 27 years.

On the face of things, Spanish society remained as rigidly hierarchical as it had ever been under Habsburg rule. At the apex, stood the two socially privileged groups, the nobility and the clergy, who between them owned more than two-thirds of all the productive land. In 1750, there were still some 800,000 individuals of noble rank, ranging from a select group of grandees and other titled aristocrats to a large mass of often impoverished *hidalgos*. Yet, the noble estate was losing its allure: increasingly wealth, not rank, was becoming the mark of social distinction, and as the century progressed many poor *hidalgos* lost their noble status altogether. In 1783, a royal decree gave permission for *hidalgos* to undertake manual labour. By 1797, the number of nobles had fallen to 402,059, that is, 3.8 per cent of the population as a whole. For all its landed wealth, the higher nobility lacked the political clout of old. With their military function now a thing of the past, the grandees were marginalized from politics by the Bourbon rulers, who preferred to recruit lesser nobles and lawyers into their service. The landowning nobles lived largely from the profits of their estates, upon which they continued to exercise seigneurial authority, and lavished much of their income on conspicuous consumption of one sort or another, and on the maintenance of a substantial domestic service. The duke of Arcos (d. 1780) is said to have employed some 3000 servants in his household. As the eighteenth century progressed, the great landowning aristocracy became the target of sustained criticism by reformers, who viewed the institution of the *mayorazgo*, or entail, which kept large estates undivided, and the still pervasive seigneurial regime as obstacles to wider ownership and much needed investment. It was not that the reformers, themselves mostly of noble stock, sought to undermine the nobility as a social group, but rather that they believed that the nobles should act for the benefit of society as a whole.

For all the restrictions placed on ecclesiastical power by an increasingly regalist government, the Spanish Church remained a wealthy and influential institution. According to the census of 1797, there were still 172,231 religious in Spain, that is, 1.6 per cent of the total population; Church property accounted for one quarter of the total income from Spanish agriculture. While contemporary reformers were critical of the Church's landowning role, which was seen to restrict access to land and investment in profitable agriculture, they also drew a clear distinction between 'useful' clergymen, who at a local level were often leading lights in the emerging Economic Societies, and the Regular Orders, Jesuits and cathedral canons who were regarded as a dead weight on society as a whole. In keeping with the times, many leading churchmen were at the forefront of a number of reforming initiatives, financing public works, providing subsidies for local industries, endowing university chairs and encouraging improvements in agriculture. The Church also supported large numbers of charitable institutions, such as hospitals, schools and poor-houses. Another current of criticism was represented by the Jansenists, a group of clergymen who took their name from a similar French group, who denounced what they saw as superstition and moral laxity and the frivolity of popular religious beliefs, and were particularly hostile to the Jesuits, the Regular Orders and the papacy.

Economic expansion, however unspectacular, and the relentless growth of the state bureaucracy, encouraged the fledgeling middle class to expand. This emerging bourgeoisie included merchants, farmers, *hidalgos* and parish priests. The development was not felt uniformly across the peninsula, for the merchant bourgeoisie tended to gravitate around major trading centres. The census of 1797 identified some 25,000 wholesale or retail merchants, most of them based in Barcelona and Cádiz. Industrial entrepreneurs, who were willing to invest in manufacturing industry, were chiefly to be found in Catalonia, where agricultural expansion and rising incomes stimulated demand. This expanding group lacked any sense of what might be termed 'class consciousness' and there is no evidence its members pursued any clear political agenda designed to favour their own interests.

Bourbon Spain remained an overwhelmingly rural society, with over 75 per cent of the population earning a living from agriculture at the end of the eighteenth century. Of the 1,824,353 *campesinos* (peasants) who are recorded in the census of 1797, nearly half (805,235) were categorized as *jornaleros* (day-labourers), 27 per cent (507,423) were tenant farmers and only 19 per cent (364,514) owned their farms outright. For many farmers, having to contend with poor soils, low rainfall, inadequate irrigation and high rents imposed by absentee landlords, agriculture was largely a matter of subsistence: there was little or no question of producing a sufficient surplus for sale locally, let alone for export. In Andalusia, where 563 landowners were in receipt of almost 15 per cent of the total agricultural production of the region, the landscape was dominated by a number of vast aristocratic latifundia, worked by an army of day-labourers who were well acquainted with the misery of rural life and were vulnerable to the pressures engendered by poverty, malnutrition and disease. At the beginning of the century, a day-labourer would typically be paid 5 or 6 reales, when a loaf of bread cost 5 and a half reales. It was a very different story in the prosperous irrigated coastal plain of Alicante and Valencia, whose market gardens, given over to the production of rice, wheat, citrus fruits, vines, nuts and olives, were a source of admiration and envy to visitors from abroad, and in Catalonia, where agricultural extension, improved irrigation systems and more intensive cultivation encouraged crop specialization, notably vines, and export-led commercial production.

Contemporaries were well aware of the deficiencies of Spain's agricultural economy. In 1765, the then fiscal of the Council of Castile, Campomanes, argued for the need to reform the conditions of land distribution in favour of peasant farmers, principally at the expense of the Church, in an attempt to overcome shortfalls in production; but his plans foundered on the rock of vested interests. In similar vein, in 1795, Gaspar Melchor de Jovellanos published his celebrated treatise on agrarian reform, in which he denounced aristocratic entail, clerical mortmain and the *Mesta* as obstacles to the greater prosperity of the individual and the state, and called for common lands to be auctioned off to the highest bidder. During the second half of the eighteenth century, various government initiatives attempted to widen access to the land and improve yields. In 1765, a free trade in grain was introduced, which it was hoped would encourage farmers to increase production, only to be abandoned in 1804 as prices soared and recurring subsistence crises caused widespread famine. Between 1766 and 1768, municipal authorities were instructed to redistribute common lands to peasant tenants, although in the event much of the property ended up in the hands of the wealthy. Successive governments ploughed large sums of money into improving irrigation systems and constructing canals, reservoirs and dams: the construction of the Canal Imperial de Aragón in the Ebro valley in the 1780s helped to bring over 30,000 hectares of land under the plough. Another means to increase land use was by the establishment of colonies in barren lands. In 1767, Campomanes instructed the intendant of Seville, Pablo de Olavide, to establish colonies along the road to Seville in the remote lands in the Sierra Morena and west of Córdoba. Over 10,000 settlers from as far afield as Germany and the Low Countries, as well as from Spain itself, were attracted to the colonies with the promise of grants of land in leasehold, rent free for the first ten years, livestock and tools. The results were encouraging: crop yields were impressive and the main centres of settlement – La Carolina, La Carlota and La Luisiana – soon became thriving communities. But the success of the Sierra Morena experiment was not replicated elsewhere. For all their statements of good intent, the reformers lacked the political will to drive through a far-reaching programme of agrarian reform which might not only have improved the lot of the individual peasant farmer, but the prosperity of the Spanish state as a whole.

If Spain's agrarian structure was largely an obstacle to economic development, her towns were equally unenterprising. Most were primarily administrative centres, the home of bureaucrats, lawyers, clergymen and absentee landlords. Described by John Lynch as 'places of inertia and routine', few experienced any notable economic or demographic growth in this period. The main exceptions to the rule were landlocked Madrid, whose population mushroomed from 11,268 in 1743 to 184,404 in 1799, by virtue of being the seat of Bourbon government, and the resurgent cities of the periphery, notably Barcelona, which underwent a marked increase in population and wealth on the back of the booming transatlantic trade and expanding manufacturing industry. In Madrid, a series of projects of urban regeneration gave the down-at-heel city a much needed face-lift. Many of the most famous urban landmarks of the city belong to the reign of Charles III: the erection of the Casa de Correos in the Puerta del Sol (1768) and the triumphal Alcalá gate (1778); and the foundation of the Botanical Garden (1781) and the Prado Museum (1785). There were also improvements in paving, lighting and sewage disposal. Citizens were instructed not to allow their pigs to roam the streets. For all the cosmetic improvements, urban poverty remained rife and the problem was exacerbated by the arrival of large numbers of beggars and vagrants from depressed rural areas. In 1785, the government tried to get to grips with the problem of vagrancy by introducing compulsory military service for unemployed young men between the ages of 17 and 26; others were sent to *hospicios*, or workhouses, which were established in some 25 towns by 1798.

Industrial activity remained chiefly based around scattered artisan workshops whose output was directed towards local or regional markets. These were largely small-scale operations in terms of technology, capital investment and labour costs, and were often subject to guild regulations. In many rural areas domestic industry, be it cloth manufacture, leather working or metal-working, represented little more than a means for impoverished farm labourers to supplement their meagre incomes. When the English traveller William Townsend journeyed through central Spain in 1786–7, he found the once-prosperous Castilian wool centres 'skeletons of towns once populous and crammed with factories, workshops and stalls, now full of churches, convents and hospitals ... destitute of commerce, supported by the church'. As the century progressed, however, demographic growth and increased overseas demand acted as a stimulus to production. For all its technological shortcomings, iron production in the Basque Country increased by 150 per cent during the first two-thirds of the century and by 1790 was exporting 4000 tons of metal goods to the American colonies. In Valencia, the local silk industry, although remaining largely artisan-based, enjoyed a notable expansion in capacity, so that by the end of the century there were over 4000 looms. However, modern factory-based industrial production remained the exception rather than the rule. Those factories that existed were mostly state-run enterprises, like the glassworks at San Ildefonso, the porcelain factory at Buen Retiro, the Royal Tobacco Factory in Seville and the vast woollen factory at Guadalajara, which towards the end of the century was employing 24,000 workers. State-financed factories were intended to act as a model for the private sector to imitate. However, not only did all of these factories fail to actually make a profit, but the advantages they enjoyed in terms of capital investment and fiscal exemption acted as a deterrent to the very entrepreneurial enterprise sought after by the reformists in government.

Catalonia was the one beacon of hope for those who believed that Spanish industry might one day compete on equal terms with her commercial rivals in France and Britain. In stark contrast to most of the rest of the country, the Catalan economy managed to break free from the corporative restraints that smothered private enterprise elsewhere, capital investment was plentifully available and profits were reinvested. The principal catalyst for industrial growth was the highly productive and commercialized agricultural sector, much of whose produce (notably brandy and wine) was exported overseas and whose profits were often invested in manufacturing outlets of varying kinds. The cotton industry, which at its height employed more than 100,000 workers, competed particularly successfully for international markets by concentrating its work-force and by adopting English technological advances, such as the Spinning Jenny, which in turn increased productive capacity. However, even the burgeoning Catalan economy was not immune to the chill winds of recession when the war of 1796–1802 destroyed most of its colonial markets.

The Bourbon governments, faithful to the mercantilist principles imported from France, sought to stimulate the national economy in various other ways. Internal customs duties between regions were removed, in an effort to create a genuinely national market; trade between leading commercial centres such as Barcelona and Cádiz was encouraged; and import prohibitions, such as that of 1757, which banned the entry of Genoese paper and silk products, were imposed in an attempt to protect local industry. Not all reforms were government led. In 1764, with royal assent, a group of Basque noblemen set up a society of *Amigos del país*, or 'Friends of the Nation', whose purpose was to encourage innovation in agriculture, commerce, industry and the arts and sciences. In the succeeding years, over 50 similar economic societies were set up in Spain and the colonies. But the longed-for economic boom failed to materialize. Spain's failure to 'take off' industrially at a time when her rivals France and England were undergoing major industrial expansion has been attributed to a number of factors. Poor communications and transport systems, which left the local economies of the interior isolated from each other and the coastal ports, undoubtedly played a part. Floridablanca drew up ambitious plans to build a new network of roads, but a lack of sufficient funds meant that only 1100 kilometres were built. Spain's failure to keep up technologically with her commercial rivals was equally significant. The bottom line, however, was the failure of Spanish agriculture as a whole to deliver the profits that would have released capital, improved living standards and increased demand. With the vast mass of the rural population living on or near the breadline, buoyant consumer demand simply did not exist. What capital was generated tended to be reinvested in other parts of the economy, in particular into property investment, or was channelled overseas. At the same time, demographic and economic growth in the peripheral coastal regions served to exacerbate the economic decline of the centre: wages in Barcelona rose at four times the rate of those in Madrid during the final quarter of the century. The ambitious projects of reform championed by Campomanes and Floridablanca promised far more than they ever delivered: large-scale economic structural change remained an aspiration rather than a reality.

SPAIN AND THE ENLIGHTENMENT

During the eighteenth century, the ideas of the Enlightenment began to circulate widely in educated circles across Europe. In broad terms, Enlightenment thinkers emphasized the importance of rational thought, unfettered by tradition, privilege or superstition, as the key to advancing the material well-being of society through legal, social and educational reform. These novel ideas percolated only slowly into Spain. Writing in 1765, the Swedish envoy Count Creutz proclaimed: 'most of Europe wallows still in shameful ignorance. The Pyrenees in particular are the barriers to the enlightened world. Since I have been here it has seemed to me that the people are ten centuries behind.' Yet, Spain was experiencing signs of increased intellectual activity, reflected in the royal foundation of academic institutions such as the National Library (1712), the Spanish Academy (1713) and the Academy of History (1735), and most notably in the writings of the essayist Benito Jerónimo Feijóo (1676–1764), whose numerous treatises, principally the encyclopaedic *Theatro crítico universal* (published in nine volumes in 1726–40), attacked Spain's backwardness and superstition, and called upon Spaniards to embrace knowledge and innovation through reasoned investigation. During the reigns of Ferdinand VI and Charles III, the ideas of the Enlightenment began to circulate more widely. Despite their prohibition by the Inquisition, the works of French *philosophes* such as Voltaire, Montesquieu or Rousseau became known to a small minority of nobles, clergy, professionals and merchants. Newspapers, such as *El Pensador* (1761–7), *El Censor* (1781–7) and *El Correo de Madrid* (established 1786), as well as the Economic Societies, helped to disseminate reformist ideas. By and large, however, it was the utilitarian rather than the political or philosophical aspects of the new tendency of thought that had greatest impact. Pragmatists to a man, 'enlightened reformers' like Ensenada, Campomanes, Jovellanos and Floridablanca did not challenge the model of absolutist monarchy, nor question the existing order of society, but sought to strengthen the state and increase the prosperity of the nation as a whole through economic progress. It was not until the 1790s, in the wake of the French Revolution, that some liberal intellectuals began to argue that the time had come for Spain to grasp the nettle of political and constitutional reform.

SPAIN AND ITS AMERICAN EMPIRE

During the first half-century of Bourbon rule, Spain's American colonies remained largely peripheral to government concerns. The War of the Spanish Succession, Philip V's Italian campaigns, and the drive to overhaul Spain's administrative and fiscal structures all ensured that Spanish political priorities between 1700 and 1746 remained overwhelmingly Eurocentric. The result of this neglect was that the frontiers of the empire came under increasing pressure from Spain's colonial rivals, transatlantic commerce remained almost wholly in foreign hands and was prey to piracy, and Spain's putative commercial monopoly with its New World colonies was steadily undermined by contraband trade. Within the colonies themselves, the power of the central administration was more theoretical than real: local government was largely the preserve of an influential creole élite of landowners, lawyers and merchants, many of whom had bought their way into office; the Church, and in particular the Jesuit Order, also wielded immense influence over colonial society.

During the reign of Charles III, the immediate priority was to ensure that the colonies were provided with sufficient military strength to protect themselves from external attack or put down internal revolts. In 1763, General Alejandro O'Reilly was sent to Cuba to organize the defence of the island; the following year two regiments were posted to New Spain; and in 1768 a regiment was garrisoned in Caracas. By 1771, land forces across the Indies numbered some 43,000 men, in addition to which local militia units were created which could supplement regular forces in time of crisis. As a consequence, the Spanish Crown was able to act with far more decision and self-confidence than had hitherto been the case. The Portuguese colony of Sacramento, at the mouth of the River Plate, which posed a threat to Spanish interests in the region, was recovered in 1776; British settlements on the Mosquito Shore in Honduras were destroyed; the successful Pensacola expedition of 1781 led to the recovery of that area and nearby Florida; and expeditions were dispatched to reinforce Spanish claims to territories in California, Sonora and Texas. As a result of the acquisition of Louisiana from the French by the Treaty of Paris (1763), Spain established control over roughly half of the territory that now forms the United States.

Militarization was accompanied by an extensive programme of administrative reform designed to bolster the authority of the Crown. The Habsburg institution of the visitation was revived so that conditions in the colonies might be more thoroughly investigated, reforms implemented and corruption uprooted. The pervasive influence of the creole élite on local government was broken by the appointment of intendants, most of them Spanish-born, to oversee local administration, and by

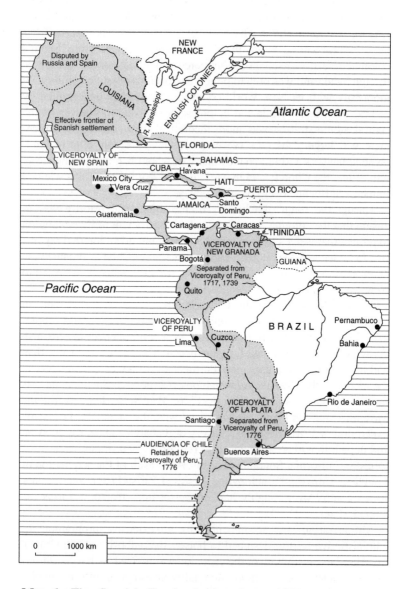

Map 6 The Spanish Empire in America, *c.*1780. Adapted from Benjamin Keen, *A History of Latin America* (Houghton Mifflin, 4th edn, 1992), p. 130.

limiting the appointment of creoles to the *audiencias* (the higher courts of justice). Steps were also taken to exploit the resources of the colonies more efficiently: a salaried fiscal bureaucracy was established to oversee the collection of excise duties; a state monopoly was established on tobacco in New Spain; and attempts were made to increase silver production. The creation of the viceroyalty of New Granada (approximating to the modern states of Ecuador, Panama, Colombia and Venezuela) in 1717 was followed by that of La Plata (approximating to Argentina, Paraguay and Uruguay) in 1776. The latter enabled the Atlantic seaboard in general, and Buenos Aires in particular, to enjoy a spectacular period of economic growth at the expense of the former nerve centre of colonial activity in South America, Lima. The authority of the monarchy over the colonial Church was enhanced with the expulsion of the Jesuits in 1767. Last but not least, the recruitment of officials who had served in America to the Council and Ministry of the Indies ensured that, for the very first time, the government in Madrid could rely upon men who had real experience and understanding of American affairs. Most notable of all in this respect was José de Gálvez, who as visitor general to New Spain (1765–71), Peru (1776) and New Granada (1778), and later Secretary of the Indies (1776–87), proved the driving force in the process of reform.

The centrepiece of colonial reform was the long-overdue restructuring of transatlantic trade. Although, theoretically, commerce between Spain and her colonies was a Crown monopoly, with all goods to and from America having to pass through the port of Cádiz, in practice Spanish control of this commercial activity had long been tenuous. For one thing, the vast majority of goods shipped to America from Cádiz were not manufactured in Spain at all: in 1689, it was estimated that of the 27,000 tons of goods legally shipped to the colonies only 1500 were manufactured in the peninsula. For another, widespread contraband traffic, organized by the British, French and Portuguese, avoided custom duties altogether. During the War of the Spanish Succession, French ships had been allowed to trade freely with Chile and Peru; and the Treaty of Utrecht had allowed the British direct access to the American markets. The recovery of this trade for the Spanish state was seen by José de Campillo, author of an influential mercantilist treatise of 1743, as the key to Spanish economic regeneration. If foreign manufactures could be kept at bay, contraband trade curbed and the commercial monopoly enjoyed by Cádiz removed, the American colonies represented a vast potential market for Spanish industry and a valuable source of revenue for the Crown. During the second half of the century, a series of reforms sought to make Campillo's theory a reality. Spain's expanding naval power ensured that the Atlantic was kept open. In 1750, Spain recovered her exclusive commercial monopoly over the American empire when the British South Seas Company sold its trading rights for the sum of £100,000. Then, between 1765, when the Caribbean colonies were permitted to trade directly with nine Spanish ports, and 1778, when the enactment of *comercio libre* allowed free trade between Spanish ports and the colonies, the Cádiz monopoly was broken for good.

The results of this liberalization of commerce were spectacular. Between 1778 and 1796, when a British-imposed blockade brought transatlantic trade to a virtual halt, Spanish exports to America tripled and government revenues from customs duty soared. Towards the end of the century, income from America accounted for some 15 per cent of total state revenues. Catalonia was the leading commercial player, exporting the products of its burgeoning agricultural and industrial sectors. While the colonial economy was still chiefly based upon agriculture, ranching and mining, the importance of commodities such as tobacco, cocoa and sugar increased markedly. Commercial companies were established, such as the Compañía Guipuzcoana de Caracas (1728), which held a monopoly on the production of cocoa until the edict of free trade in 1778. However, Spain's ambition to become a great mercantile nation depended on her exercising political control over the empire, policing the seas and being able to manufacture sufficient goods to meet demand in America. The war of 1796–1802, which brought commercial traffic to halt, followed by the disaster of Trafalgar, the French invasion of 1808 and the movement for independence in the Americas, were to destroy those hopes for good.

THE WAR OF INDEPENDENCE

The French occupation of much of the peninsula and the forced abdication of Charles IV and Ferdinand VII in May 1808 in favour of Joseph Bonaparte was greeted with unbridled fury in Spain. While the ruling classes prevaricated, a popular revolt broke out in Madrid on 2 May 1808, only to be crushed by French forces the following day, events later to be immortalized by Francisco de Goya in two of his most famous paintings. As news spread of Ferdinand's abdication and the Madrid uprising, similar revolts erupted in other towns, as loose coalitions of notables, backed by urban mobs, deposed those military governors who were Godoy's placemen, took control of government in the name of Ferdinand VII and established *juntas* (committees) through which to supervise local resistance. In September 1808, a Supreme Central Junta, under the leadership of Floridablanca, was established at Aranjuez with the aim of co-ordinating the war effort; in practices its attempts to centralize power were vigorously resisted and the various provincial *juntas* remained largely autonomous throughout the war. These provincial uprisings heralded the beginning of a savage six-year struggle, known to Spaniards as the War of Independence, to the British as the Peninsular War, and to the French merely as 'the Spanish ulcer'.

The 'patriot rebellion' was a far from homogenous movement. Those who took up arms against the French occupation included liberal radicals, committed to far-reaching political and social reform, servants of enlightened absolutism, like Floridablanca and Jovellanos, and those staunch supporters of the traditional privileges of the old regime, for whom the very idea of reform was anathema. Among the latter group was José de Palafox, who established what amounted to personal dictatorship in Zaragoza in the wake of the uprising of 1808. There was also the great mass of the population, whose enthusiastic support for the uprising was guided not only by a sense of loyalty to God, king and country, but in some cases by pent-up social discontent and hatred of the traditional seigneurial regime.

At the outset of hostilities, for all its limitations as a military force, the Spanish army acquitted itself creditably. In July 1808 a French army under Dupont was routed by the Andalusian militias at Bailén near Jaén, forcing the recently installed Joseph I to abandon Madrid and the French forces to retreat north to the Ebro. In the same month, the British government called a halt to hostilities with Spain and dispatched an army under the command of Arthur Wellesey (later Duke of Wellington) to Portugal in an attempt to prop up the Spanish rising. However, when Napoleon himself entered the peninsula in November 1808 at the head of a large army, the balance of the war quickly swung in France's favour. Madrid was reoccupied in December, the Central Junta was forced to retreat to Seville, and a British expeditionary force under General Sir John Moore was forced to beat a hasty retreat to La Coruña. In January 1810, French troops overran most of Andalusia, forcing the Central Junta to flee to the near-impregnable city of Cádiz.

With the regular Spanish Army effectively out of commission, having
suffered a series of catastrophic defeats (Uclés, Medellín, Belchite,
Ocaña, etc.), resistance was entrusted to irregular locally-based forces,
dubbed the *guerrilla*, who pinned down French occupying forces and
threatened their supply lines. Guerrilla warfare was accompanied by a
virulent anti-French propaganda campaign, which sought to inflame
patriotic feelings among the Spanish populace.

One of the last acts of the discredited Central Junta before its
members resigned in favour of a Regency Council, was to summon a
meeting of the *cortes*, as the embodiment of the sovereignty of the
people, to which deputies from all regions, including the overseas
colonies, were invited to attend. The *cortes* met in Cádiz, a stronghold
of liberalism, for the first time in September 1810. On 19 March 1812,
a constitution was promulgated, which has been described by one
writer as 'a frontal attack on the social, economic and political organization of the Ancien Regime'. Ferdinand VII was recognized as head
of state, but sovereignty was declared to reside in the people and their
elected representatives. As Article 2 of the Constitution succinctly put
it: 'The Spanish nation is free and independent and it is not nor can it
ever be the property of any family or person.' The new *cortes* would
consist of a democratically elected single chamber and numerous
constraints would be placed on the king's power. He could not, for
example, prevent the *cortes* from sitting nor dissolve it, levy taxes,
arrange treaties nor pass laws in his own name, nor absent himself
from the realm without the consent of the *cortes*. The constitution also
gave primacy to the rights and obligations of the individual citizen. No
restrictions were to be placed on personal liberty and private property;
all citizens were to be equal before the law; seigneurial rights were to
be swept away; a new system of income tax was to be introduced;
restrictions on freedom of expression were to be lifted; regional differences and privileges were to be abolished in favour of a unitary
centralized state; there was to be free primary education for all. The
material wealth of the Church came under renewed attack, but the
authority of the Church went unchallenged. Catholicism was to remain
the state religion and heresy was still to be punishable by law, although
the Inquisition, which had long been viewed in progressive circles as
an obstacle to reform, was soon to be abolished.

Not all Spaniards resisted the French invasion. In those areas where
French forces were firmly in control, some among the local élites
chose to co-operate with the new regime. Some of these *afrancesados*,

or 'frenchified ones', as they were contemptuously dubbed by the patriots, regarded the arrival of Joseph I as an opportunity to accelerate the programme of 'enlightened reform', which had begun to run out of steam during the preceding two decades. Others thought Napoleon to be invincible and pragmatically concluded that collaboration was essential if Spain's independence was to be preserved. Yet others, the majority, were driven to collaborate by simple opportunism or a desire for security. For his part, Joseph I attempted to demonstrate his own commitment to reform by issuing a series of 'enlightened decrees': the *Mesta* and the military orders were abolished; convents and monasteries were suppressed; the *Bolsa* (Stock Exchange) was established; and there were a series of educational reforms. However, the new king's power was effectively reduced to Madrid and its hinterland: he wielded no authority over the French generals in Spain, and the revenue he could raise was limited in the extreme.

After 1812, the balance of the war shifted once again. Napoleon's decision to invade Russia led to the withdrawal of a considerable number of troops from the peninsula and allowed British and Portuguese forces under Wellington, who hitherto had been cooped up in Portugal, to move on to the offensive. Victory over the French at Salamanca in July 1812 paved the way for the liberation of Madrid; that at Vitora in June 1813 prompted the evacuation of all French forces from Spanish soil, with the exception of Catalonia. In December 1813, Napoleon, under pressure on all fronts, signed the Treaty of Valençay with Ferdinand VII, which brought hostilities between France and Spain to a close and allowed for the restoration of the latter. By this time, an absolutist backlash against the radical Constitution of Cádiz had begun to gather pace. With poverty and hunger causing unprecedented levels of social unrest in the countryside, traditionalists claimed that the liberal reform programme was leading Spain to the brink of revolution. For his part, Ferdinand VII had no intention of turning himself into a constitutional monarch. In May 1814, backed by the army, the Church and the mob, he refused to recognize the authority of the *cortes* that had convened in Cádiz and declared the constitution it had promulgated in his absence to be null and void. Liberal leaders were executed or imprisoned and their property confiscated, in addition to which some 12,000 *afrancesado* families were forced into exile. Spain's first experiment with liberalism was at an end.

THE INDEPENDENCE OF SPANISH AMERICA

From a purely peninsular perspective, the policies that were implemented by Charles III in the Spanish American colonies proved a resounding success. Not only was colonial government brought more firmly under the control of the Spanish Crown than at any time since the conquest, but efficiencies in tax collection and increased customs receipts from booming colonial trade caused government revenues to rise spectacularly. However, the systematic exclusion from power of the creole élites, coupled with a growing demand among the colonies for free trade with the rest of the world, led to widespread resentment within the upper echelons of colonial society. At this stage, however, there was no groundswell of movement for independence. The crisis of the reign of Charles IV and the subsequent collapse of the Spanish monarchy were to prove the watershed. The wars with Britain in 1796–1802 and 1804–8 paralysed transatlantic commerce and forced the government to sanction neutral trade. Meanwhile, the Spanish Crown seemed unable to protect its overseas interests. When British troops occupied Buenos Aires in 1806 and 1807, the invasion was repelled not by Spanish regulars, but by a local militia raised by the municipal authorities.

The collapse of the monarchy in 1808–9 sent shock-waves throughout the colonies. In response, creoles and *peninsulares* (Spanish immigrants) followed the example of the Spanish patriots by refusing to recognize Joseph I and by establishing local *juntas* which would take over the reins of government until Ferdinand VII was restored. Public opinion was initially split between those who supported the old absolutist system and those who hoped that the Spanish government would introduce some form of political equality between the peninsula and the New World colonies. When, in 1810, news arrived of the fall of Andalusia, the defeat of Spain seemed inevitable and a plethora of revolts erupted. The restoration of Ferdinand VII in 1814, his swift abrogation of the 1812 Constitution and his refusal to countenance any measure of political reform in the colonies set the moderate loyalists in the New World on a collision course with the Spanish Crown. In 1815, Ferdinand dispatched a 10,000-strong army to America in an attempt to reimpose order. The royalist army soon fulfilled its objectives in New Granada, defeating the rebels and forcing them to retreat, but lacked sufficient men and resources to prevail throughout the continent. By 1819, the royalist 'reconquest' of the American colonies had run out of steam. In Venezuela, Simón Bolívar, supported by the *llaneros* (cowboys) of the country's plains, as well as by British money and troops, launched an offensive in the course of which he defeated the main royalist army at Boyacá (August 1819). By 1821, Bolívar had brought the entire area of New Granada under his control.

To the south, meanwhile, the United Provinces of La Plata (later to form the states of Argentina, Uruguay and Bolivia) declared their independence from Spanish rule in 1816. The following year, José de San Martín won a stunning victory over royalist forces at Chacabuco, which paved the way for the capture of Santiago and the liberation of Chile. Mexico and Peru remained the main bastions of conservative royalist support, but withdrew their allegiance to the Crown when a liberal revolt in Spain in 1820 forced Ferdinand VII to endorse the Constitution of Cádiz (see below). In 1821, Mexico along with the provinces of Central America, declared their independence from Spain. Three years later, the defeat of a royalist army at Ayacucho led to the independence of Peru and Bolivia. By that stage, only Cuba, Puerto Rico and the Philippines and a handful of small Pacific islands remained under Spanish rule.

REVOLUTION AND REACTION

The War of Independence left Spain in the grip of a profound political, social and economic crisis. The rebellion of the American colonies had cut off the supply of silver which had helped sustain state finances for the best part of 300 years, reducing the Crown to bankruptcy. Agriculture, trade and industry were in a parlous state. The ideological divisions that separated the servants of enlightened absolutism, the reformist liberals and those who sought the full restoration of the privileges and power of the aristocracy and the Church were more pronounced than ever. There were a number of unsuccessful conspiracies hatched by disgruntled members of the military who had been denied promotion, or had been forced to retire from service. Some of these malcontents began to make common cause with the liberal camp. In January 1820, some troops who had assembled in Cádiz prior to embarking on an expedition to subdue Buenos Aires, rose in revolt under the leadership of Lieutenant-Colonel Rafael de Riego and proclaimed their allegiance to the 1812 Constitution. Riego's attempted *coup* sparked a series of similar uprisings across Spain, although popular support was muted. The following March, in the face of widespread opposition, Ferdinand VII was compelled to back down and accept the 1812 Constitution.

In the wake of the Revolution of 1820, the reins of power were entrusted to a group of moderate liberals, many of them men of property and standing, who saw the 1812 Constitution as essentially unworkable and argued for the need to reach a more consensual constitutional settlement, similar to the French Charter of 1814, which provided for a power-sharing agreement between the king and the property-holding classes. Ferdinand himself, however, remained firmly wedded to the absolutist principle and rejected any such settlement out of hand. Meanwhile, the radical liberals, dubbed *exaltados*, backed by elements in the army and the urban masses, were committed to full-scale democratic reform and saw the preservation of the 'sacred codex' of 1812 as a solemn duty. These disagreements between the rival liberal factions gave rise to instability and tensions within government, while an upsurge in provincial radicalism threatened to reduce Spain to anarchy. Hostility to the liberal regime was articulated most strongly by conservatives, aggrieved by a series of anticlerical measures, such as the closure of monasteries, the abolition of the Inquisition and the suppression of tithes. In rural districts, peasant communities aggrieved by the government tax policy, and feeling the effects of the bad harvest of 1822, responded to a call to arms by the absolutists. Realizing that he lacked the power to overcome the regular army, Ferdinand VII sought military assistance from Louis XVIII of France, arguing that there was a need to stop the disease of liberal radicalism spreading across the Pyrenees. In April 1823, a French army of 60,000 men crossed the Pyrenees and was joined by a further 35,000 Spanish royalists. This time there was to be no patriotic uprising against the invader and Ferdinand VII was restored to absolute power.

The return of the absolutists in 1823 was followed by a new political crack-down on their liberal opponents. In the aftermath, some 132 liberal leaders were executed, including a number of the heroes of the War of Independence, and 435 imprisoned; thousands of army officers and civil servants who had served the liberal government were sacked and replaced by royalist sympathisers. Exiled liberals tried to foment military rebellions, but divisions within their ranks hindered effective organization and co-operation. Yet, at the same time, tensions within the royalist camp were also becoming more evident. While moderate royalists argued for the need for reconciliation and political stability, hard-line royalists, known as *apostólicos*, sought to preserve the *ancien régime* and regarded liberal ideas as anathema. Many among the *apostólicos* harboured hopes that Ferdinand III's brother, the ultra-royalist Charles, would succeed to the throne on the king's death. In May 1829, however, Ferdinand married Maria Cristina of Naples and the following year passed the Pragmatic Sanction, which restored equal rights of succession by overturning the so-called Salic Law (introduced in 1713), which had given any male heir a stronger claim than a female. Six months later a daughter, Isabella, was born to the king. But Charles was not about to renounce his own claim to the throne. Within weeks of Ferdinand VII's death in September 1833, the supporters of the Pretender, dubbed the Carlists, had raised the flag of rebellion and Spain was plunged into a new civil war.

5

Liberalism and Reaction, 1833–1931

The century that followed the death of Ferdinand VII in 1833 was marked by rapid demographic expansion, significant economic growth and far-reaching social change. In the political and economic spheres, liberalism took firm root, the structures of absolutist rule were in large part dismantled and the administrative and legal framework of a modern, centralized state was established. However, the demise of absolutism was not accompanied by sweeping political reform. Instead, a new oligarchy came into being, comprising the liberal bourgeoisie and the traditional land-owning class, which while committed to 'ordered progress' was determined to resist any attempt to introduce fundamental political or social reforms which might ultimately undermine its privileged position.

DEMOGRAPHIC CHANGE

In common with most regions of Western Europe, Spain's population grew rapidly during the nineteenth century and the early decades of the twentieth. Improvements in medicine, nutrition and sanitation helped the total population to more than double from about 11 million at the beginning of the 1830s to 23.5 million by the end of the 1920s, with a particularly pronounced increase after 1900. Average life expectancy, which had stood at 27 years in the eighteenth century, had reached 51 by 1910, while rates of infant mortality fell from about 25 per cent to 16 per cent during the same period. As had been the trend in the eighteenth century, demographic growth continued to be more pronounced in the economically dynamic regions of the periphery; by contrast, in parts of the interior, notably in Aragon, Navarre and Old Castile, the population actually declined. Further demographic growth was kept in check by recurrent food shortages, such as those which ravaged Andalusia in 1867–8 and 1880–2, and by the effects of epidemic disease: outbreaks of cholera killed over 100,000 people in 1833–5, 200,000 in 1853–6, and a further 237,000 in 1865. Rural deprivation, particularly in Galicia and Andalusia, also encouraged emigration: over one and a half million Spaniards emigrated to Latin America – principally to Argentina and Brazil – between 1880 and 1913.

AGRARIAN SOCIETY: EXPANSION AND STAGNATION

With an ever-larger population to feed, Spanish agriculture initially met rising demand by extending the area of land under cultivation, rather than by introducing new technologies and more intensive farming methods. Between 1837 and 1860, assisted by the disentailment of ecclesiastical and municipal lands, a further 4 million hectares were brought under the plough. Most of this land was given over to the cultivation of wheat, but since a good proportion of it was marginal, the soil quickly became exhausted and yields declined. As a result, between 1860 and 1880 approximately one and a half million hectares of wheat-producing land were set aside. Hindered by drought, poor soils, deficient communications, inadequate investment, rigidly traditional ownership patterns and exploitation systems, Castilian wheat growers found it hard to compete when cheap imports from Russia and North America, transported by steamship, began to flood the market in the 1880s. In 1891, the government responded to vociferous lobbying from the landowners by imposing high tariffs on wheat imports, a move that guaranteed the livelihoods of the cerealists, but removed much of the incentive to modernize. Between 1900 and 1929, however, the area of land given over to the cultivation of cereals began to expand once again and levels of land and labour productivity improved, thanks in large part to the widespread use of chemical fertilizers and the introduction of improved farm equipment.

Despite the primacy of cereal cultivation, Spanish agriculture was beginning to diversify. During the second half of the century, foreign demand for Spanish wine, sherry and brandy soared, helped in large part by the devastation caused to the French wine industry by phylloxera between 1868 and 1878. The area of land given over to the vine expanded nearly four-fold from about 400,000 hectares in 1800 to 1.5 million hectares by the end of the century, with a particular concentration in La Mancha and Rioja. By 1884, wine accounted for 45 per cent of total Spanish exports. However, the industry slumped dramatically during the early 1890s when Spanish vines themselves fell victim to phylloxera. Oranges, most of which were cultivated in the provinces of Valencia and Castellón, became a major export-earner from the final decade of the nineteenth century: between 1890–4 and 1930–4 exports increased nine-fold from 101,493 tons to 936,648. Exports of olive oil, cork and almonds also rose substantially in the second half of the nineteenth century, and there was a dramatic increase in sugar-beet production after the loss of Spain's colonies in Cuba, Puerto Rico and the Philippines in 1898.

Despite these signs of agricultural diversification, Spain's overall agrarian structure changed relatively little. Systems of land holding remained as diverse as they had ever been. At one extreme stood the Galician peasant, eking out a meagre existence from his 'pocket handkerchief' plots of land; at the other were the gangs of wretchedly poor agricultural day-labourers, who spent more than half the year unemployed, kicking their heels in large agro-towns, and the rest of the time working for a pittance for absentee landowners on the latifundia of Andalusia, Extremadura and New Castile. The prosperous, well-irrigated lands of the Levante and Catalonia, whose fruits, vegetables, nuts and wines represented a major export-earner, were a world apart from the dry-farming communities of the *meseta*, where low productivity and low levels of per capita income remained the norm. The dismantling of the traditional seigneurial regime during the 1830s and the subsequent disentailment of clerical and municipal lands, which together accounted for about a quarter of all the arable land in Spain, did little to change the overall land-holding structure: most of the lands were snapped up at public auction by existing landowners and by members of the emerging mercantile and commercial bourgeoisie, for whom land holding became a badge of social prestige. As a result, by 1900, one per cent of the population still owned 42 per cent of the cultivable land in Spain. The disentailment of the land hit the peasantry doubly hard: not only did very few have the wherewithal to purchase the lands that were sold at auction, but the distribution of municipal common lands, where for centuries small farmers had grazed livestock or gathered firewood, led to a marked deterioration of living standards for many and drove numerous peasant families to seek new opportunities in the expanding towns and industrial centres, or even to emigrate abroad. Food short-ages, chronic seasonal unemployment and extreme poverty also fuelled periodic explosions of rural unrest. In 1861, at Loja in Andalusia, some 10,000 peasants drawn from 43 villages across the provinces of Almería, Granada, Jaén and Málaga, rose in rebellion to demand land reform; in 1892, an army of farm labourers briefly seized the town of Jerez. Revolutionary anarchists, promising social justice and the redistribution of landed wealth, would find an enthusiastic groundswell of support among the depressed agricultural communities of southern Spain.

A FAILED INDUSTRIAL REVOLUTION?

Agriculture remained the dominant economic activity in Spain. In 1910, fully two-thirds of the population still lived and worked in the countryside. Slowly yet steadily, however, Spain was beginning to industrialize. After 1850, mushrooming demand for Spanish raw mate-rials, particularly iron, copper, lead, mercury and zinc, among the industrialized powers of Western Europe attracted large-scale foreign investment in Spanish mining interests, a process that was accelerated by the Mining Act of 1868. Belgian investors, for example, founded the Royal Company of the Asturias in 1853 in order to exploit the zinc deposits of that region, while a British firm acquired the Río Tinto copper mines near Huelva in 1873, which 16 years later had some 9000 workers on the payroll. Thanks to the flow of inward investment and technical expertise, mineral production increased dramatically. Between 1864 and 1913, Spanish iron ore production rose from 280,000 metric tons to 9.86 million; copper from 213,000 metric tons to 2.3 million; coal from 387,000 metric tons to 3.7 million. By 1913, roughly one-half of Spanish mining capital and 29 per cent of Spanish mining companies were in the hands of foreign investors.

Foreign investment and technical know-how, as well as the greater availability of local capital, were also decisive in introducing Spain to the railway age. The first railway line, a 29 kilometre stretch of track between Barcelona and Mataró, was inaugurated in 1848. The Railway Act of 1855 paved the way for a major phase of railway building, much of it financed by French investors such as the Rothschilds and Pereires. By 1866, when the speculative bubble burst and brought the rail-build-ing frenzy to a halt, over 5500 kilometres of track had been laid; by

1931 a national network of over 17,000 kilometres of track was in place. Several criticisms have been levelled at the Spanish rail system. In particular, the network reflected the centralizing aims of successive governments, in that a radial system linking Madrid to the provinces, rather than servicing the needs of the emerging centres of Spanish industry, was preferred. The foreign companies who funded and built most of the network were allowed to import all the necessary rolling stock and rails free of duty. As a result, the railways proved much less of a stimulus to economic growth than its promoters had anticipated. For all that, the railway revolution did help to break the isolation of local economies, bring about gradual price convergence and the creation of a national market.

Railway building was accompanied by other improvements to Spain's communications infrastructure. Between 1843 and 1868, the road network more than doubled from 8500 to 18,000 kilometres; by 1908 the figure had reached some 41,500 kilometres; and by 1931 nearly 57,000 kilometres. From 1852, steamships began to ply the route from Cuba to the peninsula; in the same year, electrical telegraphy was introduced.

Industrial development was concentrated in two main areas. In Catalonia, where factory-based textile manufacturing predominated, increased levels of capital investment and the widespread introduction of steam-powered machinery during the 1830s and 1840s helped engender a spectacular increase in cotton production and transformed Barcelona and its hinterland into 'the Manchester of Spain'. Although most Catalan industrial centres remained relatively small-scale operations, typically employing fewer than 20 men, the period also saw the foundation of large factories. The Bonaplata factory, *El Vapor*, founded in 1832, which was among the first to make extensive use of steam technology, employed some 700 workers. The introduction of new technologies unleashed a violent reaction among the urban proletariat, who feared for their jobs. The Bonaplata factory was burned down in 1836 and the introduction of automatic spinning machines prompted a series of strikes in the 1840s. A further surge of growth in the Catalan textile sector came during the 1850s when a woollen industry was established in the towns of Sabadell and Terrasa. The Catalan textiles boom drove many small low-tech workshops in much of the rest of Spain to the wall. Yet, Catalan textiles struggled to compete abroad, with the result that production was geared chiefly towards the domestic and the colonial markets. While Madrid-based liberals preached the virtues of free trade, Catalan textile manufacturers demanded state protection to save them and their work-force from economic disaster. During the second half of the nineteenth century, Catalan industrialists attempted to diversify production. *La Maquinista Terrestre y Marítima*, which produced machinery, small ships and engines, was the most important of a number of metallurgical concerns that were founded in the region at this time.

The other main area of industrial development was in the Basque provinces, chiefly in Vizcaya, whose substantial iron ore reserves were a magnet for foreign (first French and then British) investors. Only one-tenth of Basque iron ore produced went to supply local blast furnaces, but the profits obtained from mining, the importation of British coke at preferential rates (Asturian coal was of poor quality and difficult to extract), and the availability of capital from newly established local banking institutions, such as the Bank of Bilbao (1855), contributed to the development of a modern metallurgical industry during the final quarter of the nineteenth century. In 1885, the installation of the first Bessemer converter paved the way for the beginning of steel production. In 1887, the three leading metallurgical companies in the region joined together to form the conglomerate Altos Hornos de Vizcaya, which came to employ over 6000 workers. At the same time, the port of Bilbao developed into a major shipbuilding centre. By contrast, the iron-making centres of southern Andalusia, whose charcoal-burning furnaces produced 72 per cent of Spanish iron in 1844, entered into rapid decline.

Between 1877 and 1886, thanks in large part to booming exports of textiles, wine and minerals, Spain experienced a surge of economic growth. The expansionary process was brought to a halt by the agricultural depression of the late 1880s, prompting shrill calls for state protection by industrialists and cerealists alike, only to resume once again during the first third of the twentieth century, thanks to a new influx of foreign capital, a surge in demand during World War I (1914–18) and the introduction of the new technologies of the age: electricity, the internal combustion engine and petrochemicals. By the 1920s, heavy industry (shipbuilding and metallurgy) was well established in the Basque Country, at a time when foreign demand for Spanish minerals was diminishing. Light industry, notably cement, paper and chemicals, also grew rapidly. The Hispano-Suiza company, based in Barcelona, began to produce aeroplane engines and luxury cars. By 1930, when the expansionist phase came to an abrupt halt, the proportion of the work-force engaged in agriculture had fallen to 46 per cent, while 27 per cent of workers were employed in the industrial sector.

Yet, for all its achievements, Spain's industrial development between 1830 and 1930 pales into insignificance when set against the remarkable progress made by her international competitors, notably Britain, France, Germany and the United States, during the same period. To give but one example, while total Spanish production of pig-iron in 1900 amounted to some 295,000 metric tons, British blast furnaces produced over 9 million tons. This unfavourable comparison has led many historians to portray Spain's economic performance during this period as 'retarded' or 'stagnant', and even to talk of a 'failed Industrial Revolution'. Spain's putative industrial failure has been attributed to a number of factors: the relatively sluggish performance of her agricultural sector, which failed to deliver the capital needed for industrial investment and whose low levels of per capita income restricted the domestic market for manufactured goods; the loss of her overseas colonies, which deprived manufacturers of a guaranteed market for their products; a shortage of investment capital, public and private, which allowed foreign investors to create 'colonial enclaves' on Spanish soil; an excessive reliance on protectionist policies, which removed any incentive for producers to modernize; an inadequate communications infrastructure, which delayed the creation of a truly national market; and a relative lack of enterprise among Spanish industrialists and entrepreneurs.

This bleak assessment of Spain's economic performance may be challenged on numerous points. Above all, the fact that real per capita income rose by almost 80 per cent between 1830 and 1910, and that domestic output trebled during the same period, gives the lie to the view that Spain's economy was in any way stagnant during this period. Although the poverty of the soil and technical deficiencies meant that agricultural production compared unfavourably with that of Spain's main competitors (yields were roughly half those in France and Germany), output comfortably outstripped population growth throughout the period, industrial output grew by an average of 2 to 2.25 per cent a year between 1830 and 1910, and the total value of Spain's foreign trade grew by some 1300 per cent between 1827 and 1913. Besides, had foreign capital not flowed into Spain during the second half of the nineteenth century, Spanish industrial growth would undoubtedly have been stunted and her railway network would have remained on the drawing-board. The loss of Spain's American colonies, although it had a short-term negative impact on the regions traditionally involved in colonial commerce (notably Catalonia), was less cataclysmic than has commonly been supposed. What is indisputable, however, is that Spanish industrial development occurred later and at a lower intensity than elsewhere in the industrialized West. Instead of a 'failed Industrial Revolution' it may be nearer the mark to speak of a 'growth gap' between Spain and its competitors. In 1930, Spain's industrial output per person was still only 30 per cent that of Britain, 32 per cent that of France and 39 per cent that of Germany. The perennial problem was that sustained economic development was largely limited to the periphery. Lacking the capital and the domestic market to sustain large-scale industrialization, Spain was to remain a semi-developed economy until the 1960s.

For all its limitations, Spain's gradual economic expansion brought far-reaching social changes in its wake. At the apex of society, there emerged from the 1840s a wealthy and influential urban bourgeoisie of bankers, businessmen, industrialists, lawyers and generals, who forged a close alliance with the traditional land-owning aristocracy. The interests of these two groups, who together were to dominate Spanish political life for almost a century, became closely intertwined. Members of the aristocracy acquired positions of influence in large companies, while industrialists and merchants, thanks to the disentailing laws of the 1836 and 1855, became great landowners in their own right and, in some cases, were ennobled. The industrial and banking sectors came to be dominated by a handful of influential local families, such as the Guells, Muntadas, Tous, Girona and Arnús in Catalonia, and the Urquijos and Ybarras, among others, in the Basque Country.

Below the ranks of the new élite, there was an expanding lower middle class of shopkeepers, artisans, lawyers, minor civil servants, journalists and schoolteachers. It was this politically aware group that would help man the barricades when the Progressives and other radicals rose in revolt against Isabella II's government in 1854, and from which radical political organizations, such as the Democrats and Socialists would later draw much of their support. There was also a growing group of conservative middle-class Spaniards, many of them small businessmen and farmers, for whom social conformity and the preservation of traditional values were paramount.

Demographic growth, together with the twin dynamics of industrial development in the periphery and agricultural depression in parts of the interior, led many peasant families to gravitate towards the towns and industrial centres in search of employment as factory workers, miners or building labourers. This was despite the fact that poor wages, long hours (a daily shift of between 12 and 14 hours was typical), inadequate housing and sanitation meant that for most urban and industrial workers living conditions were little better than those in the countryside. By 1856, there were over 54,000 workers in Barcelona alone. In 1800, there were only 34 Spanish cities with a population in excess of 10,000 inhabitants; by 1890, there were 174. Madrid, Barcelona, Valencia and Bilbao were the chief centres of urban growth, but a similar process of expansion can be glimpsed in other provincial cities, such as Seville, Málaga, Murcia, San Sebastián and Zaragoza. Between 1857 and 1900, the population of Madrid, which throughout this period was primarily a centre of consumption rather than production, almost doubled, from 280,000 inhabitants to 540,000; that of Bilbao more than tripled, from 30,000 to 100,000 inhabitants, between 1875 and 1905.

In order to accommodate their expanding populations, towns began to demolish their walls to allow for the construction of sprawling new suburbs. In Madrid, a programme of urban improvements was introduced from 1846: new roads and squares were laid out, gas lighting and a modern system of sewers were installed, and the city supplied with clean water. New centres of entertainment, such as theatres and cafes, began to proliferate: by 1847, Madrid could boast over 60 cafes. In Barcelona, the prosperous bourgeoisie decamped to a stylish new extramural suburb, L'Eixample, which was developed from 1859. With its distinctive grid-shaped network of broad streets and stylish buildings, for which Paris was the inspiration, designed in the daring Modernist style – characterized by the imaginative use of brick, wrought iron and stained glass – by leading architects such as Lluis Domenèche i Montaner and Antoni Gaudí, this new Barcelona was a reflection of an increasingly self-confident and prosperous society. The Universal Exhibition of 1888 set the seal on Barcelona's transformation into a major European city.

CULTURAL DEVELOPMENTS

The absolutist backlash which had followed the restoration of Ferdinand VII in 1814 had condemned Spain to a long period of cultural stagnation. 'Far be from us the dangerous novelty of thinking', the authorities at the University of Cervera famously declared. On the king's death in 1833, however, there was a resurgence of cultural activity. Literary societies were established, such as the Athenaeum in Madrid (1835), which was to become both a forum for intellectual discourse and an influential centre of political debate. The 1830s also saw the re-emergence of the periodical press, principally in Madrid and Barcelona: by the 1850s, Madrid could boast no fewer than 20 newspapers reflecting different shades of political opinion, although problems of transportation and distribution limited their circulation and influence. Cultural life was further reinvigorated by the liberal émigrés who returned to Spain from England and France after Ferdinand VII's death, bringing with them the influences of the European Romantic movement. Romanticism, with its emphasis upon the primacy of emotionalism over reason, struck a particular chord with radical liberals, such as the mordant essayist and satirist Mariano José de Larra and the poet José de Espronceda, the self-styled 'Spanish Byron'. Other Spanish Romantic writers, among them Ángel Saavedra, later Duque de Rivas, and José Zorrilla, eschewed the politically progressive aspects of Romanticism, preferring to concentrate on what Antonio Alcalá Galiano termed the 'inner commotions' of the human spirit.

Spain's social, economic and political upheavals during the final third of the nineteenth century were accompanied by a dramatic explosion of cultural creativity. Influenced by such writers as Balzac, Flaubert and Dickens, Spanish novelists began to experiment with the techniques of literary realism. By far the most prolific in this respect was Benito Pérez Galdós, whose novels provide a vivid portrait of the Madrid society of his time, as well as important perspectives on Spain's turbulent recent history. Equally popular were the numerous *costumbrista* writers, such as Pedro Antonio de Alarcón and José María de Pereda, whose works highlighted the manners and popular customs of the Spanish regions. The rediscovery of the region was matched by a flowering of Catalan and Galician letters, exemplified by the poetry of Jacint Verdaguer and Rosalía de Castro respectively. The period between about 1890 and the advent of the Second Republic has often been dubbed Spain's 'Silver Age'. Its leading lights were the group of writers known collectively as the 'Generation of 98', among them Miguel de Unamuno, Pío Baroja, Antonio Machado and Ramón del Valle Inclán, who in tune with the spirit of the age sought the 'regeneration' of society by exploring the depths of the Spanish psyche. By 1930, a new artistic generation had emerged, whose leading lights included an extraordinary group of poets (including Federico García Lorca, Rafael Alberti, Vicente Aleixandre and Luis Cernuda), dubbed the 'Generation of 1927', four internationally renowned painters (Pablo Picasso, Juan Gris, Joan Miró and Salvador Dalí), and a clutch of fine composers, most notably Manuel de Falla.

Spain remained receptive to European intellectual currents. Among the most influential was the doctrine first propounded by the obscure German philosopher Karl Krause and introduced to Spain by Julián Sanz del Río in the 1850s. Krausism, with its emphasis upon tolerance, harmony and moral self-improvement, appealed strongly to Spanish intellectuals. In 1876, a leading Krausist, Fernando Giner de los Rios, who along with a group of other professors had been sacked from his post at the University of Madrid, was instrumental in founding the Institute of Free Education (*Institución Libre de Enseñanza*). The Institute sought to provide its students with a broad secular education in arts and sciences, and inculcate in them the values of tolerance and independent thought. The Institute and its Residence (founded in 1910) were to become influential centres for successive generations of Spanish liberal intellectuals. For their part, militant Catholics regarded the Institute, and the secular values it championed, as a threat to the moral well-being of society as a whole. For the most part, however, the Spanish educational system left much to be desired. Although the foundations of a national state-run education system were established, central government lacked the funds to convert the ideal into reality. By 1908, only 14,000 pupils attended state-run secondary schools, while 40,000 attended religious foundations. Education was to remain a middle-class privilege: in 1900, more than half of the adult population in Spain remained illiterate.

POLITICAL CHANGE: THE LIBERAL ASCENDANCY

Far from being simply a conflict over dynastic rights between the supporters of the 3-year-old Queen Isabella II (1833–68) and those of Ferdinand VII's ultra-royalist brother Charles, the civil war of 1833–40, known to history as the First Carlist War, was in large part a continuation of the ideological struggle that had been waged since the time of the War of Independence. Pitted against one another were, on the one hand, the liberals, committed to the political, social and economic modernization of the country, and on the other the Carlist reactionaries, who sought nothing less than the restoration of the powers and privileges of the traditional order. Support for the Pretender Charles was strongest in the conservative, ultra-Catholic regions of rural northern Spain, notably in Navarre and the Basque provinces, and to a lesser extent in the rural districts of Aragon and Catalonia. These were the regions where the influence of the clergy was most pervasive, and where attacks by centralizing urban-based liberalism upon the Church and upon the privileges of local self-government, enshrined in the Basque and Navarrese *fueros*, were bitterly resented. The Carlist cause enjoyed particularly fervent support among the secular and regular clergy, who feared that their long-held privileges were under threat and that a further sell-off of Church lands was imminent, and among the rural peasantry whose living conditions had deteriorated as a consequence of the government's economic reforms. In this respect, the Carlist insurrection was as much a violent protest against social and economic change as a defence of royalist tradition against reform.

During the first two years of the war, under the able generalship of Tomás de Zumalacárregui, the Carlist insurgents were able to bring a large swathe of territory east of the Ebro, stretching from the Basque country to Valencia, under their control. By adopting the same tactics of guerrilla warfare that had been employed during the War of Independence, the Carlists were able to keep the poorly organized government forces pinned down. But despite winning papal backing, Carlist endeavours to establish a broad-based alliance against the liberal government in Madrid came to nothing. The bedrock of Carlist support remained in the rural districts to the north and east of the Ebro; attempts to break out of their rural heartlands and capture urban strongholds such as Bilbao and Pamplona, which remained solidly loyal to the liberal cause, were unsuccessful. The failure of the ambitious 'Royal Expedition' of 1837, which reached the very outskirts of Madrid before being halted, marked the high-water mark of Carlist fortunes. Thereafter, the government began to gain the upper hand, thanks in no small part to the troops, equipment and money supplied by the British and French governments. Aware that they lacked the resources in manpower, munitions and supplies to overthrow the liberal state, moderate elements within the Carlist movement began to seek a negotiated outcome to the conflict. The Convention of Vergara of August 1839, by which the Carlist General Maroto secured an undertaking from his opposite number Espartero that Carlist officers would be permitted to rejoin the government army, and that the Basque and Navarrese *fueros* would be respected, effectively defused the revolt. By the summer of 1840, all remaining centres of the rebellion had been neutralized. Yet, the strength of religious and regionalist feeling in the conservative rural areas of the north ensured that Carlism did not entirely disappear as a political movement; further rebellions under the Carlist banner would break out in 1846 and 1872.

At the outbreak of the war, lacking sufficient political or military support with which to be able to mount a vigorous counter-offensive against the Carlists, Ferdinand VII's widow, María Cristina, who was to act as regent until their daughter Isabella came of age in 1843, had little option but to seek an alliance with a loose grouping of prominent reformist liberals. These were the Moderates (*Moderados*), who were drawn mainly from the ranks of the traditional élites, the property-holding 'enlightened classes' and the emerging industrial and commercial bourgeoisie. As a political group, they lacked any substantial following outside the towns. It was, of course, a marriage of convenience. María Cristina, like her husband before her, found the liberal political agenda profoundly unsympathetic, and while prepared to countenance certain administrative and economic reforms, she set her face squarely against the introduction of what she dubbed 'dangerous innovations' in the political organization of the realm. The Moderates, inspired by example of King Louis-Philippe of France, remained committed to the political and economic modernization of the country, but were none the less pragmatic enough to realize that for the sake of ordered progress an accommodation with the Crown had to be reached, and that the reintroduction of the radical 1812 Constitution was profoundly unrealistic. The product of this *modus vivendi* between the monarchy and the liberal élite was the Royal Statute of 1834. Drawing inspiration from the French Charter of 1814, the Royal Statute amounted to a limited exercise in democratic constitutional reform. The more radical provisions of the 1812 Constitution were either watered down or ditched altogether. The monarchy retained a 'moderating power', that is, the right to hire and fire ministers at will, and to summon or dissolve the *cortes* whenever it saw fit. The commitment to universal male suffrage, one of the key planks of the 1812 Constitution, which had enshrined the principle that ultimate sovereignty in the nation lay with the people not with the Crown, was quietly shelved. Instead, the Statute established a bicamaral *cortes*, with an upper chamber containing the grandees, bishops and other Crown appointees, and a lower one whose members were elected to office through indirect suffrage, and whose electorate, restricted to those who enjoyed an annual income in excess of 12,000 reales, constituted barely a tenth of one per cent of the total population. In short, political power, based on wealth and fitness to rule, was to become the particular preserve of an 'enlightened' middle class.

For all its limitations as a document of reform, the Royal Statute none the less committed the Spanish Crown to the cause of constitutional liberalism. But the timid reforms enshrined in the Statute came as a disappointment for those self-proclaimed 'defenders of liberty' within the liberal movement, the Progressives (*Progresistas*), the heirs of the radical *exaltados*, whose main support lay among the urban middle classes. By and large, Moderates and Progressives shared a belief in the importance of 'ordered progress' and the right of the propertied middle class to wield political power. What distinguished the Progressives, above all, was their readiness to achieve power through revolution. Thus, in the summer of 1835, a wave of radical revolts broke out in cities across Spain, as a result of which the queen regent bowed to pressure from the disenchanted Progressives, annulled the Royal Statute and appointed the Jewish financier Juan Alvarez Mendizábal as her chief minister. When, the following year, Mendizábal was dismissed, a group of rebellious sergeants confronted the queen regent at her palace in La Granja and compelled her to restore the Progressives to office.

One of Mendizábal's first actions in office was to authorize the closure of monasteries and convents, and the sale of what remained of ecclesiastical landed property, and to abolish aristocratic entail. The attack on ecclesiastical property was designed to provide the funds to allow the cash-strapped government to bring the war against the Carlists to a successful conclusion. At the same time, it was anticipated that these measures would open 'a most abundant source of public felicity, giving new life to moribund wealth', by creating both a free market in land and a new rural middle class of small landowners, which would in turn pave the way for the economic modernization of the country. In the event, most of the lands that were sold off after 1836 were purchased at public auction by existing landowners and by members of the urban bourgeoisie. For the Progressives, as for the Moderates, economic freedom and private property took primacy over considerations of social and political reform. Thus, the Constitution of 1837 slightly widened the right of suffrage by lowering the property qualification, so that some 265,000 voters (roughly 2 per cent of the population) were enfranchised, but otherwise retained many of the principal provisions of the Royal Statute.

PRAETORIAN POLITICS

The government victory in the Carlist War confirmed Isabella II on the throne, but it also represented the death-knell of Spanish absolutism, as the liberals entrenched themselves in power and liberalism as a political creed took firm root. But the war also confirmed the military as the power-brokers in the land. As Moderates and Progressives jockeyed for political influence, both factions looked increasingly towards the generals, who enjoyed unprecedented influence and prestige by virtue of their victory over the Carlists, to give themselves and their policies more credibility, and ultimately to establish themselves in power. Since the time of the War of Independence, military insurrections against the central government had become a characteristic feature of the Spanish political landscape. These early *pronunciamientos*, or declarations – so-called because disaffected army officers would seek to win support from the lower ranks by reading out a statement of their grievances – did not aim to place political power squarely in the hands of the military, but rather to provide the conditions that would bring about political change. However, unlike Riego and other lower-ranked officers who had 'pronounced' against the system in 1820, the generals of the 1840s were key players within the political system itself, prestigious figureheads or 'swords' of the factions whose views they championed. In the majority of cases, the military acted with public support, not against it, while behind a façade of constitutional niceties, civilian politicians became increasingly peripheral to the process of political change.

Typical of the new breed of soldier-politician was General Baldomero Espartero, who eventually took command of a Progressive rebellion against the Moderate government in 1840 and wrested control of the regency from Queen María Cristina. Under Espartero's rule, the right of suffrage was increased yet further, so that by 1843 over 500,000 people were entitled to vote. However, Espartero's highhanded manner, his disregard for politicians of all shades of opinion, and his willingness to rely on a small military clique to govern, alienated both Moderates and Progressives alike. An aborted Moderate rebellion in the north in October 1841 was followed by a popular revolt in Barcelona the following year. In 1843, a coalition of Moderates and disgruntled Progressives, led by General Ramón María Narváez, rose in rebellion against Espartero, who was defeated and ousted from power.

THE MODERATE DECADE

The restoration of the Moderates was to exclude the Progressives from power for the best part of a decade. The principal objectives of the Moderates were to ensure the political and social stability of the nation and encourage economic development. 'Spaniards are tired of alternatives and convulsions', declared General Narváez in 1844. Narváez was happy to leave the day-to-day direction of policy to his Moderate political allies, who cut the suffrage dramatically to just over 97,000 citizens, that is, less than one per cent of the population as a whole and resorted to wholesale election-rigging to maintain themselves in power. The Constitution of 1845 retained most of the provisions of that of 1837, but the prerogatives of the Crown were enhanced and the elected Senate was replaced by an assembly made up of appointed notables. Steps were taken to undermine the local power-base of the Progressives: elected town councils were replaced by centrally appointed mayors; restrictions were placed on freedom of speech; trial by jury was abolished; and the National Militia, which to all intents and purposes was the private army of the Progressives, was dissolved.

During their decade in office, the Moderates implemented a series of financial and administrative reforms that would create the legal and institutional framework of a modern, centralized state. These included the creation of a uniform system of taxation, which helped state revenues to almost double; the reform of the National Bank; the professionalization of the state bureaucracy; the promulgation of a criminal code; the reform of the education system, which brought universities and schools under state control; the introduction of postage stamps and the adoption of the *peseta* as the national currency. In 1851, the Moderates also signed a Concordat with the Vatican, by the terms of which the latter retrospectively accepted the sale of Church lands in return for state recognition of Catholicism as the 'sole religion of the Spanish nation', state funding for secular clergy, and confirmation of the Church's key role as educators.

Throughout his time in power, Narváez displayed a dogged determination to maintain order and keep a lid on sedition. 'I have no enemies', the general is reputed to have declared on his deathbed, 'I have had them all shot.' In 1844, Narváez oversaw the creation of a new paramilitary police force, the Civil Guard, whose task it was to maintain order in the countryside by suppressing brigandage and crushing any social unrest. At the same time, Narváez was careful to keep on good terms with the army, which by 1850 had expanded hugely to number some 150,000 men and accounted for 55 per cent of the national budget. With the support of the army, Narváez and the Moderates were able to entrench themselves in power. Yet, Narváez's strong-arm rule did not go unchallenged. The government faced mounting opposition from radical Progressives, excluded from power by the Crown; from the Carlists, who rose in rebellion in Catalonia in 1846–9; and from the emerging Democratic party, which championed the rights of the disenfranchised majority in society by calling for universal male suffrage, agrarian reform and the legalization of workers' associations. With Democratic backing, a number of military *pronunciamientos* were launched against the Narvaéz regime between 1844 and 1848, but lacking the whole-hearted support of the Progressives, many of whom feared that popular revolution would lead to anarchy, they were easily suppressed.

It was not long, however, before the unity of Narváez's government started to come under strain. The Moderate camp fragmented into at least three different competing factions, as those who held positions of power in government came under pressure from the 'Puritans' among Moderate ranks, who sought to curb the dominance of the army over government and lobbied for a broadening of political and civil rights, and those 'clerical absolutists' who sought to revive the authority of the monarchy. Once Narváez was forced from office in 1851, political opposition to the regime began to mount. The general's successor, the arch-conservative Juan Bravo Murillo, sought to put an end to the factionalism and corruption of political life and bolster the authority of the state. Plans were drawn up to reduce the electorate to a mere 25,000 and to subordinate the *cortes* to an advisory role. But Bravo Murillo's neo-absolutist agenda aroused considerable opposition among his fellow Moderates, not least among the generals, who viewed it as a threat to their own political position, and he in turn was forced from office in 1853. The following year, a *pronunciamiento* by a group of generals triggered a series of risings in Madrid and the provincial towns, supported by an uneasy alliance of Progressives, Democrats and urban workers. Seeing which way the wind was blowing, Queen Isabella saved her position by agreeing to dismiss the government and invited Espartero and the Progressives to take up the reins of power once more. The Democrats, many of whom had hoped that the rebellion would lead to the overthrow of the Bourbon dynasty and the creation of a revolutionary republican government, were suppressed.

THE 'PROGRESSIVE REVOLUTION' AND THE LIBERAL UNION

One of Espartero's first acts was to restore many of the civil liberties that had been suppressed by Narváez. The National Militia was resuscitated and locally elected town councils were restored. The Progressive government also pushed ahead with a programme of administrative reform and accelerated economic liberalization. The Law of General Disentailment, introduced by Pascual Madoz in 1855, provided for the sale of municipal common lands. A series of laws and regulations were promulgated with the aim of encouraging business enterprise and extending banking and credit facilities, while an act of 1855 gave the green light to the creation of a national network of railways.

However, the much-vaunted 'Progressive Revolution' soon ran out of steam. Deep political divisions opened up between an increasingly conservative-minded leadership, for whom the suppression of disorder took priority, and those Democrats and radical Progressives who demanded wholesale political and social reform. There was also an upsurge of violent social disorder in 1856, provoked by rising food prices, industrial recession and epidemic disease. In July 1856, a new *pronunciamiento* by General Leopoldo O'Donnell forced Espartero from power and brought an end to the Progressive regime. In its place, and in an attempt to give Spain some measure of political stability, O'Donnell founded a broad-based political grouping called the Liberal Union, whose ideology was deliberately couched in such vague terms that it might appeal to mainstream Moderates and Progressives alike. In an attempt to mollify the radical Left, O'Donnell extended the suffrage and restored some measure of press freedom.

During most of the nineteenth century, Spanish foreign policy remained resolutely defensive. The overriding priority of successive governments was to protect the few colonial possessions that still lay under Spanish sovereignty. However, O'Donnell committed Spain to a number of largely fruitless military adventures overseas, which he calculated would bolster public support for the government. Thus, between 1858 and 1863, Spanish forces assisted the French conquest of Indochina; in 1861, Spain resumed control of Santo Domingo at the invitation of its beleaguered president, then embroiled in a civil war, only to withdraw four years later; also in 1861, a Spanish expeditionary force intervened in Mexico; and between 1862 and 1866, Spanish fleets took part in the War of the Pacific. Most important of all, Spanish forces fought a successful campaign in the Morocco in 1859–60, which culminated in the capture of Tetuán. As O'Donnell had hoped, the Moroccan campaign unleashed a public outpouring of patriotic sentiment. But the feel-good factor was short-lived and the Liberal Union began to crumble, as O'Donnell faced increasing opposition from radical Progressives and the conservative Right alike. In 1863, the ruling coalition fell apart and O'Donnell was forced to resign. Rather than hand over the reins of power to the Progressives, whom she regarded as dangerous revolutionaries, Queen Isabella, who increasingly resented the constitutional restraints placed upon her by the liberals, appointed a series of reactionary court conservative governments to office.

THE 'GLORIOUS REVOLUTION' AND THE FIRST REPUBLIC

By 1868, Queen Isabella had succeeded in alienating wide sections of Spanish society. Her personal reputation had been besmirched by a series of high-profile financial and sexual scandals. The population at large was suffering the effects of severe economic recession, rising unemployment, higher taxation, renewed food shortages and soaring wheat prices. Financiers and industrialists were feeling the pinch as profits plummeted. Politically marginalized and persecuted, the Progressives entered into an alliance with a group of exiled Liberal Union generals. While radical Progressives and Democrats fomented rebellion in the main towns and set up revolutionary committees, the military, led by General Juan Prim, hero of the Moroccan campaign of 1859–60, issued a *pronunciamiento* in September 1868, overthrew the government and drove Isabella into exile.

The so-called 'Glorious Revolution' of 1868 was the prelude to what became known as the 'six revolutionary years', a period marked by acute political and social turmoil, as politicians and generals grappled to fill the political vacuum that had been left by the demise of the monarchy. The immediate problem in the aftermath of the Revolution was to establish a political system that would go at least some way towards satisfying the expectations and aspirations of Liberal Unionists, Progressives and Democrats alike. The resulting Constitution of 1869 was a compromise document, which foresaw the establishment of a revamped constitutional monarchy, yet contained sufficient radical provisions – universal suffrage for all males aged over 25, religious freedom, the right of association, the introduction of the jury system, and an end to press censorship – to command the support of the majority of the Progressives. However, while a section of the Democrats was willing to pledge support for these constitutional arrangements, which made Spain perhaps the most politically progressive country in the world at that time, the radical majority, considering that the Revolution had been betrayed, broke away in disgust and formed a federalist Republican party. In September 1869, Republicans stirred up revolt in Catalonia, Aragon and the Levante in pursuit of their revolutionary aims, only to be crushed by the government. Order having been restored, the search began for a new king. But suitable candidates were few and far between – an invitation to a member of the Hohenzollern dynasty was the spark that triggered the Franco-Prussian War – and a year would elapse before Prim finally offered the throne to a son of King Victor Emmanuel II of Italy, Amadeo of Savoy, who was proclaimed Amadeo I (1870–3) in November 1870.

Amadeo I's sojourn in Spain was to prove deeply unhappy. On the very day of his arrival in the country in December 1870, Prim was assassinated, probably at the hands of extremist Republicans. With Prim's death, the revolutionary coalition of 1868 which had brought the king to power in the first place rapidly disintegrated. The radical wing of the Progressives, under Manuel Ruiz Zorrilla, joined forces with the Democrats to found the Radical Party. This left a conservative Progressive rump, under the leadership of Práxedes Mateo Sagasta, which remained committed to the constitutional arrangements laid down in 1869 and continued to collaborate with the Liberal Unionists. When, in 1872, Amadeo allowed Ruiz Zorrilla to form a government, the Liberal Unionists withdrew their support for the monarchy. The hapless king also faced the implacable opposition of the 'intransigent' federalists among Republican ranks, who rejected the legalistic approach of the party leadership, which sought to achieve its political goals through the ballot box. Moreover, the king was rejected by the aristocratic *Alfonsistas* (those who championed the dynastic rights of Queen Isabella's 13-year-old son Alfonso), and by the Carlists, who rose in rebellion in the north-east in 1872 in support of a new pretender, the self-styled Charles VII. Taking advantage of the fact that the Spanish Army was in disarray, Carlist forces won a series of victories and by 1874 they had established what was nothing less than a separate Carlist state in the Basque Country and Navarre. However, as in the war of 1833–40, the Carlists proved unable to attract mainstream conservative support throughout the country and their attempts to break out from their rural strongholds ultimately failed.

King Amadeo also inherited a full-blown colonial rebellion in Cuba. During the first half of the nineteenth century there had been little appetite for political independence in Cuba, in large part because her economy, based chiefly upon the sugar and tobacco industries, was booming. However, the dominance of Spanish immigrants in the affairs of the colony, together with the refusal of the Spanish authorities to allow commercial freedom or any measure of local autonomy, bred resentment among the creole élite and led to the creation of a Reformist party to press their demands. When negotiations between the Reformists and the Madrid government foundered in 1867, a group of creole secessionists launched a rebellion the following year, which was not to be suppressed until 1878 and was to prove a major drain on the resources of the Spanish government.

By 11 February 1873, lacking any significant support among the political classes, Amadeo had had enough and abdicated the throne. In the absence of any viable alternative, and in the face of mass abstention by the conservative monarchists, a Republic was proclaimed. The First Republic proved short-lived, however. Quite apart from having to contend with the ongoing wars against the Cuban rebels and the Carlists, the new Republican government found it impossible to curb a mounting wave of political and social disorder. In the summer of 1873, there were a series of mutinies in the army, an outburst of violent anti-clericalist demonstrations and a rash of strikes and workers' revolts, some of them fomented by the First International. At Alcoy near Alicante, for example, the mayor was murdered and the workers seized control of the town. During that summer, with the forces of public order crumbling, and with loyal army units otherwise engaged in fighting the Carlist uprising, groups of extremist Federal Republicans established revolutionary committees in many of the towns of Andalusia and the Levante, and declared them to be self-governing 'cantons'. Most of these uprisings were quickly snuffed out, but a handful of centres, notably Málaga and Cartagena, held out for a number of months. The cantonalist uprisings convinced the army high command that Spain's experiment with Federal Republicanism had unleashed forces that threatened to plunge the nation into anarchy. In January 1874, in an attempt 'to save society and the Fatherland', General Manuel Pavía overthrew the established government and established a conservative unitary republic under General Serrano. By now, however, republicanism was rapidly becoming a discredited creed and conservative opinion began to shift towards the *Alfonsista* camp. The following December, a new *pronunciamiento*, issued by Brigadier-General Arsenio Martínez Campos, restored the Bourbon monarchy and installed Alfonso XII (1874–85) on the throne. Shortly afterwards, Martínez Campos neutralized the last remaining centres of the Carlist rebellion.

The collapse of the First Republic ensured that power would remain the preserve of the liberal oligarchy who had run Spain since 1833. It also signalled an important shift in the attitude of the military towards politics. Hitherto, generals had intervened in the affairs of state on behalf of one political party or another. The *pronunciamientos* of Pavía and Martínez Campos were different, in that, as noted above, they declared themselves to be acting 'as soldiers and citizens to save society and the Fatherland (*patria*)', and to maintain the 'harmony of the military family', which was seen to be under threat.

THE RESTORATION SYSTEM

The first prime minister of the Restoration monarchy was a former Liberal Unionist politician, Antonio Cánovas del Castillo. Cánovas's immediate priority on becoming prime minister was to establish a political system that would provide Spain with the stability that had patently been lacking since the fall of the monarchy in 1868, and to put an end to the praetorianism that had dominated political life for decades. The perennial problem was how to prevent those excluded from power from seeking to regain it via a military *pronunciamiento* or a popular revolution. Cánovas's solution to this conundrum was to devise the *turno pacífico* (literally 'peaceful alternation'), a two-party system inspired by the British model, in which the main political groupings who were not opposed to the monarchy – a Liberal party, which had absorbed into its ranks many of the Progressives, Democrats and Republicans, under Sagasta, and a Conservative party (heir to the Liberal Union) under Cánovas himself – alternated in power. The delivery of a satisfactory working majority to one party or another was achieved by the institutionalized manipulation of the electoral machine, a process orchestrated from Madrid by the Ministry of the Interior and implemented at a local level by government-appointed civil governors and mayors, and by prominent local *caciques*, or bosses, an influential group of landowners, moneylenders, government officials, lawyers and priests, whose extensive powers of patronage over such things as jobs, property disputes, contracts or even exemptions from military service created an elaborate clientelist network within the districts under their sway. Those groups that were opposed to the constitutional monarchy, notably the Carlists, Republicans and working-class organizations, were suppressed.

The Restoration System engineered by Cánovas was to survive until its overthrow by a military *coup* in 1923. It was underpinned by the new Constitution of 1876, which, like that of 1845, restored joint sovereignty between king and *cortes*, thereby allowing the monarch considerable influence over the political process. It was the king who decided whether to dismiss ministers, to veto legislation or, indeed, when the time was ripe to replace the party in power with the opposition. As Cánovas had intended, the mechanism of the *turno pacífico* successfully brought a halt to military intervention in the political process and caused the revolutionary liberal tradition to wither away. Republican *pronunciamientos* were staged in 1883 and 1886, but both were damp squibs. 'As a business the revolution is so depressed that it is impossible to gain a living by it', commented the novelist Galdós. Political stability also contributed to a period of impressive economic growth, which ensured the continuing support of the landowning, financial and industrial oligarchy. The Liberals, who remained in power during most of the 1880s, reintroduced of a number of the key 'liberal conquests' of the 1868 revolution, notably freedom of association and expression, which effectively legalized workers' organizations, trial by jury, and religious liberty, as well as the abolition of slavery in Cuba and Puerto Rico. This was followed in 1890 by a law

of universal male suffrage. The beneficiaries of this more tolerant attitude were the Carlists and Republicans, who were allowed some representation in the *cortes*.

For all its achievements, Cánovas's system has been criticized as
being both artificial and flawed. The two 'dynastic parties' were little
more than loose coalitions of notables, which lacked any coherent
political programme or ideology, beyond maintaining the status quo,
or any nation-wide party organization. In the words of Paul Preston,
'politics became an exclusive minuet danced out by a small privileged
minority'. The marginalization from the political process of non-
monarchical groups – the Republicans, regional nationalists and
working-class movements – by the ruling élites was to exacerbate
political and social tensions and stored up problems for the future.
Furthermore, the perverse influence of *caciquismo* encouraged political indifference, particularly among the illiterate rural masses, with the
result that the political education of the country and the modernization
of political parties were delayed. To the country at large, politics, with
its endemic faction-fighting and rigged elections, was increasingly
perceived as a disreputable and futile business. Even in the big cities,
where the dynastic parties found it much harder to manipulate the electorate, apathy reigned. In 1899, in Barcelona, only 10 per cent of the
electorate exercised their entitlement to vote. This, Antonio Machado
memorably declared, was a 'Spain which yawns'. This lack of grass-
roots support for parliamentary democracy would have important
consequences for the country in years to come.

THE CUBAN DISASTER

In 1898, the Restoration System was dealt a grievous blow to its
authority. The failure of the Spanish government to grant local autonomy to Cuba, in accordance with the terms of the peace settlement of
1878, led to the outbreak of a new nationalist revolt in the colony in
1895. Prime Minister Cánovas promised to defend the island 'to the
last man, to the last peseta'. Public opinion in Spain, and among the
'Spanish party' in Cuba itself, demanded a hard line against the rebels,
and the government committed over a quarter of a million troops in an
unsuccessful attempt to suppress the insurgents. Even when it became
clear to the Spanish high command that the United States – which
already enjoyed close economic ties with Cuba, and was determined to

end Spanish influence in the Western Hemisphere once and for all – was planning to intervene on the side of the Cuban rebels, and that Spain was likely to come off second best in any military confrontation, the consequences of relinquishing Cuba and its other territories without a shot being fired were unpalatable beyond reckoning. Sagasta, who resumed the premiership after the murder of Cánovas by an Italian anarchist in 1897, feared that the surrender of the Spanish empire would lead to a popular insurrection against his government. 'We went to war because we had no choice', he later explained, 'We were faced with a terrible dilemma: war with all its consequences or dishonour, and dishonour would have meant the end of everything and of us all.'

As the Spanish government had feared and anticipated, the Spanish-American War proved short, bloody and far from glorious. In May and July 1898, the Spanish fleets stationed in the Philippines (where another colonial rebellion had erupted in 1896) and Cuba respectively were destroyed by US squadrons in brief and unequal engagements. Seeing that further resistance was futile, Spain sued for peace shortly afterwards and by the terms of the Treaty of Paris (December 1898), surrendered Puerto Rico, the Philippines and Guam to the United States, while Cuba became a virtual American protectorate. In February 1899, Spain relinquished the last remnants of her once vast overseas empire when she sold her remaining archipelagos in the Pacific – the Carolines, Marianas and Pelews – to Germany for the sum of 25 million marks.

The Cuban War, which left over 60,000 Spanish dead through combat or disease, was widely regarded as a national humiliation. For *The Times* of London, the defeat meant that Spain's 'prestige as a fighting-power, by land or sea, has disappeared'. Coming at the very time when the great European powers were busily engaged in empire building overseas, the loss of Spain's last colonies was taken by many as a sign of racial and national inferiority. Blame for what came to be known simply as 'The Disaster' (*El Desastre*) was directed first at Spain's military high command and then at the 'bungling politicians' in Madrid, who it was said had failed to provide the Spanish armed forces with the resources they desperately needed in their unequal struggle with the United States. The post-mortem that followed the Cuban War went well beyond the search for scapegoats, however. In an atmosphere of collective anguish and pessimism, the call went up for the 'regeneration' of what was widely regarded as Spain's atrophied political system. 'Regenerationism' provided a language of criticism of the system that could be embraced by a whole range of political groups. Some 'regenerationists' pursued a narrowly conservative agenda, attributing Spain's ills to the disintegration of traditional social and religious loyalties. By contrast, the influential Aragonese writer and lawyer, Joaquín Costa, deplored Spain's historical isolation from the mainstream of European political and cultural thought, and called for the destruction of corrupt *caciquismo* and the urgent modernization of the country's political, social and economic structures. Above all, Costa believed that agricultural reform, linked to programmes for better irrigation systems, canals, reforestation and other public works, was essential if Spain's economic potential was to be realized and the 'living forces' (*fuerzas vivas*) of society, the apathetic lower middle classes, be allowed to flourish. However, Costa's party or, rather, pressure group, the National League of Producers, a loose alliance of middle-class farmers and tradesmen, made only a limited political impact. By 1901, Costa had come to the conclusion that what Spain required was an 'iron surgeon', a benevolent military dictator, who would remove the cancer of *caciquismo* and thereby allow the nation to flourish.

At the same time, an influential group of intellectuals, the so-called 'Generation of 98', set about examining the causes of the 'Spanish predicament' and putting forward solutions of their own for the nation's salvation. Spain's problems were not only attributed to the pernicious influence of a corrupt ruling regime, but to fundamental flaws in the Spanish character, to a loss of 'spirit and ancient virtue', or even to Spain's supposed incapacity to live up to her 'historical identity'. The general tone of these works was one of soul-searching and disillusion, summed up by Machado's aching lament: 'Wretched Castile, once supreme, now folorn, wrapping herself in rags, closes her mind in scorn.' It was not just the historical development of Spain that was being probed here, but the very essence of the Spanish soul. To borrow Gerald Brenan's memorable metaphor, it was as if Spain herself had become a patient on the psychoanalyst's couch.

OTHER CRITICS OF THE REGIME

The torrent of criticism unleashed by the proponents of regenerationism and by the intellectuals of the 'Generation of 1898' was matched by a surge in support for other protest and reform movements. Having been marginalized and largely dormant as a political force since the demise of the First Republic, the Republican movement enjoyed a revival in its fortunes. A leading figure in this revival was the newspaper editor Alejandro Lerroux. In the aftermath of the 'Disaster', Lerroux began to lay the foundations of a revolutionary Republican movement in Barcelona, which not only sought to challenge the supremacy of the dynastic parties, but also to forge an effective alliance with the working class. In pursuit of these aims, Lerroux and his supporters campaigned for workers' rights, established lay schools and trade unions, organized multitudinous picnics, and founded a network of social clubs (*Casas del Pueblo*), where workers could enjoy recreational and cultural facilities. In January 1908, however, under attack from some of his own supporters for his attempts to seek support within the army, Lerroux changed tack. Abandoning much of the revolutionary rhetoric and the virulently anticlerical propaganda which had dominated his political discourse hitherto, Lerroux founded the Radical Republican Party, which he sought to establish as a nation-wide, moderate centrist party which would campaign to reform the political system by legal means and would represent the interests of the middle class and workers alike. However, Lerroux's credibility as the champion of the working man was damaged by his notoriously lavish lifestyle, his shady business dealings and his failure to seize the initiative during the 'Tragic Week' disturbances in Barcelona in July 1909 (see below). By 1914, working-class support for the Radicals had begun to dwindle. Moreover, from 1912 the party was being challenged by a rival group, the Reformist Republican Party, founded by a group of university intellectuals, which put forward a series of practical proposals designed to bring about the political, social and educational modernization of Spain. The Republican parties constituted a highly influential and vocal pressure group, but lacking any significant support outside the main industrialized cities, they did not possess the clout to challenge the constitutional parties for power.

The final decades of the nineteenth century witnessed an upsurge in support for regional nationalist movements. In Catalonia, a resurgence of Catalan linguistic and literary activity, known as the *Renaixença* (Renaissance), which had got under way in the 1830s, contributed to a renewed sense of Catalan national sentiment towards the end of the century, as deep-seated resentment at the centralizing policies of successive liberal governments was accompanied by a growing conviction among the Catalan industrial bourgeoisie that the 'parasitic' political establishment in Madrid was draining the economically dynamic regions of the periphery. Valentí Almirall, author of *Lo Catalanisme* (1886), was among the first to give voice to Catalan political nationalism. The 'Manresa Principles' (*Bases de Manresa*), drawn up by one of Almirall's disciples, Enric Prat de la Riba, in 1892, demanded autonomy for a Catalan-speaking state within Spain. These demands were fuelled by the economic downturn which the region suffered as a consequence of the loss of empire in 1898 (the Cuban market had accounted for some 60 per cent of Catalan exports) and the failure of the Madrid government to ease the plight of Catalan businesses. Most influential of all among the nationalist forces in Catalonia was the middle-class Regionalist League (*Lliga Regionalista*), founded in 1901, whose principal aims were to secure self-rule for Catalonia and defend the economic interests of local Catalan industrialists. Under the leadership of Françesc Cambó, the *Lliga* rapidly established itself as an influential political force in the region. Catalan sensibilities were inflamed in 1905, when a mob of army officers ransacked the offices of the Catalan satirical magazine *Cut-Cut*, which had published an anti-militarist cartoon, and those of the Catalanist newspaper *La Veu de Catalunya*. The following year, the Liberal government was pressurized by the army into passing the Law of Jurisdictions, which allowed the military courts to take action against anyone who defamed the reputation of the armed forces. In indignant response, all the political parties of the region, including the Nationalists, Republicans and Carlists, forged an electoral alliance, 'Catalan Solidarity' (*Solidaritat Catalan*), which won a sweeping victory in the elections of 1907. In 1913, the Conservative government of Eduardo Dato allowed the four Catalan provinces (Barcelona, Gerona, Lérida and Tarragona) to join together to create the *Mancomunitat*, by which they were awarded a limited measure of autonomy.

In the Basque country, regional nationalism did not enjoy such deep roots as in Catalonia, nor could it boast the same distinguished literary tradition. The Basque National Party (*Partido Nacional Vasco*), founded by Sabino de Arana in 1894, was a Catholic conservative party whose nationalist ideology was built upon resentment of political centralism (exemplified by the abolition of the Basque *fueros* in 1876), an ingrained sense of racial and cultural distinctiveness from the rest of Spain, and a fear that the influx of Castilian-speaking

migrant workers (pejoratively dubbed *maketos*) to the rapidly expanding industrial heartlands around Bilbao would eventually obliterate the
Basque-speaking community altogether. Sabino's dream was of an
independent, Catholic *Euzkadi*, a rural idyll comprising all the Basque-
speaking regions north and south of the Pyrenees, in which neither the
Castilian language nor the forces of liberalism would have any place.
Yet, despite enjoying strong support among the rural peasantry and
some among the lower middle classes, the PNV was regarded with
hostility by Basque industrialists and bankers, for whom separation
from the rest of Spain was unthinkable, by working-class organizations committed to defending the rights of Basques and *maketos* alike,
and by the Carlists, who rejected its separatist aims.

The partial industrialization of Spain during the second half of the
nineteenth century was accompanied by the emergence of a number of
working-class political organizations. Inspired by the writings of the
Russian Bakunin, whose ideas were introduced to Spain in 1868, the
revolutionary Anarchist movement found widespread support among
the landless peasants of Andalusia and the industrial workers of
Catalonia. The aims of the Anarchists were clear-cut: social justice,
land reform and the destruction of the capitalist system. In the countryside, small groups incited outbursts of peasant violence against the
landowners and their property. One such group, the Regional
Federation of Spanish Workers (*Federación de Trabajadores de la
Región Española*, FTRE), founded in 1881, recruited some 60,000
members, until it was suppressed by the Civil Guard in 1884. By the
1890s, some extremists were arguing that the capitalist system could
only be broken through violent 'direct action'. This policy was manifested in numerous terrorist bombings – most notoriously that which
killed 21 theatre-goers at the Liceu Opera House in Barcelona in 1893
– and political assassinations (including those of three prime ministers). Terrorist outrages gave rise to brutal police repression of union
leaders. The 'National Labour Confederation' (*Confederación
Nacional del Trabajo*, or CNT), founded in 1910, sought to achieve its
revolutionary aims through electoral abstention and strikes, and its
evangelical zeal found an enthusiastic response among the working
class, particularly among the landless peasantry.

By far the most important of the groups influenced by Marxist
ideology was the Spanish Socialist party (*Partido Socialista Obrero
Español*, or PSOE), founded in Madrid by Pablo Iglesias in 1879; to
this was later affiliated a trade union, the 'General Workers' Union'

(*Unión General de Trabajadores*, UGT) in 1888. Unlike the apolitical Anarchists, the Socialists sought 'the possession of political power by the working class', but was gradualist and pragmatic in its actions, devoting most of its energies towards improving workers' living standards and seeking political power through the ballot box rather than through violent revolution. The chief centres of Socialism lay in the industrial centres around Bilbao, in the coal-mining districts of Asturias, and in rural Castile. Yet, the disciplined, legalistic approach of the Socialists failed to strike a chord with the majority of Spanish workers, with the result that party membership grew only painfully slowly and the PSOE had to enter into an electoral alliance with the Reformist Republicans in 1909 in order to maximize its influence.

CHURCH AND SOCIETY

The ascendancy of liberalism transformed the position of the Catholic Church within Spanish society. The liberals were far from being anti-Catholic. The constitution of 1837, like that of 1812, recognized Catholicism as the official religion of state; Mendizábal and Espartero, who spearheaded the Progressive attack on the Church, were devout Catholics themselves. Yet, the Progressives, like the Bourbon regalist-reformers before them, regarded land ownership by the 'dead hands' of the Church to be an obstacle to economic progress and were committed to reducing its wealth and power. The enthusiastic support lent by some among the clergy for the absolutist regime of Ferdinand VII between 1814 and 1820, and again between 1823 and 1833, as well as for the Carlist rebellion in 1833, caused an anticlerical backlash, particularly towards the regular orders and strengthened the determination of the liberal élite to reform the institutional foundations of the Church. Mendizábal's disentailing legislation of 1836 stripped the Church of its landed wealth. To add to the Church's woes, there was a steep decline in religious vocations: the number of religious declined from around 172,000 in 1797 to 63,000 in 1860. The secularizing policies of the Progressives also caused large numbers of religious buildings to be abandoned. In Madrid alone, 44 churches and monasteries were either demolished or converted to other uses. In 1844, the Moderates sought to heal the rift between Church and state: further sales of property of the secular clergy were suspended, although no steps were taken to reappropriate the lands that had already been sold, many of which had ended up in the hands of the Moderates themselves. The Concordat of 1851, by which the Moderate government undertook to pay the secular clergy, allowed the Church the right to acquire property and confirmed the prominent role of the clergy in education, set the seal on the reconciliation.

During the Restoration period, alarmed by a rising tide of anti-clericalism, particularly among the disaffected urban proletariat and the rural population of the south, the Church launched a determined counter-offensive designed to 're-Catholicize' the population. With the enthusiastic support of the upper classes, devotional and charitable organizations proliferated, new Catholic schools were set up and a Jesuit-run university was founded at Deusto. Religious orders enjoyed a rapid expansion in numbers. The Catholic Workers' Circles, founded by the Jesuit Father Vicent in the 1890s, were transformed into fully fledged workers' syndicates after 1912. The National Catholic Agrarian Confederation (*Confederación Nacional Católica Agraria*, CNCA), founded in 1917, which provided rural banks to its members, came to enjoy widespread influence in Castile and Navarre, and had recruited over half a million families to its ranks by 1922.

The religious question was to polarize Spanish society. The activities of 'Social Catholicism' were resented by many on the liberal Left, who considered that clerical domination of the education system was an obstacle to the modernization of Spain. The close links between the Church and the upper class, and the movement's resolutely paternalist stance, reinforced the view among the disaffected urban proletariat and the rural dispossessed that the Church and the rich were working hand in glove. There was a resurgence of anticlericalism, particularly in major urban centres. Galdós's staunchly anticlerical play *Electra* (1901) sold 10,000 copies in just two days. Although popular piety continued to flourish, there were also periodic explosions of anticlerical violence, most notably during the popular uprisings of 1869 and 1909. By contrast, for those who viewed liberalism as a threat to the very essence of the nation, and who feared that working-class militancy and regional nationalism threatened to tear the country apart, the Church represented a comforting symbol of stability and permanence.

THE CRISIS OF LIBERAL SPAIN

The climate of pessimism which engulfed Spain after 1898 may have damaged the prestige and credibility of the Restoration parliamentary system, but it did not lead to its immediate demise. The 'dynastic parties' sought to stem the rising tide of criticism by increasing the pace of reform. The Conservative Francisco Silvela, who took office in 1899, argued for the need to relax government influence over municipal councils as a means to eradicate electoral corruption and the network of clientilism (*caciquismo*) that sustained it, but his ideas were rebuffed both by the Liberals and by some within his own party. Silvela's fellow 'puritan' Antonio Maura, who took office as prime minister in 1907, spoke optimistically of carrying out a 'revolution from above', which by enlisting the support of the Catholic middle classes would rejuvenate local government and uproot *caciquismo*, thereby preventing the outbreak of a 'revolution from below'. But Maura's reformist agenda failed to win the support of the Liberals, who feared that the abandonment of the *turno pacífico* would reduce their chances of returning to power, while his overbearing, high-handed style won him many enemies. His standing was fatally damaged in July 1909, when a call-up of reservists to help defend the Spanish enclave in northern Morocco provoked a violent uprising in Barcelona. Workers' demonstrations degenerated into an orgy of anti-clericalism, in the course of which 42 churches and convents were burnt or damaged. Anarchist propaganda declared its 'indifference to the triumph of the Cross over the Crescent' and demanded that regiments of priests and friars 'who are of no use to the country' be sent to Morocco in the reservists' stead. The uprising was crushed by the army with great bloodshed, but Maura's reputation never recovered from what came to be known as the 'Tragic Week'. Shortly afterwards, the Liberals, who disapproved of the brutal repression which had followed the Barcelona uprising, allied themselves with the Republicans to force the prime minister from office.

Despite the fracturing of the political consensus that had governed Spain since 1875, the Restoration System was not yet dead. In February 1910, Alfonso XIII (1885–1931) invited the Liberal José Canalejas to form a new administration. Canalejas courted popularity with the Left by introducing a radical package of reforms designed to improve social conditions, such as the abolition of the unpopular *consumos* tax levied on foodstuffs, and he also won plaudits by barring the wealthy from purchasing exemption from military service. However, when Canalejas was assassinated by an anarchist's bullet in November 1912, the 'revolution from above' ground to a halt and the old party structure began to disintegrate. The Conservatives split between those, like Maura, who, bitter at his earlier removal from office, declared his 'implacable hostility' to the Liberals and demanded the reinvigoration of the entire political process, and the majority of the party, who remained committed to the existing order. The latter prevailed, leading to the displacement of Maura as party leader by Eduardo Dato and the latter's appointment as prime minister in October 1913. The Liberals were also beset by severe internal dissension. With the emergence of new political forces, notably the regionalists, Republicans and Socialists, the two-party Restoration System began to seem increasingly anachronistic. Old-style *caciquismo* was still alive and well in many rural districts, but in the towns governments found it impossible to 'choreograph' elections as they had done in the past. The fragmentation of the oligarchical parties made the task of government all the more difficult and forced Alfonso XIII to intervene more frequently in the political process, which in turn exposed him to the charge that he was meddling in the affairs of government.

Spain remained strictly neutral during World War I (1914–18) and enjoyed a period of rapid economic growth (particularly in the industrial and mining sectors) on the back of surging exports to the Allies. Rampant inflation, which by 1918 had reached 62 per cent, led industrial and agricultural workers to demand increased wages and improved working conditions. Levels of affiliation to workers' organizations increased dramatically as a consequence. Membership of the Socialist UGT almost doubled between 1914 and 1920, to reach 211,000 members, while the Anarcho-Syndicalist CNT achieved an even more impressive rate of growth, expanding from an estimated 14,000 members in 1914 to 700,000 by 1919.

In the summer of 1917, Spain was gripped by a new political crisis. Junior army officers, who were feeling the financial pinch as inflation rose steadily, established Military Defence Councils (*Juntas Militares de Defensa*) to press for better pay and the preservation of the system of promotion by seniority, and to demand the immediate 'regeneration' of the political regime. In Catalonia, there was a surge of support for the regionalist parties, notably the Regionalist League, and demands for home rule grew ever shriller. Encouraged by the stance adopted by the *Juntas*, a short-lived coalition of Catalan nationalists, Liberals and Republicans, known as the Assembly Movement, came together in Barcelona in July 1917 to demand fresh elections and add their own calls for 'national regeneration'. To add to the atmosphere of political crisis, a general strike was orchestrated by the UGT and CNT in August to press for higher wages, but it failed to win the support of any of the main political parties and was suppressed by the army. In the aftermath, a number of Socialist leaders were arrested, while other politicians, among them Lerroux, fled the country. The Assembly Movement disintegrated when Cambó of the Regionalist League dropped his demands for reform and instead entered into government with a coalition of Liberals and Conservatives led by Maura. As a consequence of Cambó's desertion of the nationalist cause, the influence of the Regionalist League began to evaporate and was displaced by a number of other Catalanist groups, notably Catalan Action (*Accio Catalá*), founded in 1922, which would campaign for the creation of a Catalan republic within a fully federal Spanish state.

Between 1917 and 1923 the dynastic system struggled on, but political and social divisions in Spain deepened yet further. The *cortes* was suspended on various occasions; no fewer than 15 coalition governments came and went. Revolutionary Anarchists, inspired by the example of the Russian Bolshevik Revolution of 1917, took advantage of the political instability to foment armed revolt against the established order. In Barcelona and other cities, gang warfare broke out between the Anarchists and gunmen hired by local industrialists, leaving hundreds of deaths in its wake. In rural districts, notably in Andalusia, landless peasants demanding better wages and working conditions went on strike, burned crops and called for the breakup of latifundia. In 1919 alone, there were 403 strikes and more than 4 million working days were lost. In 1921, Dato became the third prime minister to fall victim to an Anarchist's bullet. As successive governments tried and failed to get to grips with the spiral of social violence, there was a growing perception, both among Republicans and Socialists, who demanded immediate political democratization, and among the conservative classes, who remained committed to oligarchical rule, that the constitutional system was 'exhausted'. Disillusionment with parliamentary politics among the Spanish population at large manifested itself in widespread political apathy. Between 1918 and 1923, electoral participation slumped from 60 per cent to 42 per cent.

The protracted crisis revived the political role of the military which had lain largely dormant since 1874. During the 'Bolshevik Years' after 1917, the army had watched with mounting alarm as the wave of strikes and violent protests threatened to plunge Spain into anarchy, the increasingly voluble opposition parties attempted to push the parliamentary system towards full-scale democracy, and the rise of regionalist parties appeared to place the very unity of the nation in jeopardy. Where once the army had stood at the forefront of the liberal assault against absolutism, it now saw itself as the protector of national unity and the traditional social order in the land. The final straw, as far as the army was concerned, was yet another military defeat beyond Spain's shores. Under the terms of a treaty of 1913, Spain and France had divided Morocco into two Protectorates. The relatively small Spanish zone, to the north, based upon Tetuán and the coastal strongholds of Tangier, Ceuta and Melilla, encompassed the largely mountainous, arid region of the Rif and Djebala. In July 1921, in the course of operations to pacify the tribes of the Rif, Spanish forces were annihilated at Annual, as a result of which some 14,000 soldiers were killed or taken prisoner. The military defeat prompted an outpouring of national outrage and stripped the government of what little authority or credibility it still possessed. In September 1923, General Miguel Primo de Rivera, one of the most prominent critics of the old system, put the Restoration System out of its misery when he staged a *pronunciamiento* in Barcelona. Alfonso XIII, who had long since lost patience with parliamentary politics, gratefully dissolved the *cortes* and appointed Primo de Rivera as head of a military directorate.

THE DICTATORSHIP OF PRIMO DE RIVERA

The collapse of the constitutional system in Spain was symptomatic of the wider crisis in liberal democracy during the 1920s and 1930s. For the social and economic élites, both in Spain and elsewhere in Europe, authoritarian government came to be seen as a bulwark against full-scale political democracy and the rising power of the working class. Primo de Rivera's *coup* was initially greeted with enthusiasm, not only by the military, industrialists, landowners and clergy, who feared imminent Bolshevik Revolution, but by members of the 'regenerationist' intellectual élite, who had long since argued that the Restoration System was exhausted and in urgent need of renewal. Primo was the 'Iron Surgeon' Joaquín Costa had demanded, who would restore and purify a Spain which had been ruined by corrupt politicians, and would return to the ranks once his task was done. Given the turmoil and bloodshed that had gone before, most people were prepared to regard the general's more authoritarian initiatives –

the suspension of the Constitution of 1876, the curbing of press freedom and trial by jury, the outlawing of strikes, and the restriction of
political activity – as the bitter medicine Spain desperately needed if
stability were to be restored.

Primo's guiding philosophy was founded upon unswerving loyalty
to Church, fatherland (*patria*) and monarchy. Initially, his attempts to
rule by decree, supported by a directorate of fellow generals and an
admiral, and then, from December 1925, by a civil government made
up largely of lawyers and economists, met with some success. In
Morocco, Primo initially contemplated a complete Spanish withdrawal
from the Spanish Protectorate. However, when the leader of the Rif
tribes, 'Abd el-Krim, launched a military assault against the French
Protectorate in 1924, the French and Spanish authorities joined forces
to neutralize the rebellion. In September 1925, Spanish forces carried
out successful landings at Alhucemas Bay, while the French simultaneously launched an assault against 'Abd el-Krim's position from the
south. These offensives paved the way for the defeat of the Berber
tribes and the complete pacification of the Moroccan Protectorate by
1927, an achievement which won Primo considerable plaudits at
home.

On the domestic front, the regime moved decisively to restore the
authority of the central government. Political parties were marginalized though not formally proscribed; the Catalan regional government
was abolished; and the Anarcho-Syndicalist CNT and the Communist
Party were suppressed. In the economic sphere, the government's
highly interventionist policy was guided by the ideal of autarky, the
belief that Spain could flourish as a self-sufficient industrial power. To
this end, the regime sought to protect domestic agriculture and industry by imposing swingeing import tariffs. An ambitious programme of
public investment – backed by higher taxation and major public
borrowing – in roads, railways, dams and irrigation works was also
unrolled, which it was hoped would provide the stimulus for large-
scale industrial growth. Thanks in large part to the upturn in the
European economy at the end of World War I, Spain enjoyed a period
of sharp economic growth, and industrial productivity rose by an
impressive 40 per cent. State-run monopolies were established, such as
Telefónica (the state telephone company) and CAMPSA (an oil and
petrol conglomerate). The foundations of the national tourist industry
were laid with the opening of the first of the *Paradores Nacionales,* a
chain of state-run hotels.

Social policy was equally paternalist and interventionist. The Labour Code, introduced in 1926, which provided subsidized housing and medical care, on the lines of Mussolini's Labour Charter in Italy, was warmly welcomed and helped to dampen the revolutionary ardour of the working classes. There were modest improvements in working conditions. Labour disputes were settled by arbitration committees (*comités paritarios*), at which employers and workers were equally represented. And while the revolutionary CNT was suppressed, Primo for a time enjoyed the active collaboration of the Socialist UGT, whose leader, Francisco Largo Caballero, was appointed to the Council of State. The success of these various measures may be gauged from the fact that the number of strikes fell markedly during this period.

Primo's activities in the political sphere proved far less successful. The general's plans to create a new political system, in which the discredited and discarded dynastic parties would be replaced by a broad-based 'Patriotic Union' (*Unión Patriótica*), were widely criticized. His attempts to forge a new constitution, by summoning an Advisory Congress in 1927, met with failure, since most of the opposition parties refused to play any part in the proceedings. At the same time, Primo's attempts to uproot *caciquismo*, by replacing provincial and municipal governments with army officers, achieved little. After the failure of the Advisory Congress, opposition to Primo's rule began to mount. The Catalan Conservatives, who had originally offered him their support because he represented a defence against revolutionary anarchism, resented Primo's refusal to countenance any form of self-government, as well as his suppression of the Catalan language, and made common cause with the Republican nationalists. The Liberal politicians, who had been unceremoniously removed from office in 1923, demanded the restoration of parliamentary democracy. Leading Liberal intellectuals, such as Miguel de Unamuno, Ramón del Valle-Inclán, José Ortega y Gassett and Vicente Blasco Ibáñez, who had suffered Primo's authoritarianism first-hand, voiced their disapproval of the regime, while university students marched in protest at the lack of free speech, prompting the authorities to close the universities of Madrid and Barcelona altogether. The UGT withdrew its support from the regime and workers protests began to mount. Financiers, landowners and industrialists, alarmed by a deteriorating economic situation from 1929, which led to the devaluation of the peseta, denounced Primo's fiscal irresponsibility. Most important of all, Primo had lost the support of important elements within the army, which was opposed to his attempts at military reform, notably a new system of promotion based upon merit rather than longevity, and that of the king who feared that the dwindling popularity of the regime would tarnish the reputation of the monarchy. In January 1929, there were unsuccessful military uprisings in Valencia and Ciudad Real. In January of the following year, as opposition demands for Primo's removal from office reached a crescendo, the king accepted the general's resignation and Primo went into exile in Paris, where he died shortly afterwards.

Primo de Rivera's successor, General Dámaso Berenguer, pledged a return to constitutional government and relaxed most of the authoritarian controls which Primo had instituted; but the old political consensus could not be restored. Society was becoming more politicized and Berenguer found it impossible to stem the rising tide of republicanism, not only among radical groups but among many of its traditional middle-class supporters. Moreover, as Spain began to feel the full impact of global recession, the flame of workers' militancy was rekindled. By the Pact of San Sebastián, agreed in August 1930, Republicans, Socialists and radical Catalan groups forged a common alliance against the monarchy. In December, Republican elements within the officer corps launched an unsuccessful rebellion in Jaca. When General Berenguer's successor in office, Admiral Aznar, held municipal elections on 12 April 1931, the Republican parties made major gains in the main towns at the expense of their monarchist rivals, whereupon the army high command and the Civil Guard intimated that they were not prepared to prop up the monarchy by force. On 14 April, Alfonso XIII bowed to the inevitable and went into exile. Spain's second Republican experiment had begun.

6

. . . .

The Modern Era, 1931–2000

The advent of the Second Republic heralded the introduction of a fully developed democratic system in Spain. However, deepening political divisions soon emerged between the antagonistic forces of the Left, which demanded social justice, and those of the Right, which feared imminent popular revolution. In July 1936, a military *pronunciamiento* triggered a bloody civil war which was finally resolved three years later in favour of the right-wing Nationalists, led by General Franco. For the next 36 years, thanks in large part to his political acumen, his fierce repression of any signs of opposition, and, not least, the support of the army, the Church and the United States, General Franco was able to maintain his grip on power. During the 1960s, Spain underwent a process of far-reaching economic and social change, but it also experienced a growth in opposition to the regime. By the time of Franco's death in 1975, Spain's boom had ground to a halt, and many among the political and economic élites were of the view that political change was imperative if the nation were to flourish. As a result, from 1976 the structures of Francoism were gradually dismantled and the peaceful transition to democracy was accomplished.

THE SECOND REPUBLIC: 'THE REFORMING YEARS'

When the Second Republic was declared to popular acclaim on 14 April 1931, the prevailing view was that it heralded a 'new dawn' in Spanish politics. Expectations of change were enormous. For those on the Republican Left, the fervent hope was that the new government would break the vice-like grip that the forces of tradition – the army, the Church and the landowning élite – still maintained over the nation and enable Spain to develop into a modern, egalitarian, democratic society. Those on the revolutionary Left – the Anarchists and radical Socialists – were emphatic in their rejection of bourgeois democracy, but were none the less of the opinion that the overthrow of the monarchy did at least represent a decisive step along the road to social justice. For their part, the Catalan nationalists, who had long since chafed at the centralization of political power in Madrid, anticipated that the declaration of the Republic would shortly lead them on the path to self-government. Even many of those on the Centre and Right, who had not taken part in the anti-monarchist coalition of 1930, hurried to clamber aboard the republican bandwagon and agreed that a return to the status quo was not an option, although few held any clear idea as to what direction the fledgeling Republic should take.

The Provisional Government of the Republic was founded upon the same coalition of forces which had coalesced in opposition to the discredited monarchy in 1930. The cabinet was comprised largely of the members of the parties of the Republican Centre and Left, and the Socialists, although the radical bent of that cabinet was tempered by the presence of two Catholic conservatives, the Prime Minister, Niceto Alcalá Zamora, and the Minister of the Interior, Miguel Maura. The authority of the Provisional Government was reinforced by the elections to the constituent *cortes* in June 1931, which resulted in a landslide victory for the parties of the Republican-Socialist coalition. Out of a total of 470 seats, the Socialist Party (PSOE) emerged as the largest single political group with 116 deputies, while assorted regional and Leftist national parties accounted for a further 180 seats. The largest group among the Centre-Right Republicans were the Radicals, under Alejandro Lerroux, who secured 90 seats; the parties of the far Right gained only 45 seats between them.

From the very outset, the reformist aspirations of the new government were constrained by a number of factors. For one thing, the Second Republic was born at a time of severe global economic depression. Against a background of sharply declining exports, rising unemployment and falling incomes, the government – already saddled with a huge budget deficit from the profligate years of the Primo de Rivera dictatorship – lacked the funds it needed if a far-reaching programme of social reform were to be successfully implemented. Economic difficulties were compounded by political divisions. The government was made up of a plethora of parties which shared no common ideology or programme. It would not be long before this uneasy alliance of

Socialists, Leftist Republicans and conservative Catholics would break down in the face of conflicting expectations of change. The traditional élites, having chosen to abandon Alfonso XIII to his fate, were in political disarray, but few felt any great loyalty to the Republic and many were positively hostile to the radical political agenda championed by the Republican-Socialist Left, considering that it posed a direct threat both to their own interests and to those of Spain as a whole. Steering a steady course between the Scylla of popular reformist expectations and the Charybdis of engrained conservative hostility to change would ultimately prove an impossible task.

The new government sought to establish a fully fledged democratic system and to implement a programme of reform that would modernize what were widely regarded as the ossified structures of Spanish society. A new constitution, issued in December 1931, laid down the democratic framework of the new Republic. A unicameral parliament was established; the corrupt electoral practices of *caciquismo* were swept away; and women were awarded the vote for the first time. Constitutional change was accompanied by a wide-ranging programme of social reform. The government was particularly concerned to alleviate the plight of the working class, especially those landless labourers in the depressed agricultural sector, who were suffering the effects of drought and soaring unemployment. Shortly after the Republic was declared, a number of emergency decrees were issued by the Socialist Minister of Labour and leader of the UGT, Francisco Largo Caballero, and the Minister of Justice, Fernando de los Ríos: wages were raised and rents frozen; a statutory eight-hour working day for all labourers was imposed; the 'Decree of Municipal Boundaries' prevented landowners from hiring labour from outside a given municipality if any labourers within its boundaries were unemployed; a Law of Obligatory Cultivation threatened landowners with expropriation of any land they did not turn over for arable use; and, for the first time, rural wages and working conditions were to be decided by arbitration committees known as 'mixed juries' (*jurados mixtos*). Even more alarming, as far as the big landowners were concerned, the government began to draw up a law of agrarian reform by which it hoped to carry out an equitable redistribution of land among the impoverished labourers of the south.

The army was another early target of the government's reforms. The Minister of War, Manuel Azaña, sought to establish a professional army that was efficient, streamlined and, above all, politically neutral.

The grotesquely overlarge officers corps was slimmed down dramatically by retiring some 8000 senior officers on full pay; the number of divisions was halved; the Military Academy in Zaragoza, which was viewed in Republican circles as a dangerous redoubt of reactionary thinking, was closed; promotions awarded during the Moroccan wars were subjected to review, as a result of which some officers were demoted; military judicial authority over civilians was abolished; and last, but not least, all serving officers were required to take an oath of loyalty to the Republic.

The determination of the Republican-Socialist coalition to break the influence that the Roman Catholic Church wielded over society was manifested in Article 26 of the new constitution. Henceforth, the ties that bound Church and state together were to be sundered: government subsidies for the clergy were curtailed; ecclesiastical orders, which had dominated the educational system of the nation, were barred from teaching and a network of 6000 lay schools was set up; divorce was legalized; and the wealth of the Church subjected to taxation. The Church was also the object of a number of vexatious other measures: religious symbols were removed from classrooms and other public buildings; bell ringing and the traditional Holy Week processions were banned. Even worse, as far as the ecclesiastical hierarchy was concerned, full religious freedom was declared, leading Azaña to declare that 'Spain is no longer Catholic'. The hostility of the ecclesiastical hierarchy to these changes fuelled the longstanding belief on the Left that the Church was an obstacle to progress. When anticlericalist mobs in Madrid, Seville and other cities embarked on an orgy of church burning in May 1931, the government adopted only a passive response and refused to call out the Civil Guard. Azaña himself declared that 'all the convents of Madrid are not worth the life of one Republican'. The perceived anticlericalism of the government not only alienated moderate Catholic opinion and helped create the conditions that allowed the emergence of a mass party of the Right, but it led to the resignations of Prime Minister Alcalá Zamora (who was soon appointed to the presidency of the Republic) and Minister of the Interior Maura, as a result of which the premiership passed to Azaña.

The package of reforms introduced by the Republican-Socialist coalition aroused both hostility and fear on the Right. Industrialists feared further radicalization of labour and higher wage demands; major landowners viewed the agrarian reforms as the prelude to collectivization and full-blown Bolshevik revolution; the more reactionary elements among the officer corps condemned Azaña's military reforms as a calculated slight against the integrity and honour of the armed forces; the ecclesiastical establishment, led by the archbishop of Toledo, Cardinal Segura, fulminated against a godless, satanic and evil Republic which was set on the destruction of the Church. Furthermore, the willingness of the government to concede self-rule to Catalonia was damning evidence, in the eyes of the Right, that the disintegration of the nation was nigh. The Right adopted two broad defensive responses to the reformist programme of the Republican-Socialist coalition. There were the so-called 'accidentalists', for whom the 'social content' of any regime was more important than forms of government *per se*. Among them, the most prominent and outspoken was José María Gil Robles, leader of 'Popular Action' (*Acción Popular*), whose primary aim was to use legal means to obstruct the progress of the Republican-Socialist reforms through the *cortes* and to lay the foundations of a mass political party. The 'catastrophists', who included the monarchists who had formerly supported Alfonso XIII, the traditional Carlists, and an assortment of fascist groups, were convinced that nothing less than a violent insurrection would be necessary if the Republic was to be overthrown.

The government also came under intense pressure from the forces of the radical Left. Although Socialists had played a prominent part in the ruling coalition, the Anarcho-Syndicalist CNT, and especially its radical offshoot, the 'Iberian Anarchist Federation' (*Federación Anarquista Ibérica*, or FAI), founded in 1927, which resented the growing influence of the Socialist UGT, was implacably opposed to 'decadent bourgeois democracy' and argued that direct action was the only viable route to social revolution.

Agrarian reform remained a key battleground between the forces of the Left and Right. The response of the big landowners to the measures introduced by Largo Caballero had been either to ignore the government's decrees or to refuse to plant crops altogether. Meanwhile, the rural labour force, egged on by the CNT and the 'Socialist Landworkers' Federation' (*Federación Nacional de Trabajadores de la Tierra*, FNTT), affiliated to the UGT, whose membership had soared from 36,000 members in December 1931 to about 400,000 a year later, was impatient for latifundia to be broken up and collectivized, a radical step which the government would not countenance. The seeming inability of the government to grasp the nettle of agrarian reform brought tensions to boiling point. A general strike called by the FNTT in December 1931 degenerated into bloodshed, when the villagers of Castilblanco in Extremadura murdered four Civil Guards. After much wrangling in the *cortes*, an Institute of Agrarian Reform was set up by the Azaña administration in 1932 to oversee the breakup of all estates over 22.5 hectares in size. But the government lacked the funds to carry out its promises: in the event barely 90,000 hectares were expropriated in this way, outraging the landowners, but doing precious little to ameliorate the lot of the rural poor and causing severe disappointment among the parties of the Left. The timid reforms, declared Largo Caballero, were the equivalent of using 'an aspirin to cure an appendicitis'.

The question of regional self-government was another 'problem of the past' that polarized opinions in Spain. There had been a resurgence in support for Catalan and Basque regionalist parties during the early decades of the twentieth century. On the fall of Alfonso XIII in 1931, the radical Catalan party, the *Esquerra*, under Francesc Maciá, had even declared Catalonia to be a self-governing republic within a federal Spain, but had been forced to back-track. In 1932, the Madrid government sought to defuse the growing separatist clamour in Catalonia by granting a statute of autonomy to the region. Coming on top of the unpopular military and religious reforms, the statute of autonomy helped convince the 'catastrophists' on the Right that the time had come to do away with the Republic. In August 1932, even before the statute was passed, a group of insurgents, under the leadership of the disaffected General José Sanjurjo, raised the flag of rebellion, but his *pronunciamiento* failed to gather any substantial support and was easily quelled by the government.

For a time, at least, it seemed that the crushing of the *Sanjurjada*, as the failed *coup* came to be known, had given the embattled Azaña administration a new lease of life. In the aftermath of the uprising, the contentious statutes of agrarian reform and Catalan autonomy successfully completed their passage through the *cortes*. However, the government's improved standing was severely tarnished in January 1933, when a CNT uprising at Casas Viejas near Cádiz was put down with considerable ferocity by Republican Assault Guards, leaving some 22 peasants dead. The massacre provided yet further proof to those on the far Left that the government was not serious about implementing root-and-branch agrarian reform; to the right-wing press, Casas Viejas, and the mounting wave of rural insurrections that accompanied it, demonstrated that the Republic was fast degenerating into outright anarchy and that stronger 'medicine' was needed if 'social equilibrium' was to be restored. The Catholic middle class was further alienated by the Law of Religious Congregations, which removed the Church's right to teach.

By 1933, as the Republican-Socialist coalition steadily disintegrated, the Right was beginning to organize itself into a credible political force. The Spanish Confederation of Autonomous Rightist Parties (*Confederación Española de Derechas Autónomas*, CEDA), the brainchild of José María Gil Robles, was a coalition of right-wing groups, whose aim was not simply the defence of the Church against the reforms of the Left, but the creation of a conservative Catholic state. Inspired by the examples of Mussolini in Italy and Hitler in Germany, both of whom had come to government via the ballot-box, in 1922 and 1933 respectively, Gil Robles spoke of purging Spain of Socialists and 'Judaizing-freemasons' and looked forward to the day when a new state might be forged: 'Democracy is not an end, but a means to the conquest of the new state', he declared in 1933, 'When the time comes, either parliament submits or we will eliminate it.' Gil Robles's feverish rhetoric stoked up fears on the Left that a CEDA victory in the elections would lead to the destruction of democracy and the creation of a Fascist state in Spain.

THE 'TWO BLACK YEARS'

In the general elections held in November 1933, no party achieved an overall majority, but victory went to Lerroux's Radicals and the CEDA. The electoral rules, which had been designed by the Republican-Socialist coalition to prevent political fragmentation, worked in favour of those parties which organized themselves into broad coalitions. As a result, the Socialists, who had committed the tactical blunder of withdrawing from their alliance with the Leftist Republicans in order to contest the elections on their own, received a bloody nose at the polls, winning only 58 seats, despite the fact that they attracted substantially more votes than any other party; the Leftist Republicans almost disappeared as a significant political force. The parties of the Centre-Right, by contrast, which had closed ranks and contested the election in coalition, maximized their returns: the CEDA gained 115 seats and the Republican Radicals 104. Given the CEDA's implacable hostility towards the Republic, President Alcalá Zamora invited the centrist Radicals, under their leader Lerroux, to form the new administration.

The period which followed, known in Republican and Socialist ranks as the 'two black years' (*bienio negro*), was marked by deepening political and social strife. The new government, a coalition of Centre and right-wing parties, reversed some of the reforms that had been introduced by the Republican-Socialist coalition. Anticlerical legislation was repealed and the Decree of Municipal Boundaries was abolished, allowing the landowners to recruit cheap labour from outside. In December 1933, an Anarchist uprising was put down and the leadership of the CNT and FAI arrested; a general strike called by the FNTT the following June, which was followed by some 200,000 labourers, was crushed with much bloodshed. To make matters worse, in the eyes of the Left, the rebels who had participated in the abortive *coup* of 1932 were granted an amnesty.

Spain, in common with much of Europe at this time, was steadily polarizing into two hostile camps. Despite the best efforts of the Radicals to steer a moderate course, the Right was beginning to flex its muscles and Gil Robles declared that the time had come for the CEDA to take part in government. On 4 October 1934, ignoring the apocalyptic warnings of the Socialists, President Alcalá Zamora relented and the CEDA were awarded three ministerial portfolios in Lerroux's new administration. For the Socialists, already demoralized by their defeat at the polls and by the regressive policies of the new regime, which threatened to wipe out all the gains of the Republican-Socialist coalition, the decision to allow the CEDA into government was the last straw. On 5 October 1934, a general strike called by the UGT, which it hoped would bring the government to its knees and pave the way for revolution, was accompanied by a call to rise from the Catalan nationalists and the republican Left. However, the strike proved a damp squib. The government declared a state of war and called in the army to crush the strike. In Barcelona, the leader of the regional government, Lluis Companys, fearful that Madrid was about to annul the statute of autonomy, proclaimed an independent state of Catalonia, but his act of defiance was soon snuffed out. Only in Asturias, where some 40,000 miners organized themselves into a 'Workers' Alliance' (*Alianza Obrera*) and armed themselves, did the revolt hold for any length of time. The response of the government was to send in contingents of the battle-hardened Spanish Foreign Legion and Moroccan troops under the leadership of General Franco. After two weeks of fierce fighting, the Asturian rebellion was crushed, leaving 1335 dead and nearly 3000 wounded.

Viewed from the Left, the October uprising had been a desperate attempt by the working classes to defend the Republic and halt the advance of fascism; for the Right, the Asturian insurrection was proof that the forces of the Left sought to overthrow the Republic by violent revolution. Political tensions were exacerbated by the deteriorating economic situation and soaring unemployment. Having crushed the October uprising, the government was in no mood to be conciliatory and acted swiftly to bring its perpetrators to book. There were some 40,000 arrests, including Largo Caballero and the leadership of the CNT and FAI; Companys was sentenced to 30 years in prison. At the same time, the government allowed the reforms of the Azaña administration to be eroded yet further: the statute of autonomy in Catalonia was suspended; agricultural wages were cut and rents rose, families were evicted and the system of mixed-juries was abandoned, along with the remaining elements of the statute for agrarian reform.

The defeat of the October rebellion allowed the CEDA to entrench itself in power. By May 1935, the party held no fewer than five cabinet portfolios, with Gil Robles obtaining for himself the post of Minister for War. At Gil Robles's bidding, the army was purged of loyal Republican officers, while the most influential among the 'catastrophists', Generals Franco, Goded and Fanjul, were promoted to key posts. When Lerroux and the Radicals became embroiled in a series of financial scandals which forced them to resign from office and disband as a political group, Gil Robles brought down the government, calculating – incorrectly as it turned out – that Alcalá Zamora, would hand over power to him. But Alcalá Zamora, distrusting Gil Robles's intentions, preferred to dissolve the *cortes* and call new elections for the following February. The anguished Gil Robles appealed to the 'catastrophists' in the army high command to stage a *coup* to propel him to power, only to be told that the time was not yet ripe for military intervention.

Desperate to avoid the political divisions that had allowed the Right into power in 1933, the parties of the Left began to close ranks. The resulting Popular Front was a coalition embracing the various parties of the Republican Left, the Socialists and the two main communist parties: the Communist Party of Spain (*Partido Comunista de España*, PCE) and the revolutionary Communist Workers' Party for Marxist Unification (*Partido Obero de Unificación Marxista*, POUM), founded in 1935. The Popular Front went to the polls in February 1936 warning of the threat of fascism posed by the CEDA and its allies, and promising an amnesty for political prisoners and a speedy return to the reformist programme of 1931. The Right, campaigning under the slogan 'Against the revolution and its accomplices', and backed by a slick, well-funded party machine, described the election as nothing less than a struggle between good and evil, and portrayed the Popular Front as part of a Moscow-backed strategy to implement a Communist take-over in Spain. In the event, the February elections saw the Popular Front, which secured 278 deputies, emerge as victors, the Right gained 124 deputies (88 of which belonged to the CEDA). In terms of votes cast, however, it was a close-run thing. The leaders of the Right refused to accept the result and brought pressure to bear on acting Prime Minister Portela, asking him to declare a state of war. When Portela refused, Alcalá Zamora offered the premiership to Azaña.

THE ROAD TO CIVIL WAR

When Azaña assumed office in February 1936, he initially adopted a conciliatory tone, speaking of his desire to seek 'the re-establishment of justice and peace'. Political prisoners were freed and the government tried to reactivate the programme of reform that had partly been abandoned in 1933. Plans to grant a statute of autonomy to the Basque Country were also tabled. But Azaña's attempts to turn back the clock alienated radicals and conservatives in equal measure. The Socialists, split between Indalecio Prieto, who advocated a return to constitutional government, and the more radical Largo Caballero, 'the Spanish Lenin', did not join the government, leaving Azaña to form an administration based on the parties of the middle-class Republican Left. The radical Socialists and the Anarchist CNT denounced piecemeal 'bourgeois' reformism and increasingly preached the language of violent revolution. Popular expectation among the urban and rural working classes that the Republic would 'make a difference', both to their rights and their living standards, had long since given way to widespread disenchantment with parliamentary democracy. As a result, workers' militancy increased sharply: in the industrial heartlands, there followed a series of strikes seeking better wages and conditions; in the rural south, notably in Extremadura, landless peasants began to occupy the estates of the big landowners. Seemingly unable to keep control, the authority of the government suffered a further blow when Alcalá Zamora was ousted from the presidency at Socialist behest and was replaced by Azaña. Azaña's successor as prime minister, Casares Quiroga, lacked the mettle and prestige of his predecessor. Street violence and tit-for-tat murders, perpetrated by extremist groups such as the right-wing Falange and the Socialist Youth, spiralled out of control and were used by the right-wing press to justify its claim that Spain was lapsing into anarchy.

For its part, the Right, having tried and failed to have the election results overturned, began to conspire to overthrow the Republic. The government tried to reduce the risk of sedition by posting the most staunchly anti-Republican generals well away from Madrid: Franco to the Canary Islands, Goded to the Balearics, and Mola to Navarre. But it was too late. The hard core of the anti-Republican military was now beginning to coalesce around the 'Spanish Military Union' (*Unión Militar Española*), membership of which increased rapidly after the victory of the Popular Front. By this time, the Right had seemingly given up on the CEDA's legalist strategy and Gil Robles's influence had begun to wane. The rising star now was the 'catastrophist' José Calvo Sotelo, leader of the reactionary monarchist group 'Spanish Renewal' (*Renovación Española*). The conspirators, under the nominal leadership of General Sanjurjo (exiled in Portugal) and the active direction of General Mola, began to make preparations for a *coup* and won promises of support from the Falangists and the Carlist militiamen (*requetés*). Against a backdrop of worsening public disorder, whipped up the Falangists, the government seemed paralysed by indecision. The murder of Calvo Sotelo by a group of Republican police officers on 12 July 1936 was the pretext needed for the *coup* leaders to strike.

On 17 July 1936, the Spanish Army in Morocco under General Franco rose in rebellion against the Republican government, to be followed the next day by garrisons throughout Spain. The conspirators were supremely confident that, like Primo de Rivera in 1923, they would quickly be able to crush any resistance and overthrow the government. However, after three days it appeared that the insurrection had failed. The army and Civil Guard were not united; the majority of the military high command, as well as the navy and air force, remained loyal to the Republic; and the experienced Army of Africa under General Franco was stranded in Morocco, prevented by a naval blockade from crossing into Spain. To make matters worse for the conspirators, the uprising

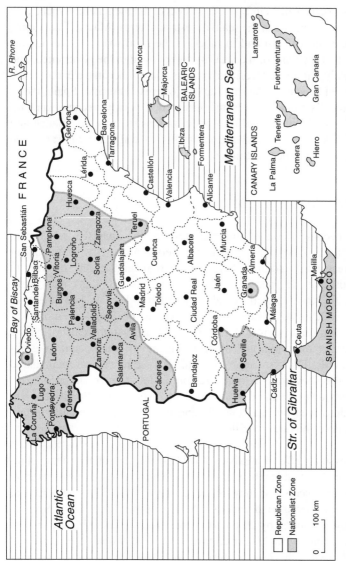
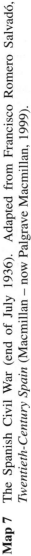

Map 7 The Spanish Civil War (end of July 1936). Adapted from Francisco Romero Salvadó, *Twentieth-Century Spain* (Macmillan – now Palgrave Macmillan, 1999).

prompted fierce popular resistance in many parts of the country. Only in the heartlands of rural Catholic conservatism (Old Castile, Galicia and Navarre) and in a few of the larger cities (Oviedo, Seville and Zaragoza), as well as in Spanish Morocco, did the rebellion meet with immediate success. In the main industrial centres (Madrid, Barcelona, Valencia and Bilbao) and in much of the rural south, the revolt was snuffed out by units of the security forces loyal to the government and by rapidly improvised workers' militias. Once it became clear that they had failed to achieve their military objectives in much of Spain, therefore, the 'Nationalists' (as the insurgents quickly became known), supported by Rightist political organizations such as the Falange and the Carlist *requetés*, had no option but to wage a civil war if the Republic was to be overthrown.

THE SPANISH TRAGEDY

It has become a commonplace to describe the Spanish Civil War in manicheistic terms as a struggle between the 'two Spains' of 'progress' and 'tradition', between 'anarchy' and 'order', or even, in the words of the poet Cecil Day Lewis, between 'light' and 'darkness'. Yet, the political agendas on either side were bewilderingly complex. On the Nationalist side were to be found a number of competing groups, from Alfonsine and Carlist monarchists fighting to preserve the traditional order, to Falangists who sought to establish a modern Fascist state. What united these forces was their shared belief that they were acting to restore law and order, suppress revolutionary anarchy and defend those interests of 'true Spain' that had been destroyed by the Republic and its lackeys. Nationalist propaganda described the rebellion as

> a desperate effort for existence itself, on the part of all the law-abiding and reputable inhabitants of the country to free themselves from the five years' tyranny of misgovernment, fraud, murders and outrages perpetrated under the Second Republic . . . If the Spanish army, supported by all the sane and uncorrupted political elements in the country, had not risen to defend their national inheritance and institutions, the Marxist revolution, instigated by greedy ferocity and determined to destroy the foundations of society, would have broken out in a few days.

The Catholic Church also weighed in on the side of the Nationalists. In a pastoral letter, the bishop of Salamanca declared the Nationalist cause to be a holy crusade, waged against the 'sons of Cain' in defence of the traditional values of the Catholic Church against the atheism, separatism, materialism and anticlericalism of the Republic.

The forces that fought in defence of the Republic were even more complex and volatile. While for the Leftist Republicans the defence of liberal democracy was of uppermost importance, Anarchists, radical Socialists (Largo Caballero's supporters) and some Communists were firmly of the view that social revolution was a priority if the war was to be won. Like the Nationalists, Republican groups used radio and posters to promote a variety of social and political messages: while the Basque and Catalan authorities laid particular emphasis on the quest for autonomy, the Anarchists preached social revolution, and the Communists the war against fascism.

From the outset of the conflict, government and rebels alike were acutely aware that international support would be vital if their cause was to prevail. Within days of the uprising, when it appeared that the *coup* might fizzle out altogether, Hitler responded to appeals for help from General Franco by dispatching German transport planes, together with supplies of arms and equipment, to help airlift the Army of Africa from Morocco into southern Spain. Mussolini, rightly calculating that the British and French were unlikely to take up arms in defence of the Republic, also sanctioned the dispatch of Italian military hardware to assist the Nationalist rebellion. By contrast, the Western democracies rebuffed Republican appeals for help to suppress the revolt. The French prime minister, the Socialist Léon Blum, was sympathetic to the Republican cause, but his coalition cabinet was divided, some ministers fearing that the war in Spain might exacerbate social tensions within France itself, or even spark a wider European conflagration. The Conservative government in Britain, although officially maintaining a neutral stance in the conflict, shared the Nationalists' conviction that a Republican victory would be the prelude to a Communist revolution in Spain, which would threaten its vital strategic and economic interests in the region. British and French attempts to 'seal off' the Spanish conflict led to the Non-Intervention Agreement of August 1936, whereby the European powers imposed an arms embargo on Spain. However, the Agreement was blatantly flouted by Germany, Italy and Portugal, all of whom continued to provide massive military and logistical support for the rebels.

The military intervention of Germany and Italy rapidly tilted the balance of the war in favour of the insurgents. Once on Spanish soil, Franco's experienced Army of Africa was able to advance rapidly through Andalusia and Extremadura. By the end of August 1936, the rebel armies controlled about one-third of the country – a vast semi-circle of territory stretching from Cádiz in the south-west to the Pyrenees – and had even begun to close in on Madrid. In the north, only Asturias and the Basque provinces remained in Republican hands. As the rebel armies advanced, they waged a systematic campaign of terror designed to cow the population into submission. At Badajoz and other places, Republican prisoners were massacred in their thousands. Behind the front lines, Falangist and Carlist death squads targeted known Republican sympathizers, including members of the Popular Front parties, trade unionists and other suspected *rojos* (Reds). The celebrated Granadan poet and intellectual Federico García Lorca, who was loathed by the Right both for his Leftist sympathies and his homosexuality, was the best known of the many thousands who died in this early purge of Republican elements. The Republican zone was not immune from this savage blood-letting either. In the aftermath of the military uprising, there was a violent backlash against the supporters of the Right, as known Falangists, conservative politicians, landowners, employers, and even middle-class Catholics who were suspected of harbouring rebel sympathies, were summarily shot. The Catholic Church, the most visible symbol of conservative opinion in the country, bore the brunt of the violence: churches were sacked or burnt down, and nearly 7000 priests, monks and nuns were killed. These murders were often the work of mobs who acted without official sanction and took advantage of the breakdown of law and order to wreak revenge on their enemies. As the war progressed, however, the restoration of government authority in the Republican zone largely curbed such violent excesses; by contrast, the systematic 'cleansing' of suspected Republican sympathizers in Nationalist-held areas continued, with official sanction, throughout the war and beyond.

That Madrid did not fall to the insurgents in October 1936, as General Mola had confidently predicted, was due partly to the ferocious resistance mounted by the workers' militias and other units who defended the capital, and more especially to the Soviet Union's decision to supply arms and military equipment to shore up the beleaguered Republic. This military assistance did not come cheap. The Republic was obliged to transfer its gold reserves (valued at an estimated $518 million) to Russia. Soviet tanks, planes and military personnel, which had begun to arrive by the middle of October 1936, were supplemented by the International Brigades, contingents of volunteers recruited by the Comintern from all over the world, who shared a determination to halt the rise of fascism. The arrival of the International Brigades (which by early 1937 numbered some 40,000 troops) and, more importantly, Soviet military equipment, kept the Republic in the war. By late November, the Nationalist offensive on Madrid had stalled. Fresh appeals to Germany and Italy for further military aid prompted Hitler to dispatch his crack air force squadron, the Condor Legion, as well as substantial amounts of *matériel*; large numbers of Italian troops (which came to number some 80,000 during the war as a whole) also made their way to Spain. With these reinforcements, the Nationalists were not only able to regroup, but to make further inroads into Republican territory. In February 1937, Málaga was captured by Nationalist and Italian forces; in the spring and summer, General Mola's army, supported by massive German and Italian firepower, overran the northern regions of Asturias, Santander and Vizcaya. Adopting the tactics of co-ordinated ground and air attacks and saturation bombing, which were later to be deployed with such devastating effect in World War II, the Condor Legion paved the way for the Nationalist advance. On 26 April, a German air raid destroyed the Basque town of Guernica killing over 1600 people, an act that was to inspire Pablo Picasso's celebrated denunciation of war, *Guernica*.

THE NATIONALIST ZONE

The initial failure of the July *coup*, and the need to fight a war on several fronts, quickly persuaded the rebel generals of the need to establish a unified command structure. In July 1936, a National Defence Committee was set up in Burgos to co-ordinate military operations. In September, General Franco, by far the most experienced and respected of the rebel leaders, was appointed *Generalísimo*, or commander-in-chief, of the Nationalist Army and head of government. Although Franco himself had proved a hesitant and cautious rebel, joining the uprising only at the very last minute, his feats of arms (from the Moroccan campaigns of the 1920s, to the crushing of the Asturian revolution in 1934, and the relief of the besieged Alcazar of Toledo in September 1936), his indispensable role as interlocutor with

225

Germany and Italy, which had secured vital military aid and prevented the rebellion from being crushed at any early stage, and, not least, his lack of any clear political leanings, had won him the acceptance and admiration of all shades of opinion on the Nationalist side. Franco's rise to power was also helped by the fact that several potential rivals had already fortuitously fallen by the wayside: the nominal leader of the *coup*, General Sanjurjo, died in a plane crash within days of the uprising; his fellow conspirators, generals Goded and Fanjul, were executed by Republican firing squads in August, and José Antonio Primo de Rivera, the founding leader of the Falange, imprisoned in a Republican jail in Alicante, would shortly meet the same fate. Once in power, Franco moved quickly to reinforce his own political authority. Other perceived rivals, such as Gil Robles of the CEDA, the Carlist Manuel Fal Conde and the new Falangist leader, Manuel Hedilla, were respectively ostracized, exiled and imprisoned. The death of the mastermind of the July uprising, General Mola, in a plane crash in June 1937 reinforced Franco's position yet further.

Franco himself was not a political animal: he was fundamentally a conservative traditionalist, who deeply distrusted civilian politicians of all shades and whose rudimentary 'belief system' was dominated by the mantra *Dios, patria, familia* (God, Fatherland, Family). Yet, once Franco was appointed head of state by his fellow generals in September 1936, he quickly became aware of the need to forge both a political ideology and a system which would give cohesion to the Nationalist state and avoid damaging in-fighting between the various factions. In April 1937, the forces who supported the Nationalist cause – the Falangists, Alfonsine and Carlist monarchists, and conservative Catholics – were amalgamated into a single political group, the 'Spanish Traditionalist Falange' (*Falange Española Tradicionalista y de las Juntas de Ofensiva Nacional Sindicalista*, FET-JONS), under Franco's leadership. The Falangists and Carlists were unhappy at their loss of political autonomy, but acquiesced in the interests of the war effort. The new political group appropriated some of the insignia, ideas and institutions of fascism. The Falangist symbol of the yoke and arrows, derived from the insignia of the Catholic Monarchs, was adopted, as was the Fascist-style salute; and the 'Vertical Syndicates', or state trade unions, which in 1938 were merged into a single state-controlled structure, were inspired by Italian Fascist models. Yet, these were largely cosmetic changes designed as a sop to Falangist thinking and as a convenient ideological framework within which Franco's personal rule might be based. The social radicalism and anti-capitalism of the original Falange were discarded; the FET-JONS would not develop a mass political movement, but remain as one among several competing political elements within the regime.

The Church hierarchy also occupied a prominent position in the political life of Nationalist Spain and helped lend legitimacy to the Francoist regime overseas. It was thanks to the efforts of the archbishop of Toledo, Cardinal Gomá, that the Nationalist state secured the recognition of the Vatican in August 1937 and professions of support from Catholic churches around the world. Nationalist ideology and propaganda drew inspiration from Spain's medieval and imperial past: the Nationalist crusade was compared to the Reconquest of the peninsula from the Moors; Franco, the self-styled *Caudillo* (or warrior chieftain), was portrayed as a latter-day El Cid waging a crusade against communism, or as a new Philip II forging the Spanish Empire anew. The Nationalist state itself, which emphasized the need to maintain the unity of the nation, was compared to the Spain of the Catholic Monarchs.

Life in the Nationalist zone was rigidly traditionalist and hierarchical. The Republic's anticlerical reforms were abolished and the Church regained its role as the guardian of the social mores of the community and nation. Women were expected to dress modestly and to adopt traditional roles as wives and mothers, or else to join the social services organized by the 'Women's Section' (*Sección Femenina*) of the Falange. Strict censorship was imposed and 'alternative lifestyles' (such as homosexuality) were not tolerated. The Nationalists waged a fierce propaganda war in Spain and abroad through radio, the press and posters through which they extolled the virtues of 'traditional Spain' and attempted to stir up anti-Communist sentiment.

THE REPUBLICAN ZONE

The July military rising was greeted with popular fury in many parts of Spain. With the government in disarray – no fewer than three cabinets were formed in the space of one day on 18 July – workers took to the streets in vast numbers to demand weapons with which to defend the Republic. In the 'spontaneous revolution' that followed, hastily improvised workers militias (using weapons either seized or distributed by government authorities) defeated the insurgents in most parts of Spain and began to displace the authority of the central government. In much of the Republican zone, political power was appropriated by a plethora of local revolutionary committees. In some areas, particularly in those where the CNT was dominant (Catalonia, Aragon and some parts of Andalusia), agriculture and industry were collectivized; public services were taken over by the workers; and workers' militias took responsibility for the upkeep of law and order, as well as playing a key role in combating the Nationalist offensive. George Orwell, who enlisted in the POUM militia in Barcelona in December 1936, was struck by the revolutionary upheaval he encountered:

> It was the first time that I had ever been in a town where the working class was in the saddle. Practically every building of any size had been seized by the workers and was draped with red flags or with the red and black flag of the Anarchists; every wall was scrawled with the hammer and sickle and with the initials of the revolutionary parties; almost every church had been gutted and its images burnt. Churches here and there were being systematically demolished by gangs of workmen. Every shop and café had an inscription saying that it had been collectivized; even the bootblacks had been collectivized and their boxes painted red and black ... Practically everyone wore rough working-class clothes, or blue overalls, or some variant of the militia uniform ...

The July revolution and the near-paralysis of the Madrid government allowed Catalonia to enjoy considerable autonomy, although co-operation between the Marxist POUM and the anarcho-syndicalist FAI and CNT ensured that it never sought outright independence. Likewise, the conservative Basque provinces of Guipúzcoa and Vizcaya, although virtually untouched by the revolutionary process experienced elsewhere, whose loyalty to the Republic was conditioned largely by their desire to obtain self-government, took advantage of the decay of central government to establish the institutions and machinery of an autonomous Basque state.

The July revolution and the fragmentation of power in the Republican zone were not uniformly welcomed. Quite apart from the Basque conservatives, for whom revolution was anathema, bourgeois Republicans, moderate Socialists and Communists argued that the war effort against the rebels was being undermined by the activities of the revolutionary parties and that the Republic could best be defended if centralized state authority were restored. As it was, although the fiercely independent, frequently ill-disciplined and often poorly armed militias had successfully halted Mola's advance from the north, they proved no match for Franco's experienced African troops. It was in an attempt to channel the revolutionary energies unleashed by the July *coup* into a united war effort and to reassert the power of the central government, that on 4 September 1936 a 'government of victory' was established under the leadership of Largo Caballero. The coalition, which contained six Socialists, two Republicans, three Communists and one Catalan and one Basque nationalist, was later joined by representatives of the CNT and FAI. Yet, for all this show of unity, political in-fighting soon re-emerged. Largo Caballero's sudden 'Damascene conversion' to the cause of bourgeois democracy was regarded with considerable cynicism by many of his fellow Socialists, who remembered his previously intransigent attitude to the governments of the Republic, while his decision to abandon Madrid and establish the headquarters of government in Valencia (November 1936) was regarded as a betrayal by many. Largo Caballero also came into conflict with the increasingly influential PCE. The arrival of large shipments of arms from Russia and the key role played by the Communist-organized International Brigades in the defence of Madrid had helped the PCE to gain considerable prestige.

The attempts of the Communists and their allies to integrate the diverse political factions that existed in the Republican zone and to contain full-blown revolution for sake of anti-Fascist unity, were to bring them into conflict with those groups who continued to argue that revolution was the precondition for the defeat of fascism. Nowhere were these political divisions more evident than in Barcelona, where on 3 May 1937 tensions between the rival factions erupted into all-out war, as the CNT-FAI and the dissident anti-Stalinist POUM struggled for supremacy against the Catalan government police and its allies. After four days of bitter fighting, which led to some 500 deaths, the CNT-FAI prevailed, but it was persuaded by its leadership to desist from further conflict. In the fall-out of the 'May days', as the internecine struggle was known, the anti-revolutionary parties seized the political ascendancy. In October 1937, the power of the CNT – and indeed the cause of Catalan autonomy – were further undermined when the central government moved its headquarters from Valencia to Barcelona. Largo Caballero was replaced as prime minister by Juan Negrín, a moderate Socialist, who allowed the Communists an enhanced role in government. Negrín was determined to galvanize the Republican war effort and was willing to suppress the volatile elements on the revolutionary Left. The anarcho-syndicalists were progressively marginalized from power, revolutionary committees were disbanded and the militias absorbed within the regular army. In Catalonia, a ruthless purge was conducted against the membership of the POUM, whose leader, Andreu Nin, was captured, tortured and later executed.

THE FALL OF THE REPUBLIC

By 1937, the tide of the war had turned decisively against the Republic. A series of major counter-offensives were launched against Nationalist positions (at Brunete in July 1937, Teruel in December 1937, and the Ebro valley in July 1938), but problems of supply soon caused these advances to run out of steam, and the better armed and better supplied Nationalist armies gradually wore the Republican forces down in a grinding war of attrition. By 1938, Republican morale was at rock-bottom. Nationalist troops had reached the Mediterranean, thereby dividing the Republican zone into two. Food shortages were commonplace. The shabby and half-empty shops encountered by George Orwell in Barcelona contrasted with a relative abundance of food in the Nationalist zone, which controlled most of the main food producing areas of the country. By the end of 1938, Madrid and Barcelona were the only major cities still in Republican hands. Negrín appealed to the Western democracies for help, but Britain and France, committed to the appeasement of Germany and Italy, were determined to avoid a wider European conflagration at all costs. While Germany and Italy increased their military support for the Nationalists, Soviet Russia anxious to seek an accommodation with Nazi Germany, began to reduce its support for the Republic and authorized the withdrawal of the International Brigades. Republican defences began to crumble. In January 1939, Barcelona was occupied by the Nationalists with hardly a shot being fired and Catalonia was overrun, as a result of which half a million refugees crossed into France. Still Negrín desperately tried to galvanize resistance, but in Madrid a group of generals, Socialists and Anarchists, led by Colonel Casado, who hoped to negotiate a peace with Franco, formed a Council of Defence, seized power from Negrín and waged a fierce struggle for ascendancy against the Communists.

At the end of March, the Republican Army surrendered. On 1 April, Franco issued his final war bulletin: 'Today, with the Red Army captive and disarmed, the Nationalist troops have attained their final military objectives. The war has ended.'

FRANCOISM TRIUMPHANT

With the conclusion of hostilities, General Franco moved swiftly to consolidate his own political authority and ensure the impregnability of the Nationalist regime. Convinced that he was the only person who could possibly hold Spain together and avoid a return to Republican 'anarchy', Franco was determined to ensure that there would be no resurgence of support for the ideals of 'decadent' liberal democracy, regional nationalism or the revolutionary Left; nor was there to be any clemency for the vanquished. Instead, the brutal purge of Republican sympathizers, which had begun in earnest immediately after the uprising of July 1936, was intensified. The Law of Political Responsibilities, enacted in February 1939, retroactively criminalized (with effect from 1 October 1934) anyone who had supported the Republic or had been affiliated to a Republican political party or trade union. The law even targeted those considered culpable of 'passivity' in the conflict. This legislation, and the supplementary Law for the Suppression of Freemasonry and Communism (March 1940), was vigorously enforced through a system of tribunals. Just how many people suffered in the wave of repression that followed is hard to establish with any precision, given that complete records of executions, imprisonments and other punishments were not kept. Current estimates suggest that between 1939 and 1945 there were upwards of 30,000 executions in Spain (although the number began to tail off after 1942–3), while a further 400,000 people were handed out lengthy prison sentences.

Extrajudicial killings were also by no means uncommon, as private individuals or members of the security forces sought to settle scores with their enemies. Many of those held in prison fell victim to the effects of hunger, torture and disease, among them the celebrated poet Miguel Hernández, who died from tuberculosis while in prison in Alicante in 1942. Other victims of the Nationalist purge were dismissed from their jobs, exiled, fined, suffered confiscation of property or loss of citizenship, or were organised into 'Labour Battalions' and forced to work on public building projects. For example, between 1940 and 1959, some 20,000 political prisoners were employed in the construction of El Valle de los Caídos (The Valley of the Fallen) north-east of Madrid, a vast monastery carved into the Gredos mountains, topped with an immense concrete and granite cross, which was designed to act as a monument 'to the memory of those who fell in the Crusade of Liberation', as well as a mausoleum for the remains of the founder of the Falange, José Antonio Primo de Rivera, and, ultimately, those of Franco himself. There was to be no memorial to the Republican dead.

A climate of fear thus pervaded post-war Spain. In order to secure a job or a ration card, citizens were required to demonstrate their loyalty to the regime by obtaining an official certificate or a letter signed by a person accredited by the authorities. An elaborate network of internal surveillance was established across the country in order to keep a lid on potential dissent, while state propaganda warned Spaniards to be on their guard against the 'enemy within'. Meanwhile, any vestigial hopes among the vanquished Republicans that Franco might soon be over-thrown were quickly dampened. The Republican government-in-exile became mired in a series of factional quarrels, while those guerrilla bands that attempted to continue the war against the Nationalist regime from mountain bases within Spain were neutralized by a vigorous counter-insurgency campaign. For the bulk of the population, trauma-tized by three years of vicious civil war, cowed by repression, and suffer-ing the effects of extreme economic hardship, there was precious little appetite for a renewal of the armed struggle between Left and Right.

Political repression went hand in hand with a policy of rigorous cultural homogenization designed to cement the unity of Spain. In local administration, education, commerce, the media and all cultural activities, the use of Basque, Catalan and Galician was prohibited. In Catalonia, the civil governor set a deadline of 15 September 1939 for all public notices, advertisements and documents in Catalan to be replaced by others in 'the national language', that is, Castilian; those institutions unable to replace headed notepaper in Catalan because of paper shortages were instructed to stamp 'Up with Spain!' (¡Arriba España!) in large red letters over the offending text. Civil servants or teachers who flouted the order faced immediate dismissal. Not only was the use of Basque, Catalan and Galician proscribed outside the home, but the ban even extended to traditional manifestations of regional culture such as music and dance. State propaganda trumpeted the notion of *hispanidad*, emphasizing the racial and cultural superiority of the Spanish-speaking world.

Keen to cultivate in the population a sense of eternal Spanish values, the regime none the less encouraged political apathy among the masses. Despite the triumphalist rhetoric, there would be no attempt to politicize the population at large as had occurred under the Republic. Meanwhile, the Catholic Church, which with the army formed one of the two principal pillars of the Franco regime, lent its enthusiastic support to a campaign of 'moral regeneration' designed to curb the anticlericalism that had taken root among the masses during the preceding decades. In the sphere of education, lay schools were abolished with the aim, as one inspector put it, of moulding Spaniards who were 'profound believers and austere patriots'. The Church also became the arbiter of public morality: divorce, contraception, abortion and civil marriage were all outlawed, and strict censorship was enforced. The Church was able to disseminate its moral message through its own newspapers, such as the influential national daily *Ya*, and its radio station COPE.

The Nationalist victory, and the Church's reassertion of its position of moral authority over the population as a whole, impacted hugely on the lives of Spanish women, in particular. Influenced, in part, by the pronatalist attitudes of the regime, which viewed an expanding population as a manifestation of national strength, and by its own deeply patriarchal view of society, the Church promoted the family as the basic unit of social stability and organization, and exalted the stereotype of the 'perfect married woman' (*la perfecta casada*), who served the nation by selflessly devoting herself to husband and home, as well as watching over the moral and spiritual welfare of her children. Various incentives, in the form of family allowances, health assistance and exemption from school fees, were offered to those large families (*familias numerosas*) which had four or more children. This cult of domesticity was accompanied by a series of legal measures designed to reinforce wives' subordination to their husbands. Males were legally recognized as the head of household, with the result that wives had to secure their husbands' permission if they wanted to enter paid employment, open a bank account, buy and sell goods, or travel abroad. Married women were also debarred from entering paid employment, although the policy was not rigorously imposed in all areas, such as agriculture. In some sectors, for example banking, women who married could be summarily dismissed.

The post-war period was brutally hard for much of the Spanish population. With agricultural production depressed and the transport system in tatters, food shortages were rife, particularly in urban areas, and strict rationing had to be introduced. It is estimated that as many as 200,000 people may have died from the effects of hunger and disease between 1939 and 1945. To these problems were added those of falling wages, spiralling inflation and a flourishing black market. As living standards deteriorated, beggars thronged the main cities and prostitution is reported to have increased ten-fold. Camilo José Cela's novel *La Colmena* (The Beehive), published in 1951, provides a gloomy evocation of the poverty and despair of post-war Madrid.

The regime attempted to breath new life into Spain's moribund economy by drawing up a 'National Programme for Resurgence'. Drawing inspiration from the policies essayed by Primo de Rivera and Mussolini, Franco's post-war economic programme was underpinned by the principles of autarky and state intervention. Direction of the economy was entrusted to the hands of military men, who saw to it that almost all areas of activity – including wages, prices and the exchange rate – were strictly controlled. Among the plethora of bodies which supervised economic activity, were the National Wheat Service, which was set up in 1937 to regulate wheat production and prices, and the Institute of National Industry (INI), established in 1941, whose task it was to encourage new manufacturing initiatives. However, the effects of these policies were disastrous. Although higher tariff barriers, import controls and the artificially high exchange rate of the peseta successfully cocooned Spanish landowners and industrialists from foreign competition, they also stifled private initiative. Agricultural and industrial production remained stagnant, traditional exports (such as wine, olive oil, citrus fruits and vegetables) slumped, and it became increasingly difficult for landowners and industrialists to import the fertilizers, machinery, raw materials and spare parts they needed to modernize. The only way the regime could find to increase agricultural yields was to encourage migrant peasants to return to the countryside and bring marginal areas under the plough once more. Between 1935 and 1945, the proportion of the total active population employed in agriculture rose from 44.6 per cent to 50.3 per cent. In short, the effect of autarky was to retard Spain's economic development: it would not be until 1954 that GDP per capita recovered to the levels of 1929.

Once the Civil War was over, the diverse political 'families' who had joined together in opposition to the Second Republic – the

Falangists, Alfonsine and Carlist monarchists, and Catholic conservatives – began to jockey for position in Franco's 'New State'. In his first post-war cabinet, appointed in August 1939, Franco tried to balance these interests by distributing ministerial portfolios among the competing factions. The armed forces also played a particularly prominent role in the apparatus of government. Between 1938 and 1957, nearly half of the ministerial posts were held by members of the military; other high-ranking officers secured influential positions in the civil service and large corporations. Franco himself remained above the fray as impartial arbiter, happy to encourage the belief that he alone could hold Spain together. It was by successfully balancing the interests of the competing 'families' that made up the Movement (as the regime became known), and indeed by encouraging their differences, that Franco was able to remain in power for so long.

SPAIN AND WORLD WAR II

The first major test of Franco's mettle as statesman came with the German invasion of Poland and the outbreak of World War II in September 1939. The Movement itself was utterly split on the issue: while the Falangists, notably the Foreign Minister, Ramón Serrano Suñer, pressed for Spain to enter the war in support of Germany and Italy, and many thousands of Spanish volunteers (the 'Blue Division') later took part in the German invasion of Russia, the monarchist lobby within the regime argued equally forcefully that Spain should seek a rapprochement with Great Britain. Franco's reaction was typically cautious. Although sympathetic to the cause of the Axis powers, Germany and Italy, and contemptuous of the 'decadent' bourgeois democracies, the *Caudillo* was in no rush to commit himself to either side, declaring Spain to be neutral in the conflict and providing minerals and other supplies to Axis and Allies alike. By June 1940, however, his position had shifted. With German forces triumphant on mainland Europe, Franco indicated a willingness to enter the war on the side of the Axis: in return he demanded territory in French Morocco, as well as massive military and economic aid with which to rearm Spain's depleted and under-equipped forces. These terms were reiterated when Franco met with Hitler at Hendaye on the Hispano-French border on 23 October 1940, by which time Spain had declared itself to be 'non-belligerent' in the conflict. But the Germans were unwilling to foot the bill for Spanish modernization and rearmament, and viewed Franco's imperialist ambitions in North Africa with suspicion, with the result that talks between the two soon foundered.

What has been aptly described as Franco's 'crab-like approach' to relations with the Axis was dictated partly by his fervent belief that his demands were entirely reasonable, given Nationalist Spain's role in crushing the 'Communist Menace' in Western Europe, but also by the need to satisfy the competing factions within the regime. By 1940, political rivalries between the Falangists, who sought greater party control over government, and the large conservative clique of Catholics, monarchists and military leaders, had reached new heights. When a group of Falangists threw a hand grenade at a Carlist gathering near Bilbao in August 1942, Franco was quick to intervene: Serrano Suñer was dismissed as Foreign Minister and one of the Falangist agitators was executed. Even when the Axis tide appeared to have turned, after the German defeat at Stalingrad in February 1943, Franco preferred to sit tight. When the heir to the throne, Don Juan de Borbón, son of Alfonso XIII (who had died in 1941), wrote to Franco in 1943 suggesting that the time had come to restore the monarchy, Franco demurred.

By 1944, however, seeing which way the wind was blowing, Franco began to court Allied favour. He emphasized his anti-Communist stance and vigorously denied that his regime was, or ever had been, Fascist. In order to reinforce this impression, the Fascist salute and some of the other Falangist symbolism adopted by the regime were abandoned and the traditional ideology of National Catholicism came to the fore. The Falangist Foreign Minister, José Felix Lequerica, was replaced by the Catholic conservative Alberto Martín Artajo. As so often, the regime would evolve not by changing its political structures, but by changing personnel according to the circumstances and requirements of the time. Franco also attempted to give the regime a veneer of constitutional legitimacy by summoning the *cortes* in 1943 and by issuing the 'Charter of the Spaniards' (*Fuero de los Españoles*), which set out Spaniards' supposed rights and duties within the regime, in 1945. This, along with the various elections that were held to municipal councils and the *cortes* in 1945–6, was an exercise in what the regime liked to call 'organic popular democracy'. But the Western powers remained unimpressed. When the United Nations was created in June 1945, Spain was excluded from membership. A Tripartite Note issued by Britain, France and the United States the following year condemned the Franco dictatorship as a Fascist regime and most member states of the UN (with the notable exceptions of Argentina, Ireland, Portugal and the Vatican) withdrew their ambassadors and called for its substitution by a democratic regime. The allies also ensured that Spain was excluded from the post-war European Recovery Programme known as the Marshall Plan. Yet, though they condemned Franco, the Western Allies had no intention of toppling him, fearing the consequences of a new military conflict and the resurgence of Communist power in Spain. By portraying the decision of the United Nations as a new foreign conspiracy to destroy Spain, by constantly reminding his factious supporters and the country at large of the consequences if the 'Red Menace' were allowed to reappear, and comfortable in the knowledge that neither the Allies nor the UN would support any external intervention to overthrow him, Franco was able to entrench himself in power. Besides, even as Spain was cold-shouldered by the UN, it could rely on the solidarity and support of Perón in Argentina and Salazar in Portugal.

In 1947, a Law of Succession was drafted which confirmed that Franco would be Head of State for the rest of his life, but stipulated that institutionally the Spanish state was henceforth a kingdom and that in the fullness of time Franco would appoint a member of the Spanish royal dynasty as his successor. The Law of Succession was designed to appease the influential monarchist faction within the government and to sideline Don Juan de Borbón, whose pronouncements against the regime were an increasing irritant to Franco. None the less, it came as something of a disappointment to those Spanish monarchists who had fondly believed that a Bourbon restoration was imminent, and to the Falangists who were opposed to monarchy *per se* and hankered after the creation of an authoritarian state. But Franco pressed on regardless. The law was approved by the *cortes* and, as if to underline Spain's democratic credentials in the eyes of the rest of the world, by a popular referendum held in July 1947.

THE 'SENTINEL OF THE WEST'

By 1950, General Franco's grip on power was tighter than ever. Within Spain, the Falangist and monarchist 'families' had fallen into line behind the *Caudillo*, despite the misgivings they harboured about Franco's plans for the succession. Internationally, Spain had been

237

diplomatically ostracized, but attitudes towards the pariah regime were beginning to shift. As tensions between the Soviet Union and the major Western powers (notably the United States) steadily increased towards the end of the decade, Spain's potential importance as a strategic bulwark against Communism in Southern Europe was increasingly recognized. The authoritarian nature of Spain's political system, which had led the world to ostracize Spain, was now conveniently overlooked and encouraged a thawing of relations. In November 1950, the UN General Assembly authorized its members to re-establish diplomatic relations with Spain, while a US delegation visited Spain and approved a loan of $62.5 million. In 1953, by the terms of the treaty known as the 'Pacts of Madrid', the United States was granted airbases at Morón de la Frontera in Andalusia, Torrejón de Ardoz near Madrid, and Zaragoza, and the naval base of Rota, near Cádiz, in return for which Spain received substantial economic aid (amounting to some $625 million between 1953 and 1957); the treaty also opened the way for US companies to invest in Spain. The treaty with the United States was not uniformly welcomed within the regime, but it marked the international rehabilitation of Spain and Franco's transformation from post-war dictator to the 'sentinel of the West', as one fawning newspaper editor put it. To crown his achievement, a concordat was signed with the Vatican in August 1953, and two years after that Spain was finally admitted as a full member into the United Nations.

Spain's international rehabilitation could not mask her deepening economic crisis. By the mid-1950s, the failings of Franco's experiment in economic autarky were plain for all to see. While American loans and increased foreign investment after 1953 had helped paper over the cracks and allowed industrial production to rise, agricultural productivity remained sluggish, for all the subsidies that had been lavished on the sector; food and fuel shortages were commonplace until rationing was abolished by the middle of the decade; and inflation had risen sharply, with the result that living standards had deteriorated yet further. Economic instability prompted a wave of strikes in support of higher wage claims. Franco was a reluctant reformer, suspicious of change and its consequences. Loosening the straitjacket of autarky was an admission of failure; economic liberalization was anathema to a man for whom control was everything. But by the latter half of the 1950s, Franco was increasingly of the opinion that if the regime was to continue, important structural changes would be necessary if Spain was to fulfil her economic potential. Accordingly, when Franco reshuffled his cabinet in February 1957, he balanced the inclusion of old-style Falangist hard-liners in the key ministries of the Interior and Foreign Affairs with the incorporation of a team of lawyers and economists to the key ministries of Agriculture, Industry, Public Works, Commerce and Finance. These technocrats, many of whom belonged to the conservative Catholic lay organization Opus Dei, represented a new breed of minister, in that, while fully subscribing to the political and social attitudes of Francoism, they were acutely aware of the need to bring about major structural reform if the transition from autarky to a full-blown capitalist market economy was to be achieved.

CHANGE AND ITS CONSEQUENCES

The cabinet reshuffle of 1957 marked a decisive moment in the development of the Franco regime. Thereafter, although he continued to exercise supreme authority, Franco was increasingly happy to distance himself from much of the day-to-day mechanics of government, leaving his trusted right-hand man, Admiral Luis Carrero Blanco, at the head of the Presidency of Government to formulate and oversee policy, while economic matters were delegated to the Economic Co-ordination and Planning Office. The latter was responsible for drawing up the Plan for Economic Stabilization and Liberalization of February 1959. The principal objectives of the Plan were to keep inflation in check and provide the conditions that would lead to rapid industrial growth and the creation of a modern capitalist economy. To achieve these 'conditions', the planners proposed, among other things, to cut public expenditure, remove agricultural subsidies, devalue the peseta and liberalize foreign investment and trade. Francoist die-hards opposed the programme, fearing that economic liberalization would lead to a resurgence of political dissent and weaken the regime's hold on power; but such was Spain's economic plight by 1959 that even Franco reluctantly concluded that reform was imperative.

In the short term, the effects of the Plan were not encouraging: industrial production slumped and unemployment soared, to reach 34.7 per cent in 1960. However, the impact of this economic downturn was soon eased by a surge in inward investment, most of it from Western European companies attracted by government incentives and Spain's low-wage work-force. Foreign exchange earnings were also boosted by Spain's rapidly expanding tourist industry, as visitors from prosperous Northern Europe began to flock to Spain's Mediterranean resorts. Between 1959 and 1963, the number of tourists to Spain increased from 4 million to 14 million; by the end of the decade the figure had reached over 30 million. The economy was further stimulated by rapid growth in the industrial and service sectors, rising exports and the remittances of the one and a quarter million Spaniards who found alternative and far better remunerated employment in the booming economies of Western Europe. These developments helped the Spanish economy to grow by leaps and bounds. Between 1960 and 1973, gross domestic product grew by an average of 7 per cent per year and average incomes trebled. 'Never has so much been achieved in so short a time', declared one of the chief architects of the economic transformation, Laureano López Rodó.

Spanish society was to experience a period of sudden and vertiginous change as a result of the so-called 'economic miracle' of the 1960s. Rising wages and improved living standards for the majority of the population meant that the 'Hungry Forties' were becoming an increasingly distant memory, even if the gap between rich and poor grew ever wider during the course of the decade. As the economic planners had intended, Spaniards were steadily integrated into a modern consumer society. While in 1960, only 4 per cent of Spanish households had a fridge, by 1973 the figure had reached 82 per cent; the proportion of households which owned a car increased from 4 per cent to 38 per cent during the same period. Rapid industrialization and the growth of the service sector gave birth to a new and rapidly expanding middle class; it also triggered massive rural depopulation. An estimated two and a half million Spaniards, one half of the total rural workforce, the majority of them from the depressed rural areas of Andalusia and Extremadura, abandoned the countryside during the 1960s and migrated to the cities or to the industrial and service centres of Northern Europe. Urban growth brought with it grave social problems, as the newcomers settled in *chabolas* (shacks) or in the jerry-built towerblocks which mushroomed around the main cities. By 1970, only 22.8 per cent of the total active population was still engaged in agriculture. None the less, mechanization, improved irrigation, a drive to consolidate fragmented landholdings, and the intensification of livestock husbandry all contributed to a rise in agricultural production.

Another consequence of the economic transformation was a gradual shift in social attitudes and behaviour. There was, for example, a gradual relaxation in the regime's policy towards women. The rapid expansion of the service sector, in particular, led the number of women taking up employment to almost double, from 2.4 million in 1960 to reach 4.6 million by the middle of the 1980s. From 1963, marriage was no longer regarded as a sackable offence; in 1975 the role of the husband as head of family was abolished.

Growing economic prosperity, as well as the ever-present threat of repression, helped to ensure the continuity of the regime. Franco himself continued to hark back nostalgically to the 'glorious Crusade' in his public addresses, but state propaganda, articulated through television, the press and the official 'NO-DO' newsreels, began to adapt its message to reflect the changing times. If hitherto it had been Franco's role as saviour of the nation that was emphasized, now Spaniards were reminded of the unprecedented prosperity that the 'peace of Franco' had provided. The regime hoped that increased affluence and the emergence of a mass consumer culture, dominated by film, television and football, would induce political apathy among the population. In fact, by the late 1960s there was a marked increase in anti-government protest, as a population whose lifestyle increasingly resembled those of its European neighbours began to hanker after the political freedoms they were denied. As the official vertical syndicates lost influence to the clandestine Communist 'Workers Commissions' (*Comisiones Obreras*, CCOO), workers protests and strikes, designed to secure better pay and working conditions, proliferated. University campuses, which underwent a considerable expansion during the course of the 1960s, became hotbeds of left-wing student protest. A new generation of ecclesiastical leaders, influenced by the liberalizing Second Vatican Council (1962–5), began to distance the Church from the regime and began to place new emphasis upon the need for social justice.

The regime was also faced by a resurgence of regional nationalism. In Catalonia, a movement of cultural revival became the focus of opposition to the regime and attracted support from a wide range of political forces. By far the most powerful challenge, however, was posed by the separatist group *Euskadi Ta Askatasuna* (Basque Home-land and Liberty or ETA) which sought the outright independence of the Basque region. Founded in 1958–9, ETA originated as a radical offshoot of the conservative Basque National Party (PNV). In 1968, it began an armed struggle against the regime. Alarmed by the rise in dissent, Franco promptly denounced the demonstrations as the work of Soviet-backed elements who were 'anti-Spain' and sanctioned an increase in repressive measures. But these failed to stem the rising tide of protest. When the regime applied for associate membership of the European Economic Community (EEC) in 1962, the Western democracies, horrified by Franco's repressive policies, rejected his overtures.

During the second half of the 1960s, the regime appeared torn in two directions. On the one hand, there were a series of timid liberalizing gestures, designed to give the impression to the world that Spain was an open, pluralist society; at the same time, the regime remained determined to suppress the growing chorus of internal dissent. The official students' union was dissolved and university lecturers who took part in pro-democracy meetings were expelled from their posts. The censorship laws were overhauled with a new Press Law (1966), which, by leaving it to editors to censor their material, was in many respects even more restrictive than before. Far from trying to establish the conditions that would allow a growing political pluralism, Franco and his closest advisors were seeking to ensure the self-perpetuation of the regime. In 1961, Franco had indicated that legislation would shortly be drawn up which would map out the structure of the post-Francoist monarchy. However, it was not until November 1966 that the Organic Law of State was finally promulgated. The Law fulfilled the promise first made in 1947, when it had been determined that Franco would be succeeded as head of state by a member of the Spanish royal family, but it also provided the institutional framework which would ensure the continuity of the system Franco had founded. In order to demonstrate Spain's democratic values, the Organic Law was approved by popular referendum. However, after further prevarication, it was not until January 1969 that Franco officially designated Prince Juan Carlos, grandson of Alfonso XIII, as his successor.

By the early 1970s, Francoism was in crisis. Although Franco considered that he had done enough to ensure the survival of the regime, famously boasting that he had left everything 'all tied down, well tied down' (*atado y bien atado*), splits had emerged between those members of the political class who favoured a gradual liberalization of policy, and the Francoist *inmovilistas*, or die-hards, within the Movement – nicknamed 'the Bunker' by the opposition, in allusion to the last days of the Nazi regime – who regarded any attempt to carry out political reform as a betrayal of the *Caudillo* himself. By now, Franco himself was suffering from the debilitating effects of Parkinson's disease and was unable to play much part in the business of government. In 1973, he withdrew almost entirely from affairs of state, appointing Carrero Blanco, for so long his loyal *alter ego*, as head of government.

Meanwhile, opposition to the regime, articulated by students, workers and even members of the Church, was on the increase. In December 1973, an ETA car bomb assassinated Carrero Blanco as he returned from Mass. Franco named the authoritarian Minister of the Interior, Carlos Arias Navarro, as the next head of government. The new government was subjected to unprecedented levels of protest from wide sectors of society and the overthrow of the Portuguese military government in April 1974 added to the expectations of change. The execution of two ETA activists and three members of the left-wing 'Revolutionary Antifascist and Popular Front' (*Frente Revolucionario Antifascista y Popular*, FRAP) in November 1975 was greeted with outrage both within Spain and abroad, and fuelled social and political tensions.

THE TRANSITION TO DEMOCRACY

General Franco died on 20 November 1975 after a long drawn-out illness. In his final political testament to the nation, which he had drawn up the previous October, he urged Spaniards to demonstrate their support for his successor, Prince Juan Carlos, and not to forget that 'the enemies of Spain and of Christian civilization are on the alert'. As Franco had planned, the institutions already in place ensured that the change-over of power was smoothly managed. Prince Juan Carlos was crowned King of Spain two days later and swore to uphold 'the principles which inform the National Movement', although he also adopted a conciliatory tone by serving notice that he would endeavour to overcome the divisions of the Civil War and seek social reconciliation. In the short term, however, there was little in what the new king said or did that suggested that he was about to become the 'motor of change'. The hard-line Arias Navarro was confirmed in office and a new cabinet appointed which, though it contained a sprinkling of reformists, namely José María de Areilza, Manuel Fraga and Antonio Garrigues at the ministries of Foreign Affairs, Interior and Justice respectively, included a good number of hard-liners too. The opposition was deeply underwhelmed by the new ministerial team, prompting the leader of the Communists, Santiago Carrillo, to jibe that the new king would be remembered as 'Juan Carlos the Brief'. For his part, the timid Arias tried and failed to steer a political course between the intransigent members of 'the Bunker', the reformists and an increasingly vociferous opposition which clamoured for a 'democratic break' with the past and an immediate transition to full parliamentary democracy. When, in June 1976, the Francoist *cortes* refused to accept the reform of those articles of the Penal Code which outlawed political activity, Arias resigned from office.

The appointment by King Juan Carlos of the 43-year-old Adolfo Suárez as the new Prime Minister came as a considerable surprise to die-hard Francoists and opposition alike. Vice-secretary of the National Movement, and former civil governor and director of state television and radio, Suárez's Francoist credentials were impeccable. Yet, it was Suárez, the supreme pragmatist, who, with the king's support, was to be the architect of the series of rapid political reforms that would establish a modern pluralist democracy in Spain. He was helped in this task by the fact that by late 1976, the majority opinion within the political establishment was that the old institutions of Francoism had served their time and that a political accommodation with at least some elements of the opposition was urgently needed. When the Francoist *cortes* passed the Law of Political Reform in November 1976, thereby effectively voting itself out of existence, it paved the way for democratic change. In a popular referendum held the following December, the government's reforms received the overwhelming backing of 94.2 per cent of those who voted. In the succeeding months, the institutions of Francoism were gradually dismantled: the *cortes* was dissolved and the National Movement disbanded; political parties were legalized, including the Communist Party in April 1977; and political prisoners were released. These changes took place against a background of an unprecedented wave of political violence. In January 1977, five Communist labour lawyers were murdered by right-wing assassins; meanwhile, ETA, which remained committed to the armed struggle for Basque independence, stepped up its campaign of violence.

On 15 June 1977, a general election was held. The election was contested by the long-established parties of the Left, notably the Socialists and Communists, as well as a number of hastily formed parties of the Centre-Right, which were made up of former Francoists, such as the ex-minister Manuel Fraga, who founded the Popular Alliance (*Alianza Popular*, AP). Suárez himself founded the Union of the Democratic Centre (*Unión del Centro Democrático*, UCD), a loose coalition of Liberals, Social Democrats and Christian Democrats. A number of moderate regionalist groups also contested the elections, such as the PNV in the Basque Country and a coalition of Catalan centrist politicians, Convergence and Democratic Union of Catalonia (*Convergència i Unió Democrática de Catalunya*, CiU), under the leadership of Jordi Puyol. The clear winners of the election were the UCD with 166 seats (34 per cent of the vote) and the PSOE with 118 seats (28 per cent). The parties most closely associated in voters' minds with the past – the Communist PCE, which secured 20 seats (9 per cent) and Fraga's AP, which won 16 seats (8 per cent) – were decisively routed.

Suárez's victory allowed him to press ahead with his programme of reform. However, as in 1931, the circumstances for his reformist government were far from propitious. The oil shock of 1973, when the price of crude oil rose by almost 500 per cent, had plunged Spain into deep recession; unemployment had soared; by 1977, inflation had reached 26.4 per cent; strikes, student demonstrations and political violence remained rife. What saved Suárez and the fragile reform process was that political leaders of all shades showed a remarkable willingness to compromise. Aware that articulating the traditional revolutionary rhetoric of the Left would be counter-productive, in that it was likely to provoke the army into issuing a new *pronunciamiento*, Socialists and Communists alike trod a careful path and dropped their insistence upon a clean break with the past, referring instead to the need for a 'negotiated break' (*ruptura pactada*). In October 1977, a series of agreements between government and opposition, known as the 'Pacts of Moncloa', bore witness to this new spirit of compromise. In an attempt to ease inflationary pressures on the economy, leaders of the Socialist UGT and Communist CCOO unions agreed to rein in excessive wage demands by their members and they also sanctioned major cuts in public spending; in return, the government promised to introduce tax reforms and a package of measures designed to create employment, although in the event it did little to carry out its side of the bargain.

The problem of regional nationalism was to prove altogether a harder nut to crack. In the short term, the government tried to assuage nationalist aspirations by establishing regional governments in Catalonia, the Basque Country and Galicia. Meanwhile, a seven-man parliamentary committee, representing most of the main currents of democratic political opinion, set about drawing up a new constitution which would not only enshrine the basic democratic rights of Spaniards, but delineate the structures of the new democratic state. In tune with the spirit of the times, the constitution which resulted from the committee's deliberations was a compromise document. The Spanish state was established as a democratic parliamentary monarchy with a bicameral legislature elected by universal suffrage. The king was recognized as Head of State and Commander-in-Chief of the armed forces, but with no authority over the Prime Minister. With the Church's blessing, Spain became a non-confessional state. While trumpeting the 'indissoluble unity of the Spanish nation, common indivisible fatherland of all Spaniards', the constitution tried to meet one of the key demands of the regional nationalists by decentralizing political power. The 'historic nationalities' – the Basque Country, Catalonia and Galicia – were awarded statutes of autonomy, with extensive powers over education, policing and tax, and the door was left open to other regions to assume a measure of self-rule. By 1983, Spain was established as a quasi-federal state, comprising 17 autonomous regions (*autonomías*), in addition to the two North African enclaves of Ceuta and Melilla.

The granting of autonomous powers to all Spanish regions, known jocularly as a policy of 'coffee all round' (*café para todos*), was regarded with suspicion in the Basque and Catalan regions, but it at least helped reassure reactionary elements within the military that the new democratic regime was not hell-bent on the destruction of the nation. On 6 December 1978, the constitution was approved by 88 per cent of the voting population. In the Basque Country, however, where memories of Francoist repression were fresh and some still aspired to outright independence, public opinion was more lukewarm and many abstained. The following March, fresh elections were held which confirmed the political ascendancy of the UCD and PSOE, which secured 168 and 121 seats respectively, while support for the AP declined.

The transition to democracy was the product of a complex series of circumstances. The growing demands for change among a young, expanding society – itself the product of the economic boom of the 1960s – was undoubtedly important, but so too was the recognition among the political and economic élites that the structures of Francoism were in decay and that political change was essential if Spain's future prosperity was to be guaranteed. In addition, there was the willingness among most of the military to countenance political change, once it became clear that democracy would not lead to revolution or to the

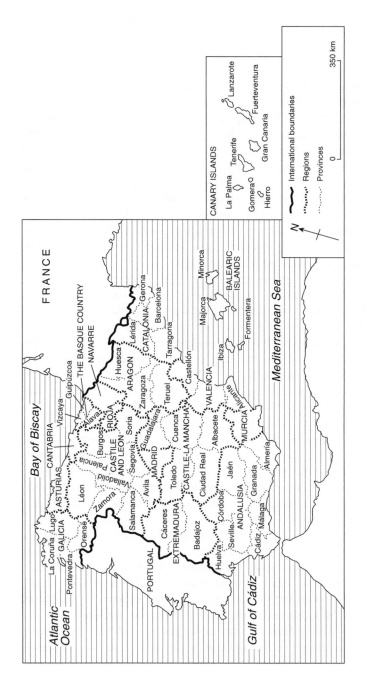

Map 8 The provinces and regions of modern Spain. Adapted from Hooper, *The New Spaniards*, p. xv.

breakup of the unity of Spain. In 1979, the Socialist leader, Felipe González, sought to allay fears that the PSOE remained wedded to the cause of social revolution, by abandoning Marxism and presenting his rejuvenated party as a modern, moderate force for change. Finally, the transition relied upon a gradual shift in mindset and political behaviour, as the population as a whole accepted that Spain's future did not lie with Francoism, and adapted to the give-and-take of party politics. The Spain of the transition bore little resemblance to that of 1931. Democracy was firmly established in the West; the religious question was no longer so volatile as it had once been; and with living standards far higher than they had been 40 years earlier, few workers shared the revolutionary zeal of their counterparts of the 1930s. Spaniards were willing to forget about their troubled past and look to the future. Once it was realized that the end of Francoism would not bring about revolution or anarchy, the vast majority of Spaniards were happy to support the peaceful transition towards democracy.

After his electoral victory of March 1979, Suárez's political position began to crumble. Spain remained mired in recession and was suffering a new wave of terrorist outrages committed by ETA and by Rightist extremists, who hoped that a breakdown in law and order would lead to a new *pronunciamiento* by the army. These difficulties contributed to an overwhelming sense of disillusion (*desencanto*) among the Spanish electorate, which had anticipated that the transition to democracy would lead to an immediate improvement in their economic fortunes. Meanwhile, the UCD, having successfully piloted Spain through the choppy waters of political change, began to break up, as the constituent parts which made up the coalition came into conflict over a whole range of policy issues, not least the impending legalization of divorce. In January 1981, considering that his position as Prime Minister had become untenable, Suárez unexpectedly announced his resignation. He was succeeded by the then Minister of Economy, Leopoldo Calvo Sotelo.

There remained those who viewed democratization as a mistake and would yearn for a return to the Francoist state. That those elements still posed a threat to Spain's fledgeling democracy, was dramatically underlined on 23 February 1981 when a detachment of Civil Guards under the command of Lieutenant-Colonel Antonio Tejero Molina stormed the Congress of Deputies – where the investiture of Calvo Sotelo as Prime Minister was taking place – and held the deputies captive at gun-point. Simultaneously, units of the Brunete armoured division seized key points in and around Madrid, while in Valencia General Miláns del Bosch declared a state of martial law and tanks appeared on the streets. A statement issued by Tejero summed up the aspirations of the conspirators in simple terms: 'the unity of Spain, peace, order and security'. That the *coup* was quickly snuffed out was thanks in large part to the timely intervention of King Juan Carlos who, as Commander-in-Chief of the armed forces, condemned the insurrection and ordered the troops to remain in their barracks.

The failure of the 23-F, as the *coup* attempt became known, marked a watershed in democratic politics. Disenchantment with the democratic process swiftly gave way to relief that the *coup* had failed and sparked mass demonstrations of support for democracy throughout Spain. There then followed a period of political flux, as the UCD, beset by infighting between its composite factions, began to disintegrate: in 1982, the Christian Democrats abandoned the party and joined forces with the AP, while the Social Democrats attached themselves to the PSOE. Suárez himself broke away to form his own political party, the 'Democratic and Social Centre' (*Centro Democrático y Social*, CDS). Simultaneously, internal feuding broke out within the ranks of the PCE. Only the PSOE, under the charismatic leadership of González, appeared to offer the dynamic political leadership that Spaniards were seeking. When fresh elections were held in October 1982, the PSOE achieved a landslide majority with 202 seats (that is, 48.4 per cent of the vote); support for the AP rose substantially to 106 seats; the UCD and PCE suffered a humiliating collapse in support, returning only 12 and four deputies respectively; Suárez's newly founded CDS secured only two seats. The following year, Socialist hegemony was reinforced when the party swept to victory in 11 of the *autonomías*.

THE TRIUMPH OF THE CENTRE

The general election of October 1982 marked an important stage in the process of political transition in Spain. The Socialist victory was not the prelude to revolution, as some on the Right had predicted. Instead, as government and opposition settled down to the bread and butter issues of parliamentary politics, the far Right dwindled as a political force and the army remained in its barracks. The principal objective of the Socialists was to implement a programme of social and economic modernization which would integrate Spain firmly within the international mainstream, help close the economic 'growth gap' with her neighbours, and bring about greater prosperity and social justice for all.

Under Socialist rule, Spain's standing in the world was transformed. Negotiations to join the European Community, which had been begun by Suárez, were resumed in the belief that membership would provide political stability, speed the process of modernization and bring improved standards of living to all the regions of Spain. It would also do away with the hoary cliché, so beloved of some on the Right, that Spain was profoundly 'different' – politically, socially and culturally – to her European neighbours. This process was not to be without pain. A policy of industrial restructuring, designed to make Spanish industry better equipped to compete in the international marketplace, caused large-scale redundancies, particularly in the steel and shipbuilding communities of the north. By 1985, as a consequence of the various measures introduced to liberalize the economy, the rate of unemployment had reached 22 per cent. That same year, after lengthy negotiations, Spain signed the Treaty of Accession and on 1 January 1986 formally became a member of the European Community, although it would be another seven years before she could enjoy full rights of membership.

The Socialists, along with other left-wing groups, had always been stoutly anti-American in their world view, not least because it had been the United States that had helped sustain Franco in power for so long. Membership of NATO was anathema, so much so that when the UCD took Spain into the organization in 1981, without even seeking parliamentary approval, it provoked a storm of criticism on the Left and prompted the Socialists to pledge to reverse the decision should they be voted into office. Once in power, however, political pragmatism prevailed. It soon became clear to Felipe González and his fellow ministers that withdrawal would leave Spain at loggerheads with many of the other member states of the EC, for whom NATO represented the corner-stone of their foreign policy. Skilfully changing tack, or performing a breathtaking U-turn, depending on your point of view, González set out to persuade his own party and the country as a whole of the need for Spain to retain membership of NATO, arguing that by doing so it would help to modernize the armed forces and thereby lessen any possibility of a new military *pronunciamiento*. Moreover, the government pledged that there would be a substantial reduction in the number of US troops in Spain and that nuclear weapons would not be allowed entry on to Spanish soil. In March 1986, González's decision was backed by a narrow majority in a national referendum.

Notwithstanding Spain's commitment to Europe and to the Atlantic alliance, attempts were also made to strengthen her political and economic ties with her former colonies in Latin America. In 1991, what was to be the first in a series of conferences of Ibero-American states was held in Mexico.

Between 1986 and 1991, thanks chiefly to the sizeable financial subsidies provided by the EC Structural Funds, increased trading activity and a surge of foreign direct investment (the bulk of it from within the EC), Spain's economy expanded rapidly. By 1992, Spain was about 40 per cent richer in real terms than she had been in 1980. On the back of this expansion, the government authorized a substantial rise in the level of public spending to provide for improved health care, unemployment benefits and pensions. It also sought to demonstrate the modern and progressive nature of the New Spain to the world by investing heavily in infrastructure, such as a high-speed rail link between Madrid and Seville, and embarking on an ambitious programme of prestige building projects, notably in Barcelona, which played host to the 1992 Olympic Games, and Seville, where the World Fair was held in the same year. The national euphoria that accompanied those events was followed by a severe economic hangover as Spain slid into recession. By 1993, unemployment had reached 24 per cent and the balance of payments deficit had increased sharply.

Thanks in large part to Spain's growing economic prosperity, the Socialists remained firmly entrenched in power. In the elections of 1986 and 1989, González again won comfortable majorities, although the share of the vote – 43.4 per cent and 39.6 per cent respectively – represented a decline with respect to 1982. He was further helped in this regard by the weakness of the opposition, as neither the far Left, which had formed a coalition, 'United Left' (*Izquierda Unida*), nor Fraga's Centre-Right AP was able to make any significant inroads into the government's popularity. By the early 1990s, however, the Socialist honeymoon with the electorate was clearly at an end. The reputation of the government was besmirched by a series of high-profile corruption scandals and levels of clientilism at all levels of government unheard of since the heyday of *caciquismo* at the beginning of the century. The charge that the PSOE was running Spain for the benefit of its own members began to stick. Among the most serious of all the scandals in which the Socialists were embroiled was the revelation that the government was implicated in the creation and financing of the 'Anti-Terrorist Liberation Groups' (*Grupos Antiterroristas de Liberación*, GAL), which had kidnapped and murdered 28 suspected ETA members or sympathizers, most of them in France. Although the PSOE still retained a core of support among the working classes, particularly in Andalusia, Castilla-La Mancha and Extremadura, it was becoming increasingly estranged from its traditional ally, the UGT. In December 1988, the UGT and CCOO unions jointly staged a one-day general strike in protest at the government's proposals for labour market deregulation. This was followed by further general strikes in 1992 and 1994. Despite the gradual deterioration in the party's standing, the resilient González won a fourth election victory in June 1993 with 38.68 per cent of the vote, but he was left without an overall majority and had to broker a pact with the Catalan nationalists to remain in power.

As the popularity of the PSOE dwindled, thanks to a combination of economic recession and a fresh wave of scandals, the Centre-Right was beginning to gain ground. In 1989, the founder of *Alianza Popular*, Manuel Fraga, whose Francoist past had always been something of a liability for his party, stood down from the leadership and AP was relaunched as the 'Popular Party' (*Partido Popular*, PP) under the able, yet deeply uncharismatic, José María Aznar. Under Aznar's leadership, the PP began a process of reorganization and rejuvenation, designed to protect the party from the slur, frequently invoked by the Socialists, that it remained firmly anchored in the Francoist past. Like González in 1982, Aznar portrayed the PP as the party of modernization and change. In the 1993 elections, the PP's share of the vote rose to 34.8 per cent; by 1996, it had won control of most of the major regions and cities. When fresh general elections were held in March 1996, after Jordi Puyol, leader of the Catalan CiU, pulled the plug on his alliance with the PSOE, the PP emerged as the largest party in Spain with 156 seats and 38.9 per cent of the vote. However, Aznar lacked an overall majority and had to seek the support of the Basque and Catalan nationalists before he could form a government.

On assuming office, Aznar accelerated the neo-liberal economic policy that had been implemented by the Socialists, reducing state intervention in the economy, privatizing public companies and further deregulating the labour market. Dependence on the votes of his Basque and Catalan allies led his administration to cede further powers to the regions. Thanks to increased economic growth, and the inability of the

PSOE to regain the trust of the electorate, the PP won an absolute majority in the elections of March 2000. Under Aznar's government, Spain has reaffirmed her commitment to further European integration by embracing European Monetary Union and the introduction of the single European currency. However, Spain's political clout within Europe has been lessened by the expansion of the EU to 15 members and will presumably be further diluted with the entry of the Eastern European states in the coming years.

THE NEW SPANIARDS

During the past 25 years, Spain has undergone a spectacular transformation. Democratic institutions have taken firm root. The Spanish economy has grown to the extent that Spain now occupies ninth position among the world's industrialized nations. The armed forces have been modernized and depoliticized, so that Spanish Army officers no longer plot *pronunciamientos*, but instead are heavily engaged supporting peace-keeping operations as far afield as Bosnia and Afghanistan, among other places. Thanks to her membership of the EU and NATO, as well as through her longstanding ties with Latin America and North Africa, Spain enjoys altogether a higher international profile than was the case during the isolationist period of the Franco dictatorship.

The rapid transformation of Spanish society, which began during the economic boom of the 1960s, has continued. Spaniards today are healthier than ever before (between 1950 and 1991 average life expectancy increased from 62.1 years to 76.94), are better educated and enjoy a higher standard of living, even if average income per head remains below the EU average. Although over 80 per cent of Spaniards still nominally declare themselves to be Roman Catholic, religious attendance is in sharp decline and the Church no longer exercises the dominance over public morality, social welfare and education that it did under Franco. The role of women in society has changed beyond recognition: divorce and abortion have been legalized and contraception is freely available; nearly 50 per cent of Spanish women now work (principally in the manufacturing and service sectors); and there has been a huge increase in the number of women attending university.

A direct consequence of increased female participation in the labour market, together with rising levels of education and the wide-spread use of contraception, has been a dramatic fall in the birth rate, from 2.91 children per woman in 1970 to 1.2 in 1998, one of the lowest rates of growth in the world. A lower birth rate and longer life expectancy have contributed to a sharp decrease in the rate of growth of the Spanish population, which by 1998 stood at about 39.1 million. By contrast, there has been an increase in immigration, from North Africa and Latin America in particular. Meanwhile, the depopulation of the countryside has continued apace, fuelled by a continuing decline in the proportion of the working population employed in agriculture – from 22 per cent in 1977 to 8.7 per cent in 1996 – and a correspond-ingly steady growth in the service sector. With the notable exception of Madrid, the population of the interior is in decline, particularly in the regions of Aragon, Castilla-León, Castilla-La Mancha and Extremadura.

The quarter-century since Franco's death has witnessed an explo-sion of Spanish cultural creativity. That is not to say that under the dictatorship cultural life was moribund. On the contrary, the period saw the emergence of a number of talented novelists, such as Camilo José Cela, Miguel Delibes and Juan Goytisolo, and film-makers, like Luis García Berlanga and Carlos Saura, who, notwithstanding the restrictions imposed by censorship, vividly conveyed the social fabric of the period. What has changed most markedly since 1975 has been that state funding for the arts has increased substantially and that cultural resources are no longer the élitist preserve of Madrid and Barcelona: provincial capitals now boast their own museums, art galleries, theatres and orchestras. Today the volume and variety of cultural expression is immeasurably greater than it was under Franco and Spanish artists enjoy an altogether higher international reputation. The films of Pedro Almodóvar are universally acclaimed; some Spanish actors can be found rubbing shoulders with the glitterati of Hollywood; numerous novelists, painters, sculptors, musicians and dancers are admired and fêted far beyond Spain's shores. The devolu-tion of power to the regions has been accompanied by a recovery of local identity and the Basque, Catalan and Galician languages have enjoyed a renaissance.

Yet, one must avoid the temptation to view the New Spain through rose-tinted glasses. At the beginning of the twenty-first century, Spain is confronted with any number of intractable problems: social and economic inequality; substantial disparities in regional development;

high unemployment and rising levels of crime and drug abuse, to name only a few. Moreover, despite the best intentions of the 1978 constitution, relations between central government and the regions remain deeply problematic. One consequence of devolution, indeed, has been to encourage regionalist feelings in areas where there had previously been none, as can be seen by the rise of local parties in such places as Andalusia and the Canary Islands. Even the smallest *autonomía* of them all, La Rioja, now has its own assembly, flag and anthem. But it is the Basque problem, more than any other domestic political issue, that most exercises politicians in Madrid. Since 1975, over 800 people have been killed by ETA. Despite the fact that the Basque Country now enjoys more extensive powers of self-government than almost any comparable region in Western Europe, local politicians continue to press for the right to self-determination and ETA's commitment to the armed struggle remains undiminished. In 1998, the Pact of Lizarra between the Basque nationalist parties paved the way for a declaration of a ceasefire by ETA; but hopes that a peace process would lead to the resolution of the 'Basque problem' once and for all were shattered just 14 months later, when a return to violence was announced. Tensions between the centre and the periphery remain as strong as they have ever been, as Spaniards continue to come to terms with the legacy of their past.

GLOSSARY

afrancesado 'Frenchified person'; a supporter of the regime of Joseph Bonaparte (1808–13).

alcabala A sales tax, first levied by Alfonso X of Castile.

aljama A district or ghetto inhabited by Muslims or Jews.

AP Alianza Popular (Popular Alliance): Centre-Right party founded in 1976 by former Francoist ministers led by Manuel Fraga.

arbitristas Writers, active from the reign of Philip II onwards, who drafted *arbitrios* or proposals for political and economic reform.

autonomía One of the 17 autonomous regions that make up the modern Spanish state.

caballero villano 'Commoner knights'; men who enjoyed the privileged status of a noble by virtue of possessing a horse and military equipment, and carrying out military service.

caciquismo System of political clientilism and electoral corruption, run by local political bosses (*caciques*), which underpinned the Restoration System of 1875–1923.

Caudillo Chieftain or military leader; the title by which General Franco was widely known.

CC.OO Comisiones Obreras (Workers' Commissions): Communist-led trade unions which came into being in the late 1950s and were legalized in 1977.

CDS Centro Democrático y Social (Democratic and Social Centre): Centre-Left party founded by Adolfo Suárez in 1982.

CEDA Confederación Española de Derechas Autónomas (Spanish Confederation of Autonomous Rightist Parties): coalition of Catholic right-wing parties founded in 1933 and led by José María Gil Robles.

CNT Confederación Nacional del Trabajo (National Labour Confederation): anarcho-syndicalist trade union founded in 1910.

colegiales An élite group of university graduates, drawn from the higher ranks of the aristocracy, who dominated the hierarchy of government, the judiciary and the Church from the sixteenth century.

conversos Converted Jews or their descendants.

convivencia 'Living together'; a term applied to the peaceful coexistence of Christian, Jewish and Muslim communities in the medieval peninsula.

corregidor Royal-appointed civil governor (first appointed in the fourteenth century) with administrative, judicial and political responsibilities in the major Castilian towns.

cortes A representative assembly convened by the Crown; Parliament.

encomienda In Spanish Colonial America, the grant of authority to a Spanish settler over a group of Indians.

ETA Euzkadi Ta Askatasuna (Basque Homeland and Liberty): Basque separatist movement founded in 1959.

exaltados A group of radical liberals, active from 1820, who were committed to democratic reform.

excusado A tax on clerical property, introduced in 1567.

FAI Federación Anarquista Ibérica (Iberian Anarchist Federation): Anarchist group founded in 1927.

FNTT Federación Nacional de Trabajadores de la Tierra (National Federation of Land Workers): the agrarian section of the UGT.

fuero A charter of laws, privileges and liberties applied to a particular town, region or social group.

golilla A group of Spanish bureaucrats, many of whom were university-trained lawyers of *hidalgo* (q.v.) stock, who stood at the forefront of the reformist initiatives implemented by the eighteenth-century Bourbon monarchy.

ḥājib Chief minister to the emir or caliph of al-Andalus.

Hermandad Brotherhood or association first instituted by the towns of medieval Castile to protect them and to keep the peace.

hidalgo A nobleman; a member of the lesser nobility.

jornalero Landless agricultural day-labourer.

Jund **Army** one of the areas of al-Andalus settled by Syrian soldiers after 741.

juro Annuity paid out of state revenues for loans to the Crown.

letrado University graduate in law, many of whom were recruited into the state bureaucracy or the ecclesiastical hierarchy.

Mesta Royal-chartered corporation of sheepowners established by Alfonso X of Castile *c*.1260.

millones From 1590, a tax levied on basic consumer items, such as meat, wine, vinegar and oil.

Morisco A baptized Muslim.

257

Mozarab A Christian living under Muslim rule in al-Andalus; a Christian whose lifestyle incorporated Muslim habits and customs.

Mudejar A Muslim living under Christian rule.

muwallad A Muslim of Iberian origin.

parias Tribute money paid by Muslim rulers to Christian states.

PCE Partido Comunista de España (Spanish Communist Party): founded in 1921.

POUM Partido Obrero Unificado Marxista (Workers' Party of Marxist Unification): revolutionary Marxist party founded in 1935.

PNV Partido Nacionalista Vasco (Basque Nationalist Party): Basque nationalist movement founded by Sabino de Arana in 1895.

PP Partido Popular (Popular Party): founded in 1989; successor of Alianza Popular (AP) (q.v.).

pronunciamiento A military *coup*.

PSOE Partido Socialista Obrero Español (Spanish Socialist Workers' Party): founded in 1879.

quinto One-fifth tax levied by the Spanish Crown on all American bullion and precious stones.

Reconquista Christian reconquest of Muslim Spain and Portugal.

remença Catalan peasants subjected to seigneurial domination who could only obtain liberty on payment of a large sum of money.

requeté Carlist militiaman.

ricos hombres The high nobles of medieval Castile and Aragon.

ṣaqāliba Slaves of Slav or Northern European origin, many of whom were recruited into the army or civil service of the caliphate of Córdoba.

taifa The Muslim successor states that emerged after the collapse of the Umayyad caliphate in the early eleventh century.

tercio Elite regiment in the Spanish Army.

thughūr Frontier zones of al-Andalus bordering on Christian territory.

turno pacífico Literally 'peaceful alternation'; term used to describe the Restoration System of 1875–1923.

UCD Unión de Centro Democrático (Union of the Democratic Centre): coalition of Centrist groups founded by Adolfo Suárez in 1977.

UGT Unión General de Trabajadores (General Workers' Union): Socialist-controlled trade union founded in 1888.

valido Chief minister or favourite to a king.

CHRONOLOGY

*c.*800,000 BC	*Homo antecessor* established in the Sierra de Atapuerca
*c.*100,000–40,000 BC	Middle Palaeolithic period. Neanderthals settle in the Iberian peninsula
*c.*40,000–10,000 BC	Upper Palaeolithic period. Neanderthals displaced by Cro-Magnon humans
*c.*15,000 BC	'Magdalenian' cave paintings in Asturias and Cantabria
*c.*5000–*c.*2500 BC	Neolithic period
*c.*2500–*c.*1700 BC	Copper Age
*c.*1700–*c.*1200 BC	Early Bronze Age
*c.*1200–*c.*700 BC	Middle and Later Bronze Ages
*c.*800 BC	Foundation of Cádiz by Phoenicians
*c.*700–*c.* 500 BC	Realm of Tartessos flourishes in southern Iberia
*c.*575 BC	Phocaean Greeks found trading settlement at Ampurias
237 BC	Foundation of Carthaginian Empire in Iberia
218 BC	Carthaginian attack on Sagunto, leading to outbreak of Second Punic War
206 BC	End of Carthaginian rule in Iberia
197 BC	Roman Hispania divided into two provinces, Citerior and Ulterior
147–39 BC	Rebellion of the Lusitani against Roman rule
134–33 BC	Siege and sack of Numantia
45 BC	Victory by Caesar over Pompey at *Munda* brings power struggle between the two to a close
c. 27 BC	The Emperor Augustus divides Hispania into three provinces: Baetica, Lusitania and Tarraconensis

25 BC	Foundation of *Emerita Augusta* (Mérida)
19 BC	Conquest of Cantabria brings the entire peninsula under Roman rule
AD 98–117	Reign of Trajan, born at Italica, near Seville
117–38	Reign of Hadrian, also from Italica
171–3	Moorish raids on Baetica
260–69	Hispania forms part of an independent 'Gallic Empire'
c.262	Franks and Alamani sack Tarragona
c.284	The Emperor Diocletian divides Hispania into five provinces: Gallaecia, Carthaginensis, Tarraconensis, Lusitania and Baetica
312	Conversion of Emperor Constantine to Christianity
409	Alans, Sueves and Vandals invade Spain
416–18	Visigoths campaign in the peninsula on behalf of the Roman Empire
429	Hasding Vandals invade North Africa
430–56	The Sueves dominate the peninsula, with the exception of the north-east
456	The Visigoths under Theoderic II (453–66) invade the peninsula and overthrow the kingdom of the Sueves
466–84	Reign of King Euric, who completes the Visigothic conquest of the peninsula
507	Battle of Vouillé: collapse of the Visigothic kingdom in Gaul
511–48	Visigothic kingdom under Ostrogothic authority
551	Revolt of Athanagild (554–68) against Agila (549–54) allows Emperor Justinian I (527–65) to establish a Byzantine enclave in the south of the peninsula
569–86	Reign of King Leovigild, who reunites most of the peninsula under his rule
585	Leovigild conquers the Suevic kingdom in Galicia
589	Third Council of Toledo: conversion of the Visigoths from Arianism to Catholicism
c.600–36	Episcopate of Isidore of Seville

624	Suinthila (621–31) expels the Byzantines from the peninsula
654	King Reccesuinth (649–72) issues the Visigothic law code known as the *Liber Iudicorum*
694	King Egica (687–702) orders the enslavement of the Jewish population
710	Death of King Wittiza (702–10) leads to war for the succession
711	Muslim invasion of the peninsula leads to defeat of King Roderic (710–11); Achila (710–13) rules in the north-east
711–20	The Visigothic kingdom is overrun by Muslim forces
718(?)	Asturian revolt against the Muslims
732 or 733	Charles Martel of the Franks defeats the Muslims near Poitiers
740s	Berber revolts in the peninsula and North Africa
756	'Abd al-Raḥmān I (756–88) establishes an independent Umayyad emirate in Córdoba
778	The Franks are defeated at Roncesvalles
801	The Franks capture Barcelona. Formation of the Spanish March
c.818–42	The supposed remains of St James are discovered at Compostela
824	A second Frankish defeat at Roncesvalles leads to the creation of an independent kingdom of Pamplona (later known as Navarre)
851–9	Martyrdom movement in Córdoba
881–917	Rebellion of 'Umar ibn Hafṣūn against the Umayyad emirate
929	'Abd al-Raḥmān III (912–61) proclaimed first Umayyad caliph of Córdoba
981–1002	Ascendancy of al-Manṣūr in al-Andalus
1009	Deposition of Hishām II (976–1009) leads to the outbreak of civil wars in al-Andalus and the emergence of the *taifa* states
1031	Extinction of the Umayyad caliphate
1037	Kingdom of León annexed by Ferdinand I of Castile (1035–65)

c.1063	Ferdinand I initiates annual donative of gold to the abbey of Cluny
1085	Conquest of Toledo by Alfonso VI of León-Castile (1065–1109)
1086	Almoravid invasion; Alfonso VI defeated at Sagrajas
1090–1110	Almoravid conquest of the *taifa* states
1094	Capture of Valencia by Rodrigo Díaz, El Cid (d. 1099)
1118	Alfonso I of Aragon (1104–34) conquers Zaragoza
1134	Death of Alfonso I of Aragon leads to re-emergence of an independent kingdom of Navarre
1137	Dynastic union of Aragon and the county of Barcelona
1143	Independent kingdom of Portugal recognized by Alfonso VII of León-Castile (1126–57)
1145–47	Collapse of Almoravid authority in al-Andalus
1146–73	Almohads bring al-Andalus under their control
1147	Christian conquest of Lisbon and Almería
1148	Christian conquest of Tortosa
1158	Foundation of the Military Order of Calatrava
1170	Foundation of the Military Order of Santiago
1195	Almohads defeat Alfonso VIII of Castile (1158–1214) at Alarcos
1212	Christian victory over the Almohads at the battle of Las Navas de Tolosa
1213	Defeat and death of Peter II of Aragon (1196–1213) at Muret leads to the collapse of Aragonese power in south-west France
1220s	Demise of Almohad power in al-Andalus
1229–35	Conquest of the Balearic Islands by James I of Aragon (1213–76)
1230	Definitive union of the kingdoms of Castile and León by Ferdinand III (1217–52)
1232–45	James I of Aragon annexes the kingdom of Valencia
1236	Ferdinand III of Castile captures Córdoba

1238	Muḥammad ibn al-Aḥmar (1238–72) establishes the Nasrid kingdom of Granada
1248	Seville falls to Ferdinand III
1258	Treaty of Corbeil between James I of Aragon and Louis IX of France
1264	Mudejar uprising in Andalusia and Murcia
1275–1344	Merinid intervention in the peninsula
1282	Conquest of Sicily by Peter III of Aragon (1276–85)
1295	Treaty of Anagni: James II of Aragon (1291–1327) agrees to cede Sicily to the Angevins and is recompensed with Sardinia and Corsica by Pope Boniface VIII
1340	Alfonso XI of Castile (1312–50) and his allies defeat a joint Granadan-Merinid army at the Río Salado
1348	The Black Death
1369	The Trastámara dynasty seizes power in Castile
1385	John I of Castile (1379–90) is defeated by the Portuguese at Aljubarrota
1388–89	Treaties between Castile, Portugal and the house of Lancaster bring the Iberian phase of the Hundred Years War to a close
1391	Outbreak of pogroms in many towns of the peninsula
1412	The Compromise of Caspe: the regent of Castile, Ferdinand of Antequera, designated king of Aragon
1442–3	Alfonso V of Aragon (1416–58) conquers the kingdom of Naples
1453	Execution of Álvaro de Luna
1465	Henry IV of Castile (1454–74) deposed in effigy at the 'Farce of Ávila'; civil wars in Castile
1469	The marriage of Isabella of Castile and Ferdinand of Aragon
1478	The Inquisition is established
1479	Dynastic union of the kingdoms of Castile and Aragon

1492	Fall of the Nasrid kingdom of Granada. Expulsion of the Jews from Spain. Christopher Columbus discovers the New World
1494	Treaty of Tordesillas demarcates Spanish and Portuguese spheres of influence in the Atlantic and the New World
1497	Conquest of Melilla
1499	Mudejar rebellion in Granada
1503	Victories at Cerignola and Garigliano bring Naples under Spanish rule
1512	Annexation of the kingdom of Navarre to Castile
1516	The Habsburg Succession: Charles I (1516–56) accedes to the throne of Spain
1519	Charles V elected Holy Roman Emperor
1520–1	Revolt of the *comuneros*
1521	Hernán Cortés captures Tenochtitlan and destroys the Aztec empire
1525	Victory over France at the battle of Pavia
1532–3	Conquest of the Inca empire by Pizarro and Almagro
1556	Abdication of Charles V and succession of his son Philip II (1556–98)
1561	Madrid established as the capital city of Spain
1568–71	Morisco rebellion in Granada
1571	The Christian Holy League, under the command of Don John of Austria, defeats the Ottoman fleet at Lepanto
1572	Revolt of the Netherlands
1580	Portugal annexed to the Spanish Crown
1588	Failure of the Spanish Armada
1591	Rebellion of Aragon
1598	Death of Philip II and succession of Philip III (1598–1621)
1609	Twelve Years Truce signed with the Dutch. Expulsion of the Moriscos from Spain
1619	Beginning of the Thirty Years War
1621	Death of Philip III and succession of Philip IV (1621–65)

1626	Olivares publishes the Union of Arms
1639–40	Spain suffers naval defeats at Dutch hands in the Channel and Brazil
1640	Revolts in Catalonia and Portugal
1648	The end of the Thirty Years War: Spain recognizes the independence of the United Provinces of Holland
1659	The Treaty of the Pyrenees brings 24 years of conflict between Spain and France to a close
1665	Death of Philip IV and succession of Charles II (1665–1700)
1668	Spain recognizes the independence of Portugal
1700	Death of Charles II marks the end of the Habsburg dynasty in Spain. Succession of the Bourbon Philip V (1700–46)
1702	Beginning of the War of the Spanish Succession
1704	English and Dutch forces capture Gibraltar
1707	Philip V abolishes the *fueros* of Aragon and Valencia
1708	Britain captures Minorca
1713	The Treaties of Utrecht and Rastatt (1714) bring the War of the Spanish Succession to a close. Philip V is recognized as king of Spain, but surrenders his territories in Gibraltar, Minorca, the Netherlands, Italy and Sicily
1716	The Decree of *Nueva Planta* sweeps away the autonomous powers of Catalonia
1724	Philip V abdicates in favour of his son Louis I, only to resume the throne the following year upon the death of the latter
1739–48	The War of Jenkins' Ear
1746	Death of Philip V and succession of Ferdinand VI (1746–59)
1759	Death of Ferdinand VI and succession of Charles III (1759–88)
1762	Spain enters the Seven Years War against Britain. By the Peace of Paris (1763), Spain surrenders Florida to Britain, but acquires Louisiana from France

1766	'Uprising of Squillace' in Madrid is followed by disturbances in many Spanish towns
1767	Expulsion of the Jesuits from Spain and the empire
1778	Free trade allowed between Spain and the American colonies
1779–83	Spain lends support to North American rebels against Britain
1783	The Peace of Versailles restores Florida and Minorca to Spanish rule
1788	Death of Charles III and succession of Charles IV (1788–1808)
1793–95	War with the French Republic leads to the loss of Santo Domingo
1796–1802	Spain and France wage war against Britain and Portugal
1797	Britain captures Trinidad
1798	Disentailment of ecclesiastical properties begins
1804–8	Resumption of hostilities with Britain
1805	The British under Admiral Nelson defeat the French and Spanish fleets at Cape Trafalgar
1808	The 'Tumult of Aranjuez' in March is followed by the abdication of Charles IV and the succession of Ferdinand VII (1808–33). The French military occupation of Spain provokes a popular uprising against the French: beginning of the War of Independence. Charles IV and Ferdinand VII are obliged to cede the throne to Emperor Napoleon, who in turn confers it upon his brother, Joseph Bonaparte
1810	The *cortes* of Cádiz convenes
1810–24	Independence of the Spanish American colonies, with the exception of Cuba and Puerto Rico
1812	The Constitution of Cádiz is promulgated: Spain becomes a parliamentary monarchy
1813	Defeat at the Battle of Vitoria at the hands of British, Portuguese and Spanish forces leads

	to the evacuation of French troops from Spanish soil, with the exception of Catalonia
1814	Ferdinand VII restores absolutist rule
1820	A liberal revolt compels Ferdinand VII to accept the 1812 constitution
1823	A French army helps Ferdinand VII to reimpose absolutist rule
1833	Death of Ferdinand VII. Outbreak of First Carlist War (1833–40) allows the liberal supporters of the late king's daughter and successor, Isabella II (1833–68), to enter government
1835	Juan Mendizábal is appointed prime minister and enacts the sale of ecclesiastical lands
1840–3	Regency of General Espartero, who leads the Progressives to power
1843–54	The Moderates hold power and lay the legal and institutional framework of a modern, centralized state
1854–6	Espartero and the Progressives hold power. Programme of administrative reform and economic liberalization. Disentailment of municipal common lands enacted and work begins on a national network of railways (1855)
1856–63	General O'Donnell serves as prime minister. He founds the short-lived Liberal Union
1868	A coalition of Liberal Unionists, Progressives and Democrats stage the 'Glorious Revolution', forcing Isabella II to renounce the throne
1868–78	Colonial rebellion in Cuba
1869	Constitutional monarchy established
1870	King Amadeo I (1870–3) invited to take the throne
1873	Amadeo abdicates. First Republic proclaimed. 'Cantonalist' revolts staged by Federal Republicans
1874	Brigadier Martínez Campos restores Alfonso XII (1874–85) to the throne

1875–1923	The Restoration System. Through the *turno pacífico*, devised by Cánovas del Castillo, Conservative and Liberal parties alternate in power through managed elections
1879	Foundation of Socialist Party (*Partido Socialista Obrero Español*, PSOE)
1885	Death of Alfonso XII and succession of Alfonso XIII (1885–1931). Regency held by Queen María Cristina until 1902
1888	Foundation of Socialist trade union, the 'General Workers' Union' (*Unión General de Trabajadores*, UGT)
1892	The 'Manresa Principles' give voice to demands for Catalan autonomy
1894	Foundation of Basque National Party (*Partido Nacional Vasco*, PNV)
1898	Military defeat by United States leads to loss of Spain's last colonies in Cuba, Puerto Rico and the Philippines
1909	'Tragic Week' in Barcelona is marked by widespread rioting and church burning. Collapse of the *turno pacífico*
1910	Formation of the anarchist-syndicalist union, the National Labour Confederation (*Confederación Nacional del Trabajo*, CNT)
1917	Widespread political unrest: general strike by UGT and CNT; army officers establish Military Defence Councils; Catalan Assembly movement
1923–30	Dictatorship of General Primo de Rivera
1931	Alfonso XIII abdicates after the parties of the Republican-Socialist coalition make major gains in municipal elections. The Second Republic is declared
1932	General Sanjurjo launches failed *pronunciamiento*. A Statute of Autonomy is granted to Catalonia
1933	José Antonio Primo de Rivera founds the Falange. The Right is victorious in the November general elections

1934	Workers' revolt in Asturias is crushed
1936	The Popular Front wins the general elections (16 February); military uprising in Morocco and Spain (17–18 July) leads to the outbreak of civil war; a 'government of victory' is established under Largo Caballero
1937	General Franco unites the Falange and other Nationalist groups (18 April); violence breaks out between the CNT, the POUM and the Communists in Barcelona (3 May); General Mola's army overruns the Basque Country, Santander and Asturias (April–October)
1938	Nationalist forces reach the Mediterranean and divide the Republican zone into two
1939	Nationalists capture Barcelona (26 January) and Madrid (28 February); Nationalist victory in Civil War (1 April)
1940	Franco and Hitler meet at Hendaye
1941	Death of Alfonso XIII. Don Juan de Borbón heir apparent to the throne
1945	The Charter of the Spaniards issued
1946	Diplomatic boycott of Spain by UN
1947	Franco declares Spain to be a kingdom
1953	Spain signs 'Pacts of Madrid' with the USA and a Concordat with the Vatican
1955	Spain allowed to join the UN
1957	Recruitment of Opus Dei technocrats to the cabinet marks the beginning of a programme of economic liberalization
1959	Stabilization Plan. ETA founded
1966	Organic Law of State enacted
1969	Prince Juan Carlos is designated as Franco's successor
1973	Prime Minister Carrero Blanco assassinated by ETA. Economic recession
1975	Death of Franco (20 November). Juan Carlos I crowned king
1976	Adolfo Suárez invited to form a government. The Political Reform Act paves the way for the transition to democracy

1977	Legalization of the Spanish Communist Party. First democratic elections held (15 June), won by Centrist UCD. 'Pacts of Moncloa' between government and opposition
1978	A new constitution is approved by national referendum
1979	Autonomy is granted to the Basque Country and Catalonia. General elections reinforce the political ascendancy of the UCD
1981	Resignation of Suárez. Tejero leads an abortive military *pronunciamiento* (*23–F*)
1982	Spain joins NATO. Disintegration of the UCD. The PSOE, led by Felipe González, wins the general election with a landslide majority
1986	Spain joins the EC. Membership of NATO is approved by national referendum. Felipe González wins a new term in office
1989	The PSOE wins a new election victory, but with a weakened mandate
1993	The PSOE wins the general election but is required to seek the support of the Catalan CiU to form a government
1996	The conservative Popular Party, led by José María Aznar, wins the general election and forms a government with the support of the CiU and PNV
1997	Spain joins the European Monetary Union
2000	Popular Party wins the general election with an overall majority

SELECTED FURTHER READING

It would be a daunting task to compile a detailed bibliographical essay on the history of Spain. What follows here, rather, are merely some brief suggestions for further reading which will enable the enquiring reader to pursue a particular theme or era in more depth.

GENERAL WORKS

General overviews spanning the entire course of Spanish history are few and far between. R. Carr (ed.), *Spain: A History* (Oxford, 2000), written by a team of nine leading historians, is to be warmly recommended. Although in some respects now dated, there is still much of interest in S. G. Payne, *A History of Spain and Portugal*, 2 vols (Madison, 1973); P. Vilar, *Spain: A Brief History* (Oxford, 1977); and in the relevant chapters of P. E. Russell (ed.), *Spain: A Companion to Spanish Studies* (London, 1973). Readers of Spanish are encouraged to sample F. García de Cortázar and J. M. González Vesga, *Breve historia de España* (Madrid, 1994); and J. P. Fusi, *España. La evolución de la identidad nacional* (Madrid, 2000).

THE PRIDE AND ORNAMENT OF THE WORLD: PREHISTORY TO AD 1000

On the Prehistoric period in Iberia, M. C. Fernández Castro, *Iberia in Prehistory* (Oxford, 1995); and R. J. Harrison, *Spain at the Dawn of History: Iberians, Phoenicians and Greeks* (London, 1988) are particularly useful. A number of important books on Roman Hispania have appeared in recent years. See above all, S. J. Keay, *Roman Spain*

(London, 1988); L. Curchin, *Roman Spain: Conquest and Assimilation* (London, 1991); and J. S. Richardson, *The Romans in Spain* (Oxford, 1996). On the Germanic invasions and the Visigothic kingdom in Iberia, see E. A. Thompson, *The Goths in Spain* (Oxford, 1969); P. D. King, *Law and Society in the Visigothic Kingdom* (Cambridge, 1972); E. James (ed.), *Visigothic Spain: New Approaches* (Oxford, 1980); R. Collins, *Early Medieval Spain: Unity in Diversity, 400–1000*, (2nd edn, London, 1995); and K. Baxter Wolf (trans.), *Conquerors and Chroniclers of Early Medieval Spain* (2nd edn, Liverpool, 1999). On the Muslim invasions and their aftermath, see R. Fletcher, *Moorish Spain* (London, 1992); R. Collins, *The Arab Conquest of Spain, 710–797*, (rev. edn, Oxford, 1995); and H. Kennedy, *Muslim Spain and Portugal. A Political History of al-Andalus* (London, 1996). On the emerging realms of the Christian north, Collins, *Early Medieval Spain* is the best starting-point. R. Collins, *Spain: An Oxford Archaeological Guide* (Oxford, 1998) contains a wealth of information on the civilizations of the Iberian peninsula from the Copper Age to the twelfth century.

THE ASCENDANCY OF CHRISTIAN IBERIA, AD 1000–1474

For a general overview of the period, see G. Jackson, *The Making of Medieval Spain* (London, 1972); J. F. O'Callaghan, *A History of Medieval Spain* (Ithaca, 1975); and D. W. Lomax, *The Reconquest of Spain* (London, 1978). These may be supplemented by B. F. Reilly, *The Contest of Christian and Muslim Spain, 1031–1157* (Oxford, 1992), and, by the same author, *The Medieval Spains* (Cambridge, 1993). J. N. Hillgarth, *The Spanish Kingdoms 1250–1516*, 2 vols (Oxford, 1976–78); and A. MacKay, *Spain in the Middle Ages: From Frontier to Empire, 1000–1500* (London, 1977) provide excellent introductions to the evolving societies of Christian Spain. On Muslim al-Andalus, see L. P. Harvey, *Islamic Spain 1250–1500* (Chicago, 1990); R. Fletcher, *Moorish Spain* (London, 1992); and H. Kennedy, *Muslim Spain and Portugal: A Political History of al-Andalus* (London, 1996). On Aragon, see T. N. Bisson, *The Medieval Crown of Aragon: A Short History* (Oxford, 1986). On the life and times of El Cid, R. Fletcher, *The Quest for El Cid* (London, 1989) is the indispensable guide. *Christians and Moors in Spain*, 3 vols (Warminster, 1988–92) is an illuminating collection of original sources in translation: vols 1 and 2 are edited by C. Smith, vol 3 by C. Melville and A. Ubaydli. Equally stimulating is O. R. Constable (ed.), *Medieval Iberia: Readings from Christian, Muslim, and Jewish Sources* (Philadelphia, 1997). E. M. Gerli (ed.), *Medieval Iberia: An Encyclopedia* (New York, 2003) is a superlative work of reference.

THE UNIVERSAL MONARCHY, 1474–1700

J. H. Elliott, *Imperial Spain 1469–1716* (London, 1963); and H. Kamen, *Spain 1469–1714: A Society of Conflict* (2nd edn, London, 1991) are far and away the best introductions to this period. On the Catholic Monarchs, F. Fernández-Armesto, *Ferdinand and Isabella* (1975); and J. Edwards, *The Spain of the Catholic Monarchs 1474–1520* (Oxford, 2000) are sound and authoritative. J. Lynch, *Spain 1516–1598: From Nation State to World Empire* (Oxford, 1991), and, by the same author, *The Hispanic World in Crisis and Change* (Oxford, 1992) are immensely useful on the Habsburg monarchy. On the reigns of Charles V and Philip II respectively, see M. Fernández Alvarez, *Charles V* (London, 1975); and H. Kamen, *Philip of Spain* (New Haven, 1997). On the seventeenth century, see R. A. Stradling, *Europe and the Decline of Spain* (1981), and, by the same author, *Philip IV and the Government of Spain, 1621–65* (1988); and H. Kamen, *Spain in the Later Seventeenth Century, 1665–1700* (London, 1980). An excellent introduction to the development of Spanish society is provided by J. Casey, *Early Modern Spain: A Social History* (London, 1999). On the Spanish American empire, see M. A. Burkholder and L. L. Johnson, *Colonial Latin America* (2nd edn, Oxford, 1994). J. H. Elliott, *Spain and its World, 1500–1700: Selected Essays* (New Haven, 1989) is packed with important insights.

THE ENLIGHTENED DESPOTS, 1700–1833

The outstanding work in English on the eighteenth century is J. Lynch, *Bourbon Spain, 1700–1808* (Oxford, 1989). H. Kamen, *The War of Succession in Spain, 1700–15* (London, 1969) provides a good guide to the impact of that conflict on Spanish affairs. See also H. Kamen, *Philip V of Spain: The King who Reigned Twice* (New Haven, 2001). On political developments down to the death of Charles III,

W. N. Hargreaves-Mawdsley, *Eighteenth-Century Spain, 1700–1788: A Political, Diplomatic and Institutional History* (London, 1979) is a reliable guide. D. R. Ringrose, *Spain, Europe, and the 'Spanish miracle', 1700–1900* (Cambridge, 1996) provides important insights into Spain's economic development after the Bourbon succession. On the period from the War of Independence to the death of Ferdinand VII, the first four chapters of R. Carr, *Spain, 1808–1975* (2nd edn, 1975) are immensely valuable; they may be supplemented by C. J. Esdaile, *Spain in the Liberal Age: From Constitution to Civil War, 1812–1939* (Oxford, 2000). On the War of Independence itself, C. J. Esdaile, *The Peninsular War: A New History* (London, 2002), is the best account. On the impact of the ideas of the Enlightenment in Spain, see R. Herr, *The Eighteenth-Century Revolution in Spain* (Princeton, 1958).

LIBERALISM AND REACTION, 1833–1931

The best guide to this immensely complex period in Spain's history is R. Carr's monumental *Spain, 1808–1975* (2nd edn, 1975). The same author's *Modern Spain, 1875–1980* (Oxford, 1980) provides a clear and concise overview. To these works may be added C. J. Esdaile, *Spain in the Liberal Age: From Constitution to Civil War, 1812–1939* (Oxford, 2000); C. J. Ross, *Spain, 1812–1996* (London, 2000); and J. Alvarez Junco and A. Shubert (eds), *Spanish History since 1808* (London and New York, 2000). The role of the army is explored by C. P. Boyd, *Praetorian Politics in Liberal Spain* (Chapel Hill, 1979). F. Lannon, *Privilege, Persecution, and Prophecy: The Catholic Church in Spain, 1875–1975* (Oxford, 1987) is the essential guide to the position of the Church in Spanish society. D. R. Ringrose, *Spain, Europe, and the 'Spanish Miracle', 1700–1900* (Cambridge, 1996) is valuable on economic developments. On the crisis of 1898, see S. Balfour, *The End of the Spanish Empire* (Oxford, 1997). On the dictatorship of Primo de Rivera, see S. Ben-Ami, *Fascism from Above: The Dictatorship of Primo de Rivera* (Oxford, 1983).

THE MODERN ERA, 1931–2000

There are a number of useful introductions to this period. Especially good are R. Carr, *Spain, 1808–1975* (2nd edn, 1975), and, by the same author, *Modern Spain, 1875–1980* (Oxford, 1980); F. J. Romero Salvadó, *Twentieth-Century Spain: Politics and Society in Spain, 1898–1998* (London, 1999); and J. Alvarez Junco and A. Shubert (eds), *Spanish History since 1808* (London and New York, 2000). There are numerous authoritative accounts of the period of the Second Republic. Particularly recommended are G. Brenan, *The Spanish Labyrinth* (Cambridge, 1943); G. Jackson, *The Spanish Republic and the Civil War* (Princeton, 1965); S. G. Payne, *Spain's First Democracy: The Second Republic, 1931–1936* (Madison, 1993); P. Preston, *The Coming of the Spanish Civil War* (2nd edn, London, 1994); and G. Esenwein and A. Shubert, *Spain at War: The Spanish Civil War in Context, 1931–1939* (London and New York, 1995). Amongst the vast literature on the Spanish Civil War, H. Thomas, *The Spanish Civil War* (3rd edn, London, 1977) ranks among the most impressive. P. Preston, *The Spanish Civil War* (London, 1986); and S. Ellwood, *The Spanish Civil War* (Oxford, 1991) are commendably lucid and concise. P. Preston, *Franco: A Biography* (London, 1993) is a magisterial account of the life and career of the *Caudillo*. Considerably shorter, but immensely useful none the less, are S. Ellwood, *Franco* (London and New York, 1994); and J. Grugel and T. Rees, *Franco's Spain* (London, 1997). On the transition to democracy, see R. Carr and J. P. Fusi, *Spain: Dictatorship to Democracy* (2nd edn, London, 1981); and P. Preston, *The Triumph of Democracy in Spain* (London, 1986). On modern Spanish society, J. Hooper, *The New Spaniards* (2nd edn, Harmondsworth, 1995) is highly readable and thought provoking.

INDEX

INDEX